THE
TRUDEAU
DECADE

About the Editors

Rick Butler was born in Toronto and raised in Nova Scotia. He was educated at Mount Allison University in New Brunswick, Carleton University in Ottawa, and the University of Sussex in Brighton, England, where he received his M.A. in politics. He returned to Canada at the age of 23 as a university professor and taught in that capacity for seven years before devoting himself full-time to writing and producing. He has recently produced films for the National Film Board and TV Ontario as well as a record album combining Ottawa's Peace Tower carillon with the sounds of the Canadian Brass.

Jean-Guy Carrier was born in Welland, Ontario, and raised in Québec. During a varied journalistic career he has worked for newspapers, radio and television, and was a press secretary to NDP leaders David Lewis and Ed Broadbent. He has written three novels as well as a number of short stories and a fourth novel is underway. With his wife Linda he operates a sugarbush farm-restaurant near Québec City.

THE TRUDEAU DECADE

EDITED BY

Rick Butler
& Jean-Guy Carrier

1979

Doubleday Canada Limited,
Toronto, Ontario

Doubleday & Company, Inc.,
Garden City, New York

Library of Congress Catalog Card Number 78-22730

First edition

Printed in Canada by Webcom Limited

The articles and editorials in this book are reprinted by permission.

Canadian Cataloguing in Publication Data

Main entry under title:

The Trudeau decade

Bibliography: p. 393
ISBN 0-385-14806-2 bd.   ISBN 0-385-15543-3 pa.

1. Canada—Politics and government—1963-
—Sources. 2. Trudeau, Pierre Elliott, 1919-
I. Butler, Rick, 1946-   II. Carrier, Jean-Guy, 1945-

FC625.T78   320.9′71′0644   C79-094327-1
F1034.2.T78

PREFACE

This is a book about a man, a decade, and the writers who chronicled them.

The decade from 1968 to 1978 has already emerged as the most turbulent and significant period in Canada's post-World-War-Two history. It is a period that has produced intense and wide-ranging political change—the flowering of Canadian and Quebec nationalism, the establishment of legal equality for the French and English languages after more than 100 years of Confederation, the trauma of the FLQ kidnappings and the War Measures Act, diplomatic recognition of China, the abolition of capital punishment, the birth and unexpected victory of the Parti Québécois, the fall from grace of the RCMP, the televising of Parliament, the substantial growth of the Prime Minister's Office, and a steady parade of M.P.'s and Ministers entering and leaving public life through the revolving door of federal politics. Through it all Prime Minister Pierre Elliott Trudeau remained firmly at the centre—to the delight, confusion, outrage, disillusionment, but never the boredom of press and public in Canada and abroad.

Canadians buy more than five million newspapers and periodicals daily. The Spiro Agnews of public life come and go, but the "nattering nabobs of negativism" he delighted in denouncing just seem to write on. The volumes that have been written about the Trudeau decade in the Canadian and foreign press are the basis of this book.

Over the past year we have sifted through stack upon stack of newspaper back issues, and miles of microfilm to select some of the most original and informed articles, editorials, cartoons and photographs covering the Trudeau decade. Many reprinted articles from Québec, East and Western Europe, China and the USSR appear for the first time in English translation here. In addition to having much of the journalism of the decade collected in one place, we think the reader may gain a fresh perspective on Canada by seeing the country through the eyes of the foreign editorial writers and journalists represented in these pages.

How did we decide what to reprint and what to leave in the archives? For the Canadian press, newsworthiness of stories as measured by the frequency of press coverage was the main criterion. Apart from selecting the best writing wherever it appeared, we have also attempted to maintain a broad regional representation. The foreign material has been drawn from the files of the Public Archives in Ottawa and the Department of External Affairs clipping service. We were pleasantly surprised at the amount of coverage Canada receives in the world press, and have tried to present the most unstereotyped of this material. Articles describing Canada's "swinging" P.M. or the vastness of the great northland tended to stay in the files.

Thanks are due in several directions—to untiring research assistants Karen Laurence and Linda Marchand, to Rick Archbold, our lucid editor at Doubleday, to translators Hugh Faulkner, Jin-Tiong Tan, and Margarete Maurach, to St. Paul University for its support, to the Public Archives and the Department of External Affairs for making their files available, and to the many newspapers, magazines, and columnists who granted permission to reprint their words. We also feel acknowledgement is due directly to Pierre Elliott Trudeau who shaped so many of the major events of 1968-78.

Rick Butler and Jean-Guy Carrier,
February, 1979.

CONTENTS

THE
TRUDEAU
DECADE

CHAPTER 1

INTO POWER

O*f the three "wise men" who entered federal politics in 1965 Pierre Elliott Trudeau was the most reluctant. The Liberal party of Lester Pearson, ruling awkwardly with a minority in the House of Commons, sought rejuvenation through new recruits. Mr. Pearson held strongly to the principle of alternating French and English Prime Ministers. As well, he had the foresight to know that separatist agitation in Québec, still a fringe movement, was the expression of the province's profound dissatisfaction with the status quo. The Québec representation in the government was tired, and not up to the challenge Mr. Pearson saw coming. New blood would strengthen the federal hold on Québec and reinforce the party in that province, thus improving Liberal chances of staying in power and gaining that elusive majority.*

In a break with the tradition of cronyism that had governed the selection of federal politicians from Québec, Mr. Pearson's advisors looked beyond the usual collection of lawyers and civic politicians. Among those approached was Jean Marchand, then President of the Confederation of National Trade Unions and one of the leading figures in the Québec labor movement. Marchand was not only a promising candidate for the eventual succession but was also important because of his circle of friends. Gérard Pelletier, a leading journalist and political activist, was one of these. Another was professor Pierre Elliott Trudeau, known to political and intellectual circles for his writing in Cité Libre.

Québec was in full flight, revelling in its "Quiet Revolution." Marchand, Pelletier and Trudeau had perceived one crucial fact: the nationalist aspirations that were toppling institutions and changing the inner structure of Québec society would one day shift in the direction of Confederation with equal impatience. They shared the belief that the federal system would only survive if it recognized and accommodated the aspirations of French-speaking Canadians.

It was on this basis that the team of Marchand, Pelletier and Trudeau entered federal politics and were duly elected as part of the Liberal minority in 1965. In Québec the arrival of what Claude Ryan called the "three doves" was greeted with a great deal of hope. It was felt their presence would ensure that

Québec's voice would be heard at the highest levels of decision-making. Elsewhere in the country their arrival went largely unnoticed.

Pierre Elliott Trudeau began to attract attention upon his elevation to the cabinet, as justice minister, in the spring of 1967. Québec's editorial writers, most of whom had known the three men since the forties, had from the start of their adventure into politics, identified Trudeau as the man to watch. The rest of the country began to receive that message as he was taken increasingly under Prime Minister Pearson's wing.

On December 14, 1967, Lester Pearson announced that he would be resigning as Prime Minister, and scheduled a leadership convention for the following April. The power vacuum thus created quickly attracted a large number of Liberal heavyweights eager to replace Mr. Pearson at the head of the cabinet table. First to declare, on January 9, was former Québec provincial cabinet minister Eric Kierans. He was followed (in order) by Transport Minister Paul Hellyer, Minister of National Health and Welfare Allan MacEachen, Consumer and Corporate Affairs Minister John Turner, at 38 the youngest candidate, External Affairs Minister Mitchell Sharp, and Agriculture Minister J. J. Greene. On February 16, 1968, Justice Minister Pierre Elliott Trudeau announced that he too was a candidate. With the entry of Trade Minister Robert Winters on February 28 the field was complete.

When the Prime Minister had announced his intention to retire in December, Trudeau's name was not included among the front runners in the race to replace him. Mitchell Sharp and Paul Martin, the party veterans, were considered strong contenders, as were younger veterans Paul Hellyer, Allan MacEachen, and John Turner. Mr. Trudeau's political fortunes rose with astonishing speed in the next eight weeks, mainly due to two factors: his impressive debut as a tough regotiator who faced down Québec Premier Daniel Johnson at the nationally televised federal-provincial conference in Ottawa in February, and his apparently uncontrived ability to charm the media, particularly television, and the public they serve. By January Mr. Trudeau was not only good television, he was also hot press copy.

The Trudeau Image

THE TELEGRAM, *Toronto*
January 30, 1968
EDITORIAL

Justice Minister Pierre Elliott Trudeau is rapidly emerging as the most exciting, lucid and perhaps fearless of the candidates who will be seeking the national Liberal leadership.

The fact that he hasn't yet declared himself doesn't really matter.

To all intents and purposes, he's already a contender. There's no reason to doubt that, after the federal-provincial constitutional conference starting Feb. 5, he'll be officially in the race.

The impact he made by his scintillating performance before the Quebec Liberal Federation in Montreal will easily place him among the top two or three aspirants for Prime Minister Pearson's job. Certainly, he will have the strongest power base from which to spring. The majority of Quebec delegates will likely be firmly united behind him.

Until a relatively short time ago, Mr. Trudeau, who is 47, and in politics just over two years, wasn't very well known across Canada. But events of recent date have changed that.

His far-reaching amendments to the Criminal Code just before Christmas; his visits to the provinces during the past month in connection with the coming constitutional conference; and the manner in which he projects over television, have made his name a household word.

His forthright rejection of "special status" for Quebec, and of the "two-nation" concept of Confederation, has won him a lot of friends both in English and, ironically, in French Canada.

It took courage to make the speech he did in Montreal during the weekend.

Mr. Trudeau, a lawyer, and bilingual, is of French-English ancestry. This, in itself, should help to make him acceptable to both of Canada's founding races.

Whether he's selected as the successor to Mr. Pearson, however, he has done Canada a great service. He has emerged as

the French Canadian leader in support of federalism. The fact
that he's spoken out in favor of federalism is bound to win him
much respect.

Mr. Trudeau showed further courage when he said that he's
prepared to fight his battle on the hustings in Quebec. He
speaks with eloquence and passion on this subject.

Just as Robert L. Stanfield has blossomed as an attractive
national figure for the Conservatives, Mr. Trudeau is proving
to be equally appealing to the Liberals. Strangely enough, the
two, even though dissimilar in mannerism and appearance,
hold similar views on some important matters.

Both are champions of Confederation and of maintaining a
united Canada. The two are anxious to offset the extremist
views of those who would upset this pattern.

Since he was elected national leader, Mr. Stanfield has
emerged as the English-speaking spokesman for constitutional
unity, but with a recognition of certain bilingual and bicultural
concessions for French-speaking Canadians outside of Quebec.
Now Mr. Trudeau is emerging as the spokesman for French
Canada who holds the same view.

It's only in Quebec, of course, that a French-speaking leader's views in this connection would have any effect and impact
in offsetting the stand taken by separatists.

It's apparent that Messrs. Stanfield and Trudeau are deeply
concerned with the problems of today and tomorrow. It's obvious, too, that they're prepared to fight to offset the built-in
prejudices against French and English that have existed for so
long both in English and in French Canada.

The quality of Canadianism espoused by Mr. Stanfield, and
obviously shared by Mr. Trudeau, is the kind that will make
this a better and more united country.

A Non-Candidate's Advantages

THE GLOBE AND MAIL, *Toronto*
January 31, 1968
GEORGE BAIN

There's an advantage in remaining a non-candidate for the

party leadership, as Justice Minister Pierre Trudeau might have observed at any time of the day or night over the weekend in Montreal: a non-candidate doesn't have to stand around in a hospitality suite looking like the head-greeter in a saloon.

The hospitality suite is one of the truly awful inventions of modern politics—a suite of rooms filled with red-faced, perspiring people, all of them smoking and drinking and asking one another what do they think heh?

All of them drinking, that is, except the host.

He's standing out in the middle of the room with his hand out, greeting a lot of people he never laid eyes on before, and stiff as a new boot with the effort to be seen in an aura of amiability, sincerity and sober rectitude. (This is no small trick because, as time goes on, the first and last may tend to become fiercely contradictory.)

At one point on the Saturday night, he was seated on the dresser in a room that could hold comfortably one-quarter the number of people who were in it, talking with students about the law, particularly the law relating to the sale of marijuana, censorship and obscenity, and hate literature.

It was all very free-and-easy, a discussion more than a question-and-answer session, and the students (most of whom seemed to be English-speaking) appeared well satisfied with what they got.

As has been reported already in plentiful detail, Mr. Trudeau's greatest acclaim was for his outline of the choices which are available to Quebec, with the arguments (as he saw them) for and against each.

This was an impressive performance, the whole thing carried off with great style, mostly in French but with several interpolations of English, and with the assistance only (and not much of that) of notes. Mr. Trudeau, of course, is a lecturer and here he was in his own field of special interest, but it was all beautifully clear and well-ordered—and some of the comments had little barbs on them.

The audience at the Sunday morning session grew as the morning went along; it was greatest for Mr. Trudeau, who was the fourth of four speakers. This in part undoubtedly reflected nothing more than that all the delegates had not leapt to greet the dawn; conventions tend to become late-night affairs (see above). But it also undoubtedly reflected a good deal of curiosity to see and hear the Justice Minister. It was quite an ovation he got at the end—enough perhaps to persuade a man to run.

Image Unleashed

SOUTHAM NEWS SERVICES
February 13, 1968
CHARLES LYNCH

Is Pierre Elliott Trudeau really real, or is he merely an invention of the news media?

It is a question that will be argued for the duration of the Liberal leadership race.

And if Mr. Trudeau becomes prime minister, it may be argued even more heatedly in the course of his regime.

Should he win and be found wanting (a possibility that bothers many, including apparently Mr. Trudeau himself), the toilers of press, radio and television could wind up being accused of having tricked the public by overselling him.

That in itself would be a switch since the usual accusation against us is that we destroy public men, and prime ministers in particular.

The line between reporting a bandwagon and actually getting aboard it, is a fine line, indeed, and there is no doubt that the massive reporting of Mr. Trudeau's moves in recent weeks has given tremendous momentum to his candidacy.

But is it being overdone?

Or are we really witnessing a political phenomenon of a kind not seen in Canada since the Diefenbaker mania of 10 years ago?

A very nice-sounding lady called up to ask if it could really be true, as she gathered from the papers and TV, that the only thing worth reporting from the weekend Ontario Liberal meeting in Toronto was that Mr. Trudeau showed up and shook hands with a lot of people.

Her point was that she was quite prepared to jump for joy over Mr. Trudeau, if Mr. Trudeau turns out to be worth jumping for joy about, but that first of all she wanted a chance to judge the other candidates. She wanted to know what they had to say in their speeches—and, she said, she would continue to want to know as the contest moved along.

Mr. Trudeau's rivals in the race would surely agree with this nice-sounding lady, and they must yearn for a piece of the publicity action he is getting.

Any politician would.

He himself is playing it very cool, as witness his reaction when he showed up at the Toronto meeting. In the boil of excitement, he was asked what he thought about the crowd reaction. He said it was very gratifying, "provided it's spontaneous and not staged."

Well, as he must have known, it was a combination of both. It was staged—to the extent that his supporters persuaded him to show up and provided a setting for him. It was spontaneous —to the extent that the crowd really wanted to get a look at him.

Mr. Trudeau said he only showed up because a few people had asked him to. But this was a bit cute since wild horses couldn't get Pierre Elliott Trudeau to show up anywhere if he didn't want to.

All his life he has been the bane of program chairmen who booked him for speeches or learned papers only to have him fail to show, either through absentmindedness or simply because he had found something more diverting to do.

Once he did show up in Toronto, and the crowd responded to his appearance, the press and the cameras went into action, and the other candidates might as well have gone home.

People want to know about him. And the more they find out, the more they seem to want to know.

He himself has the substance to sustain their interest because I have yet to meet anybody who has met him, or heard him, and failed to be impressed.

So many of our public men leave even their supporters with that letdown feeling, but Mr. Trudeau, at least at this early stage of his political career, is not in that number.

For myself, I should have preferred Manpower Minister Jean Marchand as a Quebec candidate in the race, and said so.

Others said the same, but there was little response from the public—and even less from Jean Marchand himself.

The Leadership Race and the Problem of Québec

LE DEVOIR, *Montréal*
March 2, 1968
EDITORIAL BY CLAUDE RYAN

It is too early to measure the final worth of every candidate. However, it is not too early to remind candidates of certain critical questions which it would be useless for them to avoid. Among them there is one that stands out by its complexity and urgency: It is the question of what place will be assigned to Québec in a renewed Canada.

All candidates are presently of one voice on bilingualism and all sing vaguely egalitarian refrains. On these questions, all candidates are remarkably in agreement. There is no discernible difference of opinion on the question of bilingualism between Mr. Trudeau, Mr. Sharp, Mr. Martin, Mr. Hellyer and others. The theme of linguistic equality accounts, however, for only part of the problem of equality between two social groups. This equality also has a political dimension, which inevitably calls up the problem of Québec. It is on this second question as much as on the first, that we should probe the ideas of the candidates.

From this point of view, one candidate elicits more interest than the others, if only because he is presented as "the French Canadian candidate for Québec." This is Mr. Pierre Elliott Trudeau. On the basic question the thinking of Mr. Trudeau runs counter to that of the present government of Québec and of all the Opposition parties, including that of Mr. Lesage. The minimum that any Québec party must commit itself to is a renewed federalism comprising a more or less defined special status for Québec. Mr. Trudeau seems to find this minimum unacceptable.

The candidate doesn't, of course, speak as categorically as a few months ago when he denounced as "vulgar unknowns" those who foresaw a distinct status for Québec. He has even let slip glimmers of compromise in certain recent statements which have, unfortunately, not been heeded. But by and large, the

position of Mr. Trudeau remains what it was. The least that
one can say is that his position raises serious reservations
amongst nearly all politicians active on the provincial scene.
We are not the least bit interested in the verbal skirmishes that
have occurred between Mr. Trudeau and Mr. Johnson on particular points.

That Mr. Trudeau has spoken of the "lousy French" and
Mr. Johnson of "Lord Elliott" seems irrelevant in both cases
and cannot inspire from us two lines of commentary.

What we are much more concerned about and what the rest
of Canada must be made perfectly aware of is that on the
question of the status of Québec there exists a serious conflict
between Mr. Trudeau and Mr. Johnson and thus, between Mr.
Trudeau and a trend of political thought that extends, in
Québec, far beyond the limits of the Union Nationale.

If Mr. Trudeau wishes to avoid the appearance of fighting
with Mr. Johnson on secondary issues, if he wishes to avoid the
appearance of bowing before the Leader of the Québec government, we would suggest he follow a very simple course.

All he has to do is take paragraphs 81 to 90 of the Laurendeau-Dunton report and tell us clearly what he thinks. If he
rejects the method of dealing with equality proposed by the
Royal Commission (which takes into account the political dimensions of the problem), then he has to know right now that
he will encounter serious and increasing difficulties in Québec.

If, on the other hand, he accepts this method of dealing with
the problem, it is in his own interest to say so immediately
since this could create a more positive view of his candidacy in
Québec. That is the crux of the divergence between Mr. Trudeau and Mr. Johnson. If this divergence is not dealt with
satisfactorily, English Canada risks, if Mr. Trudeau becomes
Leader of the Liberal Party, being alone in putting its faith in
the Messiah it will have chosen. Among the other candidates,
only one other, Mr. John Turner, has said anything pertinent
on the question of Québec.

In a speech given in Toronto on February 19, the Minister of
Consumer Affairs demonstrated that he was ready to accept
the problem in its real dimensions. "Québec," said Mr. Turner,
"represents in a way the homeland of a people.... We cannot
treat Québec like any other province.... I don't mean that we

have to scuttle Canada, or reduce the power that the central government has over the control of the economy or in providing leadership for the country. But we must understand that Québec is the homeland of 83 percent of French Canadians and as such, has special problems."

Mr. Turner will have to draw certain practical conclusions from his premises. But he has at least faced the problem correctly. He has not tried to hide from an obvious reality.

English Canada is sorely tempted at this point to believe that the future of this country can be assured if linguistic rights are extended from ocean to ocean. It wants to be told that once this problem will have been resolved, the problem of Québec will disappear by itself.

Such a view seems to us a dangerous illusion. Even if it seems ridiculous and unrealistic to only take into account the criterion we have just examined for the selection of the next Liberal Leader, the position of each candidate on the question of Québec must remain a principal point in the choice to be made by the delegates. Otherwise, they will only put off until later and risk seeing grow worse, problems which are already at a critical stage.

Old Guard Backlash

THE EDMONTON JOURNAL
April 2, 1968
EDITORIAL

The word whispered in Ottawa now is that "stop Trudeau" deals are on.

The quite remarkable way that this man has shown a wide appeal to the Canadian people may be frustrating and hurting the hardcore politicians with the smooth machines. But even if they can swing their delegates—which seems doubtful—such cynical backroom dealings should be avoided. Canadian political institutions are held in low enough esteem by the people without lowering them even further.

The choice of Mr. Trudeau as leader is almost certain to

mean that he will lead the Liberal party in an election which can be expected this year. All the other leadership candidates represent the greyness of orthodoxy.

Mr. Trudeau brings to the political scene a freshness, a new approach, something clearly different from what we are used to in Canada. He is something new. . . .

Struggle for renewal

THE MONTREAL STAR
April 3, 1968
RAMSAY COOK

Pierre Trudeau, paradoxically, is both clearest and most imprecise. He refuses to offer a panacea for every problem. Yet he is unquestionably the most liberal candidate, both in his skeptical attitude to ready-made solutions, and in his determination to measure every proposal against the yardstick of human liberty. He rejects the rhetoric of nationalism in all of its forms, whether it implies a special status for Quebec or policies of economic nationalism for Canada. He instinctively asks: Will it work? He thus irritates the nationalists in all parts of Canada.

He is a man convinced that the country is moving rapidly, more rapidly than its people realize, into a new age, one in which old answers rapidly grow obsolete. It is not his nature to be imprecise, yet he knows that if Canadians want a renewed and viable country, it would be misleading to offer them a complete blueprint evolved in a short seven weeks of furious campaigning.

Canadians in all parts of the country have discovered in the last six weeks something which André Laurendeau of *Le Devoir* perceived more than a decade ago. "What is best in Trudeau," the Montreal editor wrote, "besides his technical competence, is his taste for freedom. He demands its risks and its advantages. A remarkable personality has revealed himself." That personality has raised the Liberal leadership campaign from the level of dull mediocrity to one of excitement. M. Trudeau might just do the same for the country, if the delegates to this week's convention can be persuaded.

The Trudeau of the Image Makers

THE FREE PRESS, *Winnipeg*
April 4, 1968
MAURICE WESTERN

Ottawa—Mr. Mitchell Sharp, having read the handwriting of the pollsters on the political walls, has hastened to do homage and to turn over his organization to the anointed of the television establishment.

We are in the midst of events without precedent in Canada although they will appear less strange to students of modern American politics, of the Willkies and Kennedys. Mr. Pierre Elliott Trudeau enters the convention an overwhelming favorite although he is the least known of all the major candidates and a virtual newcomer to public life. Some veterans, mindful of the ways of popular assemblies, are sceptical. Not so fervent Trudeau followers, now confident that the band-wagon is rolling and that nothing can stop it from carrying him in triumph to a Saturday coronation.

It must all puzzle Mr. Trudeau, author of the following extracts selected for his campaign literature:

"The only constant factor to be found in my thinking over the years has been opposition to accepted opinions ...

"The tyranny of public opinion seeks to impose its domination over everything. Its aim is to reduce all action, all thought and all feelings to a common denominator. It forbids independence and kills inventiveness; condemns those who ignore it and banishes those who oppose it ... "

Without doubt Mr. Trudeau himself is now the beneficiary of a select opinion represented by television and its allies. Well before the polling revelation of The Way It Is, our screen personalities had been referring to the minister of justice as the "acknowledged" front-runner. Who had done the acknowledging, they did not explain. Then private television, with the zeal of a soap company, began to plug a program featuring Mr. Trudeau and a star from Seven Days, timed, interestingly enough, for the edification of delegates on the first evening of the convention. So it has gone.

There is no suggestion that Mr. Trudeau sought unfair advantage. What he did, in a most amusing way, was to suggest, at the time of his announcement, that his candidacy was more or less the invention of toilers for the newspapers and television. Our intent, he surmised, was to play a huge joke on the Liberal party.

Thus was launched the new politics. How it differs from the old, except in TV images, has not yet been explained; our stars seldom worry about details. Mr. Trudeau represents the new Liberalism. He may give conventional answers but they cause no anguish to his fervent supporters since he sometimes states them in unconventional ways. He is the innovator; the leader of a new generation: according to one respected commentator, "light-years" ahead of other candidates.

The standard criticism brought against the "old" Liberalism was that it was a huge umbrella spread over a coalition of all sorts of opinions. It is difficult in a transcontinental federation to build a successful party on a narrow, dogmatic basis; one important reason why the CCF (to the anguish of some old loyalists) had to die and to find reincarnation as the NDP. But since this was the reproach of critics, we can presumably look forward to something different from a party led by a former, outspoken critic, Mr. Trudeau....

The tensely-anticipated convention opened in Ottawa's Civic Centre on April 4, with Prime Minister Pearson's farewell speech. Two days later the voting began, and even on the first ballot, it was apparent that Pierre Trudeau's campaign appeal was not a passing creation of the media: Trudeau 752, Hellyer 330, Winters 293, Martin and Turner 277, Greene 169, MacEachen 165, Kierans 103. Trudeau's strength rose to 964 votes on the second ballot, and at this point thanks to an inquisitive microphone the country heard Judy LaMarsh pleading with Paul Hellyer to throw his support behind another front runner lest that "bastard" Trudeau should win. Hellyer refused, and by the fourth ballot Trudeau had both a majority (Trudeau 1203, Winters 954, Turner 195) and a new job.

Press reaction was swift and almost universally positive, in Canada and abroad.

On to Trudeau's "Just Society"

THE OTTAWA CITIZEN
April 8, 1968
EDITORIAL

April 6, 1968, will stand in future time as one of the decisive dates in Canadian history.

Whether it will mark the opening of a new chapter of constructive work, of achievement, of excellence, or of something contrary to those present hopes, remains for the unfolding of the story. But there can be no doubt that when 1,203 out of 2,365 delegates to the Liberal convention cast their votes on the fourth ballot in favor of Pierre Elliott Trudeau, they made a decision to embark on an adventurous and challenging approach to the future of this nation.

The alternative—safety and a nonpolitical conservatism—was rejected, although a very substantial minority of the delegates showed their preferences for this option by marking their final ballots for Robert Winters. The Citizen believes the convention was right to reject that choice. Like all great enterprises, this one has its dangers. But unless this country sets its goals high and broad, it will remain indefinitely a quiet backwater of mediocrity or it will shiver into futile fragments.

Mr. Trudeau, now the prime minister-designate, crystallizes his goals for Canada in a phrase: "the just society." It is a worthy call to action. It implies not only justice for individuals and for collective groups of Canadians, both ethnic and regional, who have known something less than justice in the past. It implies also justice for other peoples whom Canadian action may affect: potential immigrants to Canada and the citizens of foreign countries in which Canadian foreign policy may have some impact.

Like the retiring prime minister, the next one tests his actions against high standards of moral and intellectual excellence. He can therefore expect to be judged against this kind of standard. His candidacy for the most powerful office in the land has been so unusual and so dramatic that it has bathed him in a shining moment of favorable publicity worthy of Camelot. He cannot expect this idyll to continue long.

Mr. Trudeau is a man of great personal courage and candor. He has a swift, abrasive tongue and a ruthless wit. He will never be an ambiguous or passive force in public life, and the division between the desire for serenity and the urge for adventure that Saturday's vote revealed within his own party will not make it easy for him to weld the Liberal party into a cohesive instrument at the service of his admirable objectives.

Our wish for the new prime minister is that he will be able to achieve his just society, within the limits of the possible and the time framework of his own lifetime. Prophecy is risky, but those of us who have encouraged and supported Mr. Trudeau's candidacy are committed to risk in a good cause. Therefore we endorse the final words that Lester Pearson addressed to the Liberal convention on Saturday night as he congratulated the new leader:

"He will lead a government that will do great things for Canada, our beloved country."

LE DROIT, *Ottawa*
April 8, 1968.
EDITORIAL BY MARCEL GINGRAS

In this column, long before Mr. Trudeau's bid for the leadership and rumours of Prime Minister Pearson resigning, and even before the Conservative party crisis that saw the departure of Mr. Diefenbaker, we have expressed again and again the view that the time did not seem right for the election of a French Canadian as leader of either major federal political party. And looking back on those statements today we don't feel any need to apologize—you don't have to make excuses for an opinion arrived at in all honesty and sincerity. However, on Feb. 12 of this year we wrote on Mr. Trudeau's possible candidacy: "If Mr. Trudeau were to make a run for it and get elected leader of the Liberal party, he can count on our support whenever he is working for justice for the French Canadians."

Today, we are happy to repeat this commitment to Mr. Trudeau, but with one additional proviso: he has our support whenever he is working for justice for *all* Canadians. We are quite certain this is exactly what he intends to do, but we are just afraid that this job will be more difficult for him to accomplish than it would be for an anglophone because, no matter how fair his actions may be, they may be interpreted by English Canadians as being unduly favorable to the French.

To help dispel this fear we can only repeat that Mr. Trudeau's conception of federalism is exceptionally sound and fair. It can be summarized in a few words: federalism is based on shared powers and shared obligations. It should not be excessively centralizing nor dangerously decentralizing. The man who will be Prime Minister of Canada in a few days understands this very well, as we saw recently on television when he pointed out that if you want to live in a country you have to be prepared to get in there and fight like everyone else. He added that he didn't believe in a province closing in on itself and opting out of the battle because it's afraid of the strength of its adversary.

In the days, weeks, and months ahead we will have many opportunities to discuss Mr. Trudeau, but for the present we reiterate our congratulations to him and to the other candidates who ran for the leadership. We've just emerged from three days of political frenzy and competition that can only take place in a free country, where democracy is more than an empty word.

A New Political Era

LA PRESSE, *Montréal*
April 8, 1968
EDITORIAL

More than the Conservatives in Toronto last September, the federal Liberals in Ottawa have turned over a new leaf. By his behavior, by his style and ideas, Pierre Elliott Trudeau appears as the herald of a new political era, very different from the past.... If the April 6 election holds the promises that are indicated, he will be able to accomplish great things for his party and for the country, providing that he knows how to surround himself with a team combining the ability to move ahead and experiment.

Liberals Vote for New Image

THE GAZETTE, *Montréal*
April 8, 1968
EDITORIAL

The fact that the Liberals have chosen as their leader a man who has been a member of the party for only some three years is a phenomenon without precedent in the history of the Liberals, or of any other party in Canada. Mr. Trudeau himself, in his press conference yesterday, said that he realized that one of his chief difficulties would be to reconcile the party as a whole to the sudden rise of a newcomer. But he went on to say, and quite rightly, that he was "not exactly an upstart, banging his way to the top of the party." He did not choose himself to be Prime Minister; he was chosen. He was caught up in a movement that was not really of his own making. . . .

We Had to Pick Him—He Was So Patently What the Public Wanted

THE TORONTO STAR
April 8, 1968
PETER C. NEWMAN

Much more was won at the Civic Centre in Ottawa Saturday night than the right to succeed Lester Pearson.

What was won was the right of a new generation to be represented by one of its own. Pierre Elliott Trudeau is the first Canadian Prime Minister born in this century, a man whose perspective on history is rooted in the experience of our own times.

In a country whose population is becoming increasingly young and urban, the Liberals have gained a young, urban leader. Though the party's choice of Trudeau superficially appears to have been a daring step into the unknown, it is not really that far removed from Liberal tradition.

For one thing, it maintains the party's historic alternation between French and English leaders—a prerequisite that Trudeau alone could have satisfied. For another, the Liberals during this century have always chosen as their leaders men who have not worked their way up through the party, but who joined it close to the top. In this respect, Trudeau follows the precedents set by Mackenzie King, Louis St. Laurent and Lester Pearson.

Also, given a choice, the Liberal party has always opted for the reform candidate as it did this time with Trudeau.

Though much has been made of Trudeau's radicalism; he is probably less a radical than a reformer. His inclination has always been toward pragmatic solutions.

It is not so much his ideas as his unorthodox style which has made him appear such an abrupt break from the tradition of Canadian prime ministers. Who would have thought that in this hide-bound Presbyterian country an acceptable leader could while away the anxious time of his testing in the convention's ballot booths by tossing grapes in the air and catching them in his teeth?

His attraction to the English-speaking is a mysterious force; he fascinates us because he is so totally unpredictable. The whole house of cliches constructed by generations of politicians is demolished as soon as he begins to speak.

"For the West, where the French are feared because they are unknown," says Pat McGeer, a B.C. MLA and convention delegate, "Trudeau lives and breathes the answer to the Quebec problem. People can transfer their worries about national unity to him. In his very person, he gives us all a feeling that the second culture in Canada is precious to preserve."

The Pearson-Diefenbaker feud of the last decade has focussed attention on leadership as the critical element in federal politics. Canada's future—not just the prospects of its political parties—seems now to hang on our leadership question. In a hundred small groups on a hundred earnest evenings in the past few years. I've heard Canadians say to each other: "What this country needs is a leader."

It now begins to look as though it might have one.

The choice of Trudeau represents a unique opportunity for the revival of the Expo spirit that did so much for the Canadian psyche. Just as the great Montreal fair changed the way we look at ourselves, Trudeau could be the agent of a revival of Canadian political values, the end of the alienation that has removed most of the young generation from active involvement in our political process.

Trudeau's Victory

THE BRANDON SUN
April 8, 1968
EDITORIAL

It says something good about this country that it can have Pierre Elliott Trudeau as its prime minister. We can know what kind of a prime minister he will be only by watching him perform in the office: he may flop miserably; he may be great. But for the moment, the real significance of the next prime minister is the fact that he could be elected at all.

Think of this: think of a people told so often that they are dull and cautious that they began to believe it themselves, and these people choosing as the prime minister a man who is anything but dull, anything but cautious: a young man, a bachelor—the first since Mackenzie King, whom he resembles not at all; an intellectual; a vicious critic, at times of the Liberal party; a man thought by so many people to be a socialist that the fact he is not one was less important than the charge, by the time of the Liberal convention; a man, above all, whose style and personality are in direct contradiction to everything Canadian politicians have been over the years. Whether or not Pierre Trudeau is a good prime minister, the important thing is for now that the Canadian people would call upon him to serve.

It means, perhaps, that we have stopped being deadly dull serious about being Canadians, and have instead come to find pride, even joy, in our identity. We saw that joy in Centennial year, in Expo. We stopped worrying about our bicultural identity and began to have fun with it. We stopped worrying about Canada; we relaxed and began to enjoy it. . . .

A Refreshing Choice

THE EDMONTON JOURNAL
April 8, 1968
EDITORIAL

The Liberal Party has, we think, made the correct decision in choosing Pierre Trudeau as leader.

More than any of the other candidates by far, he is a man of his age who offers a chance to bridge the gap between the two major language groups in Canada. . . .

The Liberals, with due thought, gave the country what it is looking for—something new.

It took some courage. To have played it safe would have been wrong for the party and wrong for the country. Pierre Trudeau is new and exciting. He is short on experience, but experience, in itself, is only proof of time serving.

The result of the convention should be approved by all Canadians.

The New Man

THE WHITEHORSE STAR
April 8, 1968
EDITORIAL

There's one thing about getting Pierre Elliott Trudeau as the next Prime Minister of Canada . . . the man has style.

Even from this distance we could sense the excitement of having a new, younger and different type of man at the helm. Suddenly the fist pounding, arm waving politicians seemed pretty old fashioned, and the young, ever-so-dynamic ones seemed phoney.

He Has a Harder Race to Run

THE PROVINCE, *Vancouver*
April 8, 1968
EDITORIAL

Pierre Elliott Trudeau comes to power with perhaps more expected of him than was expected from any of Canada's 14 other prime ministers—including the visionary John Diefenbaker of 1958. It is a burden any man would find difficult, if not impossible, to bear.

When matched against the standards he has set for himself, any career that marks him merely as a better prime minister than most would be a failure.

He has set himself a goal that nobody in democratic politics has yet achieved. It is "the triumph of reason over passion in politics." That goal is itself a paradox. He can achieve it in a democracy only if he is passionately supported by those who agree that pure reason is the answer.

But the implication in Mr. Trudeau's style, for the many who support him, is that he will bring a trained, uncluttered mind to bear on all these problems.

He knows, however, and frankly says, that there are no final answers to the perennial problems. Any man does well who finds right answers for his time and place.

In Mr. Trudeau's time and place there are more questions, and of greater complexity, than ever before. What exercise in reason can avoid the effects on Canada of the agonies to the south and the war far to the west?

Paul Martin told the convention in Ottawa: "Democracy is not a system where truths are implemented by philosopher-kings." He is right, thus far in history. To prove him wrong in future would mean another Quiet Revolution, this time on a national scale. The next few months should be crucial; we await them eagerly.

New Pilot

THE VICTORIA TIMES
April 8, 1968
EDITORIAL

A vast responsibility has been thrust upon a man whose intellectual complexity, strange detachment even in the midst of a chanting, cheering crowd, and complete bi-culturism are still not fully understood by many of those who voted for him.

That is why the word "gamble" was heard so often at the convention, even from enthusiastic Trudeau supporters. But for a majority of the voting delegates it was a gamble which in the end had no acceptable alternative: Pierre Elliott Trudeau emerged as the most likely pilot for the uncharted waters that lie ahead of Canada, the most likely catalyst for the national unity which every candidate stressed as our greatest need; and the man most likely to beat Mr. Stanfield and his Conservatives in the next general election. . . .

Mr. Trudeau presumably is well aware of what he faces. In accepting his election, he thanked the people who had made "this choice so important to the future of our country." There could be no doubt of the virtual unanimity of the ovation which greeted him as the final vote was announced. It was equally obvious, in that throng of predominantly young Canadians, that a watershed in our history had been crossed.

The changes, of course, will not be immediate. The colorful kaleidoscope of the convention hall; the mad, jigging dance of the placards; the pounding, hypnotic chants of the cheering blocs—these are only memories and echoes today. The practicalities of power must now be recognized: fundamental changes in national life tend to set their own pace. But a basic alteration in course has been made; a new style has been injected into Canadian political life, and the Trudeau era could prove to be one of the most momentous in our history.

The Importance of Mr. Trudeau

THE GUARDIAN, *Manchester*
April 8, 1968
EDITORIAL

The new Canadian Prime Minister, Mr. Pierre Trudeau, is a French-Canadian. In the present tense climate of relations between the two communities in Canada, this is perhaps the most significant fact. Canada has had French-Canadian Prime Ministers before, but never at a time of such importance to the survival of the nation as today.

A few years ago the advantage of having a French-Canadian at the top would have been that it helped to interpret their position to the English-speaking majority across Canada. But that job has now largely been done. The recent Royal Commission on Biculturalism and Bilingualism reminded Canadians that the historical promises to the French-Canadians have gone unfulfilled. A Constitutional Conference is now trying to redeem them by seeing among other things that French is allowed as an official language wherever there are enough speakers to justify it.

The importance of Mr. Trudeau now is that he may be the last man available to prevent Quebec from seceding. In the last few months the secession movement has gained strength, as one of Quebec's leading figures, Mr. Rene Levesque, has come out in its favour. He has argued a cogent case for an independent Quebec, linked economically with the rest of Canada in a Common Market. To many French-Canadians separatism now looks like a much more respectable and feasible option than before. As a persuasive Federalist, Mr. Trudeau is more likely to be able to stop this trend than any English-Canadian. He had better be, for the decision seems nearer than ever.

Canada's New Man

THE TIMES, *London*
April 8, 1968
EDITORIAL

The choice of Mr. Pierre Trudeau as the new Canadian Prime Minister and leader of the Liberal Party shows an awareness of the need for unity in Canada that is driven home by external warnings as well as by internal pressures. General de Gaulle's disruptive cries from the distance are not the most pressing danger to which Canada feels it necessary to respond; indeed, they have been partly forgotten. But across her long border are the tensions and riots in the United States which Canadians must take as warnings of what can come if disunity is not countered and cured in time.

In choosing Mr. Trudeau to succeed Mr. Lester Pearson the Canadian Liberals have embarked their hopes in youth, verve, and intellect rather than tested political or business expertise. Mr. Trudeau has been in the Liberal Party for only three years, in Parliament a little less, and Minister for only two. Four months ago he was hardly known to Canadians outside Quebec.

Mr. Trudeau's assignment is to head off Quebec separatism. The great weakness of Mr. Diefenbaker's and Mr. Pearson's administrations was in their lack of outstanding French Canadian Ministers. Mr. Pearson deliberately wooed and won the handful of Quebec Federalists of which Mr. Trudeau is the best known and probably the most radical, though Mr. Marchand and Mr. Chrétien have played an essential part in attacking the Duplessis regime. Mr. Trudeau developed his belief in federal institutions which—all language difficulties apart—offers the French Canadians the whole country for a home. He also came to distrust the authoritarian motives of many Quebec statists. This credo—the assertion of French Canada against Quebec—he has set out with a force and lucidity which has delighted English Canada and won more admiration in Quebec than is avowed.

New Trends?

PRAVDA, *Moscow*
April 23, 1968
EDITORIAL

A new Prime Minister has been sworn in in Canada. P. Trudeau has relieved L. Pearson, who has resigned, and the composition of the new Liberal Government has been announced.

Though Trudeau has not yet officially announced the programme of his Cabinet, some organs of the Western press are already speculating about the political plans of the new Canadian Premier. The *New York Times*, for instance, referring to authoritative Ottawa circles, asserts that Trudeau has declared his intention to revise Canada's foreign policy. Discussing the purposes of such a revision, the newspaper points out that Trudeau's "intention" is to take Canada out of London's and Washington's sphere of influence and strengthen relations with other countries.

Evidently a strong need to find some new independent lines in foreign policy has been felt in Canada for a long time. This is because more and more right-thinking Canadians have begun to realize the difficult position their country finds herself in because of the "special" relationship with its powerful southern neighbour. This finds expression above all in deep penetration by American monopolies of Canada's economy. Under Washington's influence, Ottawa sometimes has to follow a foreign policy line of the USA which is contrary to the interests of the Canadian people. This situation caused the London *Times* to compare Canada's foreign policy with "the pursuit of a chimaera."

A characteristic example is the position of Pearson's government in the Vietnam question. While officially maintaining a policy of neutrality in the conflict and even trying to assume the role of peace-maker, it has at the same time done nothing to stop the growing deliveries of Canadian armaments and war equipment to the USA army in Vietnam. The Canadian press has revealed that many of the country's citizens are fighting freelance in the American army against the Vietnamese people and, also, that Canadian representatives on the International

Control Commission, which supervises the implementation of the Geneva Agreements on Indo-China, are engaged in spying for the USA. All this not only did nothing to raise the prestige of the former government but was an important factor in the growth of its unpopularity.

Comments in the majority of Western press reports on possible changes in Canada's policy are restrained. One thing, however, is clear from them: the country is confronted with the need to take a serious decision. Only time will tell to what extent Trudeau's government will be able to steer Canada's foreign policy in the direction of greater independence.

On April 20 Lester Pearson resigned from the government and Pierre Elliott Trudeau became Canada's fifteenth Prime Minister. One of his first acts was to dissolve Parliament and call an election for June 25, 1968.

Early in the campaign it became clear that Mr. Trudeau's strongest attribute in the minds of many editorial writers and commentators was what they regarded as his ability to deal with Canada's internal political divisions. As a forthright, if somewhat rigid champion of federalism, Mr. Trudeau was quickly able to put Conservative leader Robert Stanfield and NDP leader Tommy Douglas on the defensive, and gain excellent press coverage in the process.

Trudeau: A Bright New Chance for Ottawa to Tell Its Side of the Story to Quebec

MACLEAN'S
June, 1968
EDITORIAL

One of the commonest arguments against Pierre Elliott Trudeau as Prime Minister of Canada was his alleged "rigidity" toward Quebec. Premier Daniel Johnson used every private channel of communication to let Liberals know that he could get along with "any candidate except Trudeau," and opponents took advantage of these messages to protest their readiness to "negotiate" with the Union Nationale on constitutional issues.

Consciously or not, they were in our opinion less than candid. In practice, we believe, any federal prime minister would—and should—be as "rigid" as any other.

Premier Johnson's demands for his provincial government are well known. They have been spelled out in official documents at two recent top-level conferences, and they are demands no federal government would accept. He wants, among other things, "control" of immigration, a decisive voice in monetary policy, a complete monopoly of social-welfare legislation, international recognition of Quebec as sovereign in matters of provincial jurisdiction (which include not only education but water and other natural resources) and finally the transfer of residual powers (*i.e.*, those not actually listed in the Constitution) from federal to provincial authority. These stipulations differ very little from those of René Lévesque, the chief difference being that Lévesque admits (quite rightly in our view) that they could not be obtained under a federal system but require outright separation.

Premier Johnson is not to be talked out of these demands. It has been his hope, rather, to meet a federal prime minister who could be talked *into* them.

We trust no prominent member of any federal party at the present time is flabby enough to meet Premier Johnson's specifications for the ideal federal negotiator. It seems obvious to us that to grant his demands would mean the end of Canada as an effectively functioning nation.

Equally obvious is the danger of deadlock—the danger that this head-on collision between two groups of politicians might become, as it has not yet become, a collision between two major groups of Canadian citizens. Therefore it is urgent that the federal case be presented not just to the provincial government but directly to the people of Quebec, in their own language and by one of their own. This has not been adequately done since Ernest Lapointe died, 27 years ago. The man best equipped to do it now is Pierre Elliott Trudeau.

It is for this reason, more than for any other, that we applaud the Liberal Party's choice of Prime Minister Trudeau, and in no endeavor do we more earnestly wish him success.

Trudeau Challenges Quebec

THE PETERBOROUGH EXAMINER
May 10, 1968
EDITORIAL

To anyone who does not have an opportunity to observe at close range the actions and attitudes of Quebec Premier Daniel Johnson, Prime Minister Trudeau's determined stand over the province's international aspirations may seem out of all proportion to the seriousness of the offence. After all, it might be pointed out, Quebec wanted only to participate in a French-language education conference (in Gabon, and later in Paris) that held little interest for Canada as a whole. As education is under provincial jurisdiction, why should Ottawas object?

Actually, as was attested in the government's position paper and in the 75-page booklet published by Mr. Trudeau Wednesday, the scrap goes much farther than that. As the prime minister sees it (and he has been in a position to observe Mr. Johnson close-up for some considerable time), Quebec is deliberately flouting the constitution in order to establish precedents that would ultimately become part of the constitution. "It's not a mere bickering over some section of the constitution," says the prime minister. "When you reach a stage when provinces can determine for themselves how they will act in international matters, and when they want to erect this into a constitutional and international theory, then you're destroying the country."

This is tough talk. Mr. Trudeau is accusing Premier Johnson of endangering Canadian nationality. As he pointed out, Lester Pearson, when he was prime minister, had sought to bring about a compromise by having the Quebec education minister attend the Paris conference as head of a Canadian delegation,

but his suggestion was rejected. As Mr. Trudeau sees it, therefore, Premier Johnson doesn't care a whit how the federal
government views the constitutional legality of his government's actions: so far as the constitution goes Mr. Johnson will
determine what is right and what is wrong. . . .

Not being constitutional experts, perhaps, many Canadians
have not thus far shared Mr. Trudeau's grim appraisal of the
situation. He himself attributes this "to a spirit of tolerance and
fair play that is characteristic of Canadians." With his detailed
explanation of Ottawa's position Wednesday, he gives us a
clearer understanding of what is at stake, of what the fuss is all
about. More importantly, the prime minister has declared the
controversy to be an election issue in a direct challenge to Tory
Leader Robert Stanfield's less critical assessment of the situation.

Clearly he is inviting a showdown between Ottawa and
Quebec City, between Mr. Stanfield and himself. In Quebec,
which the Liberals must hold if they are to stay in power, it
may very well become *the* issue with the voters being asked to
declare themselves either for Ottawa or, in effect, for Quebec
City. It is a dangerous ploy but a courageous one. Elsewhere in
Canada it may not be the sole issue in the campaign (hopefully
there will still be room for economic issues) but it will be an
important one.

Whether he is right or wrong to seek a direct confrontation
with Premier Johnson over the issue, Prime Minister Trudeau
has spoken with great honesty and forthrightness and has
made his position crystal clear. It will be up to Mr. Stanfield
and Mr. Douglas to do the same—and the voters can then
decide for themselves.

Trudeau Policy Sample

THE GUARDIAN, *Charlottetown*
June 4, 1968
EDITORIAL

External Affairs Minister Sharp has announced that an election manifesto on foreign policy by Prime Minister Trudeau is being summarized for use by every Liberal candidate in the election. The manifesto sets out, in 10 pages, Mr. Trudeau's program for a major "reassessment of Canada's internal posture," and it is intended for use in every constituency as "a declaration of intentions should the government win the election."

Perhaps this will make clearer what the Prime Minister means by his recent reference to one phase of his foreign policy proposals which has puzzled most authorities on the subject. This is his offer of extending recognition to Communist China while, at the same time, continuing to take into account that there is a separate Chinese government in Formosa. As explained by Mr. Sharp, this "is not a Two China policy—it is a One China and a separate government of Taiwan." Since Red China has refused to come into the United Nations on any such basis, it is not likely that it will thank Mr. Trudeau for his kind offer. . . .

Mr. Trudeau made his phoney policy statement on his tour of the Western provinces, where they're anxious to sell more wheat to Red China and where it sounded good. But on analysis it just doesn't mean anything.

Mr. Stanfield showed in his speech here last night that he is more concerned about issues of real moment to Canada, and especially to this Atlantic area. Good stuff for an election manifesto, too, without a word of doubletalk about the China business.

QUEBEC L'ACTION, *Montréal*
June 5, 1968
EDITORIAL BY LAURENT LAPLANTE

Prime Minister Trudeau is trying in vain to spread his popularity throughout the Québec countryside.

Granted the results of the last Gallup poll seem to indicate

that the Liberals are on their way to their greatest victory in 20
years, but the Gallup poll, as different analyses have shown,
has a tendency to treat countries and provinces as whole enti-
ties. This type of polling does not permit a precise evaluation
of what is one of the greatest imponderables in any election
campaign—regional disparity. Our politicians themselves talk
of plans to eliminate or at least reduce economic disparities
among regions, but they don't seem to realize, on the other
hand, that the same disparities exist on the sociological level as
well.

People who like shortcuts will obviously conclude that rural
Québec has remained as it was 200 years ago. They even
repeat the old saying "Québec is more backward than the
other provinces."

They will bring up again the injustices of the electoral map
which leaves to the cities bare representation, even if city
dwellers today represent three-quarters of the population. . . .

We don't contest these explanations, poor as they are, nor
deny that they contain part of the truth . . . But we do say at
the same time the semi-urban areas must be given different
political treatment.

These areas are used to a different kind of political contact
and they guard their right to look at problems simply . . . Mr.
Trudeau, according to different reports, remains in the eyes of
Quebecers outside Montreal more an object of infinite curiosity
than a political leader.

Montrealers, in a certain sense, remain insular. Their island
alone suffices. Moreover, they willingly believe that the way
they see things should be applicable everywhere in Québec.

Outside Montréal, the pace slows down. Quebecers are
barely beginning to think in terms of 10-storey buildings when
Montréal is adding to its laurels a world exhibition and National League baseball franchise. . . .

But don't be mistaken. The man who suits Montréal does
not always suit the whole of Québec, and Montrealers aren't
always right.

Pierre Trudeau:
A Modern Man for Canada

THE TORONTO STAR
June 18, 1968
EDITORIAL

Are a majority of Canadians willing to take a chance on Pierre Trudeau?

That is what the Liberal party is asking in this election; that is really the question that will decide the election on June 25.

It is an unsettling experience for many Canadians to be asked to vote for this unusual and enigmatic man, to take a chance on the future rather than cling to the past. But, judging from the crowds that flock to see and hear Mr. Trudeau, it is exhilarating as well.

The Prime Minister did not formally come into the Liberal party and the House of Commons until 1965. His period as minister of justice was really too short for anyone to assess clearly his qualities as a practical politician much less as a leader.

And his decision to call an election immediately after being elected leader of the Liberal party made it impossible for the party to produce a detailed election program. The program the Liberals do have to offer has been put together literally on the run.

Yet what has emerged in the campaign is a man so compelling that what might have been decisive issues in a normal election battle—economic growth, national unity, foreign policy—have almost been submerged in the love-hate turmoil that surrounds him.

In this last week of the campaign, however, it is possible to make some assessments of Mr. Trudeau's political thinking and the kind of government he would lead.

Apart from any other political virtues, the Prime Minister's

clearcut stand on the paramount issue of English-French relations entitles him, in The Star's judgment, to the support of the
Canadian people.

Mr. Trudeau is determined there shall be only "one Canada" with equality for all provinces and special status for none.
But he is firm, as well, in the belief that French-speaking
Canadians should have the right to use their own language
everywhere in the country where their numbers warrant it.

This is a clear, precise policy on a matter of fundamental
importance to the future of Canada, a policy which in our view
is preferable to the fuzzy doubletalk of the Conservatives and
NDP.

In areas of economic and social reform, Mr. Trudeau has
been more coldly realistic than many reform-minded Liberals
would like. He has been branded as a "Socialist" by some of
his critics, but it may well be that he will prove to be too
conservative.

We have reservations, for example, about his cautious attitude toward the Carter commission report on tax reform and
toward the Watkins report which suggests ways in which we
can derive more benefits at less cost from American investment
in this country.

But he is prepared to go ahead with medicare, while the
Conservatives would delay it. And he supports the concept of a
Canada Development Corporation although he offers no details as to how the government-sponsored investment fund
would operate.

Mr. Trudeau's bill dealing with divorce, abortion and homosexuality is in the great liberal tradition of freedom of the
individual and he has shown courage in defending it against all
comers.

In this campaign, the Prime Minister has broken with tradition by making few promises, certainly none where heavy expenditures, and consequently increased taxation, may be involved.

For many politicians, a campaign without promises would be
unthinkable. But Mr. Trudeau has spoken to the voters with
unusual candor, dealing with them as intelligent men and
women, and has thus raised the quality of political debate in
this country.

We find ourselves attracted to Mr. Trudeau because he is a
thoughtful, articulate man, probably one of the most brilliant,
joyous intellectuals that have ever appeared in Ottawa. His
cool, logical mind—along with his obvious charm and wit—
would make any Canadian proud to have him speak for Canada at home or abroad.

Above all, Mr. Trudeau is a contemporary man; alive to the
challenge of what Canada can become; prepared and committed to its future as one, united country.

These are the qualities, this is the man, The Star believes
Canadians should be willing to take a chance on as the next
prime minister.

The Man for the Future

THE GLOBE AND MAIL, *Toronto*
June 20, 1968
EDITORIAL

It is improbable that there is a single person in Canada who
really dislikes Conservative Leader Robert Stanfield. He is the
embodiment of rectitude, conservatism and caution. It is possible to have great confidence in him as an individual. It is
possible, too, to have confidence in a number of the men who
are running on his ticket—men like Davie Fulton, Duff Roblin
and Dalton Camp.

Where Mr. Stanfield has failed is in creating the conviction
that his followers form a team and that he could provide that
team with dynamic leadership. Divisions are to be expected in
both the old-line parties, with their stretch of views from far
left through centre to far right. But it is usual—at least in this
country—for them to present during election campaigns a disciplined pose, not a false pose but one that reflects the consensus
of the party.

With the Conservatives this has simply not been the case.
Some of their best volleys have been reserved for each other,
and their fury that the Liberals observed this has only con-

firmed that the divisions do exist. The Conservative campaign
has lacked zest, focus and, strangely, organized purpose.

It has been different with the Liberals. True, the spotlight
has been upon Prime Minister Pierre Trudeau. But in almost
all his appearances—as in Toronto yesterday—Mr. Trudeau has
been at pains to show that he speaks for a group, and not a
group drawn only from the old establishment but one with a
considerable infusion of bright young people.

The argument most frequently made against him is that he is
unknown, that we have no long-term record of Mr. Trudeau as
an administrator, that we can't be certain how he will react in
any given situation.

But perhaps it is one of the facts of life in the Sixties that
Canada no longer needs the great certainties that are largely
born of fear; Canada is willing to adventure. It may be that
what Canadians see in Mr. Trudeau is this new side of themselves, a readiness to gamble on the unknown, to move into
areas not explored before. . . .

Former Prime Minister Lester Pearson knows Mr. Trudeau
well, and in the brief spate of campaigning he allowed himself
this week he was generous to his successor. Mr. Trudeau, he
said, is exciting, energetic, dynamic, but he is also "a man of
good, cool judgment and I feel happy leaving the country and
the Government of Canada in his hands . . . I think of him as a
very wise, mature, intelligent patriot. He has been loyal to the
language, the culture and the traditions of Quebec but he has
put above all of that his loyalty to Canada. Everything's going
to be all right and I can sit back and enjoy my retirement."

Then he added, "This man is a truly outstanding person. He
is a man for all seasons but especially a man for the season of
tomorrow."

That, we think, is what Canadians have intuitively grasped
about Mr. Trudeau.

THE OTTAWA JOURNAL
June 21, 1968
EDITORIAL

Trudeau is a vivid and strong character, with much personal
enchantment.

But, remembering we are choosing a Prime Minister, he is basically an unknown man with unknown policies. His Gallic shrug says "we'll see" in a way which, though momentarily attractive, leaves an elector little to vote for or against. He can be disarming as temptation but he doesn't arm us!

Is the country in a mood of careless rapture (or despair) wherein it wants to cast off its troubles and put in a man with orders just to live dangerously and hope for the best?

Trudeau seems a bit of a "loner." In these crucial times, should we gamble on a man whose well-stocked mind may be brilliant and courage great—but whose skill at teamwork is unknown?

A sturdier and more careful journey into the future would be led by Robert Stanfield. He will not lunge for acclaim, he will not let himself be deluded that the time has come for a kind of dictatorship of conviction and personality.

It is something to have been Prime Minister of a province for twelve and a half years and to have resigned that office to the obvious regret of his province. When Stanfield became Conservative leader in 1948 there were but seven Tories in the legislature. By 1956 he won the election with 24 in 1960 he had 27, in 1963 he had 39 and by 1967 he had 40 out of 46. The old province of Nova Scotia is a canny judge of a man's ability to govern sensibly.

Electing a Government and Prime Minister calls for sterner stuff than putting two dollars on a long-shot or granting an Oscar for best performance in a shopping centre. Even the stout cry of "full speed ahead and damn the torpedoes" will not do if one is choosing a nation's policies and parliament.

Pierre Trudeau would be a good man in Opposition but in these times it is Stanfield we would rather have in the seat of final responsibility.

Why I'm So Uneasy . . .

SOUTHAM NEWS SERVICES
June 21, 1968
CHARLES LYNCH

In the topsy-turvy world of political analysis, there is a place for the deliberate fence-sitter, and the more emotional things become, the greater the premium on detached observation.

I readily confess that in the case of Pierre Elliott Trudeau, detachment is difficult—just as it was, for a different set of reasons, with Lester Pearson.

My own criticisms of Mr. Pearson were expressed more in sorrow than in anger against a background of long and deep admiration. Criticisms of Mr. Trudeau may be no more than a reaction to the Hallelujah Chorus about him and a raspy feeling that the Man from Montreal needs critics more than he needs admirers and fawning disciples. . . .

Those of us who are nearly half a hundred years old have wondered if our generation would ever come into its own in Canadian politics. Mr. Trudeau is a member of that generation, with a flair for beckoning the young rather than following the old.

We have lamented dull-wittedness in our politicians, and Mr. Trudeau is anything but dull-witted.

We have deplored cliches, and bush-leaguery, and plays on words, and evasiveness, and officialese, and pompousness in high places.

Flashes of the best in John Diefenbaker, and Lester Pearson, and Tommy Douglas, and the Vaniers, and Jean Drapeau, and the Dalton Camp of 1966 and the Robert Stanfield of 1967, have given us a taste for more.

Along comes Pierre Elliott Trudeau, scoring on every point, and the obvious course, taken by so many, would be to throw the old hat in the air, breathe a prayer of thanks for the workings of a benign providence, and follow Pierre to glory.

Looking back on my stuff in 1958, I find that's what I did, along with just about everybody else, in relation to John Diefenbaker. In 1960, I did almost the same with John F. Kennedy.

Neither man worked out quite as I expected.

Leaders, it seems, never do.

Being human, they have quirks and flaws in judgment that come as a surprise that shock and shake their followers.

Having observed Nikita Khrushchev and Chairman Mao, one becomes jaded with the cult of personality.

If I were asked to invent a politician who would come closest to Canada's needs and desires in 1968, he would come awfully close to Pierre Elliott Trudeau.

Maybe that's why I'm so uneasy about him.

The Rights of Man

THE MONTREAL STAR
June 22, 1968
EDITORIAL

Today's issue of The Montreal Star carries our last comments of the federal election campaign. The voting is on Tuesday. We do not publish on the Monday. Here then is our final word. We are for Trudeau.

Whether we are for the traditional Liberal party, we are not so sure. Had Winters or Hellyer been elected as Pearson's successor last April, the chances are at least even that we would have supported Stanfield in this campaign, for Stanfield, of all the Conservative leaders of the last how many years, is the man who seemed to us most clearly to present a good, an intelligent, a moderate and worthy conservative point of view.

But Trudeau is something different. If he wins on Tuesday, we do not know, any more than anyone else does, what his performance will be. He has conducted a campaign unlike any other in the history of federal elections. He has made no specific pledges, but he has made one overwhelming promise — that he will take a new look at everything from the point of view of a man who is aware of 1968 and of the future.

He regards "a hundred years of injustice" as a theme empty of purpose. He seeks a century of promise: forward, not back. He has given the Canadian people a sense of participation, of belonging to something, which no other public man has done in living memory.

We hazard the guess that he has been able to do this because he believes so deeply in the rights of man, in the worth of the individual. In so doing he has removed or at least weakened the curse of faceless anonymity which is bred by the big, modern city. You do not hear Trudeau talk about the great "collectivities" of modern society. He hates them.

Each man, each woman, he believes to be a person of individual rights with hopes and aspirations different in varying degree from everyone else. Thus he restores to each of us a sense of individual worth. We are no longer insignificant members of a mob, all running in the same direction because our leaders tell us to.

This, we imagine, is his secret. When he talked in Toronto of the ancient city states and their citizens this was his message to us, more urgent and much more important than it was to the Athens of the golden age. He would like to see us create our own golden age—1968 model. He does not tell us what we should do or what he will do. He asks us to be ourselves, to make ourselves worthy of what, within ourselves, we feel we can do, each man, each woman separately.

He is not going to do it for us. He wants us to do it ourselves, to release us from servility to mass machines created by others, from the dominance of self-appointed élites who think they know better than we do what is good for us.

This is the essence of the Trudeau doctrine. This is the heart of his "One Canada" theme. The common ground he wants us to find is common ground based on the rights of man which found their first modern expression in the French Revolution before it was subverted and destroyed by centralizers and tyrants. This is why we would like to see him have his chance, to see him try to develop his "Just Society" or at least a society more just than we have had.

Canadians Hear the Truth ... from a Bilingual Patriot

THE SUN, *Vancouver*
June 24, 1968
EDITORIAL

Canada has never had another national election quite like this one and almost certainly never will again. Who would have thought that this staid democracy could be galvanized by a

smilingly enigmatic intellectual with a pared-down program
illuminated by bleak words of mostly unpalatable truth?

His unspoken slogan could have been the street phrase: "I
kid you not." No temporizing, no sliding away, no circumlocu-
tions. This is pretty shocking stuff, not to be told what you
want to hear.

The budget? He'd balance it.

More social services? You can't afford them.

Housing? You're better off than most places so don't expect
any favoritism.

Regional disparity? He'd tax you for others' benefit.

Depressed shipbuilding? Your own fault and subsidies aren't
the answer.

Seaway workers' wage demands? The offer you've got is fair
and reasonable.

Economic and social injustices? He'll fix them but no faster
than possible.

Wheat prices? You grow the stuff to be sold at the best
prices we can get.

New taxes? Not if he can help it.

In his own phrase, Prime Minister Pierre Trudeau doesn't
think the people want to be conned. If they do, by inference,
they'll have to vote for someone else. This is a new kind of
politics with a vengeance. . . .

This is a bold man and a tough one, and Canada has not seen
his like. Who will say that these are not the very qualities
demanded by the times, when the next prime minister will be
charged with the survival of the nation and the economic
security and advancement of its people?

If Mr. Trudeau has deliberately stressed these facets of his
nature it is probably because he senses that Canadians are in
the mood for strong government. So he says that he is a
pragmatist with the daring to do what must be done.

But he is much more than that. So far, in his brief career as
minister of justice, Canadians have had only quick glimpses
into the range of his mind and the depths of his character.
They have seen enough to know, however, that he has compassion for human frailty and a commitment to personal liberty as
instanced by his sponsorship of criminal code amendments and

a bill of rights. Most of all, perhaps, he is a patriot whose fluency in both of Canada's main languages has given him a better insight than most citizens into the enduring worth of the bicultural community of Canada.

With all of this goes a mentality which seems uniquely equipped to adapt to the tides of change now sweeping world society. Millions of Canadians, but especially the young, have perceived this flexibility in him and responded to it intuitively. He reminds them of the late Senator Robert Kennedy's quotation:

"Some men see things as they are and say 'why?' I dream things that never were and say 'why not'?"

When the voters as a whole come to weigh Mr. Trudeau's attributes for leadership in the privacy of the polling booths tomorrow, they too may say "Why not?"

When the final results were counted on June 26, Canada's six-year experience with minority government had decisively ended. The new House of Commons standings were: Liberals 155, Conservatives 72, NDP 22, Social Credit 14, Other 1. Under Pierre Trudeau the Liberals had captured 45 percent of the vote, compared to a humbling 31 percent for the Conservatives.

The Liberal majority which would begin the Trudeau decade was an expression of the belief that intelligence and style could transcend the insoluble problems of the past. With the afterglow of Expo and the initial excitement of the Trudeau victory still being felt, Canada entered her second century of nationhood on a psychological high unprecedented in her history.

The People Choose

THE CAPE BRETON POST, *Sydney*
June 26, 1968
EDITORIAL

Although at the moment of writing many results are still to arrive it is not too early to congratulate Prime Minister Tru-

deau and the Liberal Party for the mandate that they have
received from the Canadian people. Also to be congratulated
are Mr. Stanfield and the other opposition leaders who have
fought a good campaign. The election must have caused a
number of surprises to both the uninitiated and the experts.
The defeat of Duff Roblin, the Stanfieldmania of the Atlantic
provinces, the weight of vote for the NDP in the prairies and
of the Creditistes in Quebec—does Real Caouette lose something in translation?

The Liberal party will have a majority government, the lack
of which they have so long bewailed. Will the nation's business
now proceed with the utmost expedition? But the real crisis of
Canadian politics has not yet been resolved. The regional im-
balance stands out starkly. Neither party can be truly called a
national party and the strength of the parties still stands with
the affluent centre. Opposed to them and expressing more than
just local support for Mr. Stanfield are the Atlantic provinces.

If Mr. Trudeau is to lead the whole nation he must recognize
that the disparaties in the voting trend are an indication of
economic disparaties that exist within the nation. They are now
his duty to solve.

LE SOLEIL, Québec
June 26, 1968
EDITORIAL

In Quebec one cannot avoid interpreting the Liberal victory as
an indication that the Union Nationale has lost much of its
momentum ... and we see again that Quebec is not one but
two provinces; one which is Montreal and voted en bloc for
the Liberals, and the other of which Quebec City is sort of a
capital and extends over the entire eastern province excluding
the Gaspe area.

LA PRESSE, *Montréal*
June 26, 1968
EDITORIAL

From one coast to the other—except for Newfoundland which thumbed its nose at the Liberal party—it was the victory of Pierre Elliott Trudeau ... The Liberal party waged a passionate, exciting battle: fascination for the leader was the motor in this conquest of power. What is essential now is to use this victory for the common good and to initiate an era of uninterrupted progress, of stability in harmony.

THE RECORD, *Sherbrooke*
June 26, 1968
EDITORIAL

The conservative French-Canadians in the Eastern Townships have repudiated another prime minister, this time a Liberal one. And again, the protest has polarized around Creditiste candidates who capitalized on the distrust and distaste Mr. Trudeau's policies on abortion and homosexuality aroused in many rural and small-town French-Canadians in this part of the country.

Canada Votes Confidence in Trudeau

THE GAZETTE, *Montréal*
June 26, 1968
EDITORIAL

Prime Minister Trudeau has succeeded in winning the prize that has eluded all contenders through the last three general elections: he has won a clear majority over all his opponents. The long era of minority government has been brought to an end.

It may be said that such an achievement is all the more remarkable for a man who has had so brief a career in public life, and who called the general election before his performance as leader could be demonstrated. But what might have been a source of weakness has become in fact his greatest strength.

Being new, and having been involved so little in the frustrations and disappointments of Canada's political past, he has been able to offer the fresh hope. He had given no hostages to political fortune.

The customary method of the opposing parties in a general election has been to attack the record of the government that is going to the voters to ask for re-election. The record of the Pearson administration has been actively attacked in this campaign, and it has been open to attack on many fronts. But Mr. Trudeau has had a part in that record so brief and so limited that he has remained practically immune from the failings of his own party.

What is far more, he has been able to draw to himself the country's hopes for national unity. These hopes have become concentrated in him, in an almost mystical sense. What he has virtually promised is that national unity can be achieved by and through himself.

At a time when the country has been beset by doubts and misgivings, and weary with the slow and groping processes of negotiation, Mr. Trudeau has offered a united Canada, not only by hope and by dream, but almost by an act of will.

The emotional attraction of such an appeal, spoken across the country with resourcefulness, insistence and courage, has evoked a profound response from the uneasy and the worried. Everyone may now hope that what has been promised may now be brought to pass, that this appeal to unity will inspire the united spirit, that the power will be used with wisdom.

Against this appeal, Mr. Stanfield failed to make headway. Part of his failure may have come from the fact that he conducted his campaign with a greater consciousness of the practical problems of working out national unity. His emphasis on the need for reconciliation inevitably gave the impression that the difficulties were many, that nothing but long and patient negotiation could hope to reach an understanding.

Such an approach brought little relief for those who wished to be confronted not with slow and intricate procedures but with a sense of national uplift and confidence. In fact, Mr.

Stanfield's approach, slow and cautious and painstaking failed
to make much impression either on English-speaking Canada
or on French-speaking Canada.

His astonishingly firm hold on the Atlantic region came
from his own position as a Nova Scotian and from his long
and effective record as a maritime premier. He not only swept
the maritimes but even made deep inroads into the very heart
of Smallwood's territory.

Once beyond the Atlantic region, however, the failure of his
campaign became apparent. His position was eroded in
Quebec. The doubts in that province about Mr. Trudeau and
the Liberal regime found their expression in a resurgence of
the Créditistes. In Ontario the Progressive Conservatives retreated, and then saw the decline of their nearly complete
ascendancy in the west.

Prime Minister Trudeau has been given a clear mandate to
face tremendous problems. And perhaps no other Prime Minister, except in wartime, has had to face problems so many, so
urgent, or so complex. In addition to the central problem of
unity, there is the strike in the Seaway, and the threatened
strikes in the railways and in the Post Office. There is the need
to settle these disputes without launching another wave of
inflation.

There is the need to come to grips with inflation generally, a
problem still feverish and uncured. There is the need to control
the government's spending, to raise the country's lagging prod-
uctivity, to ease the shortage of housing, to improve the condition of the country's depressed areas, to take action against
encroaching pollution of air and water.

All these problems, and many more, have been sitting on the
doorstep, waiting for the campaign to end. The Prime Minister,
with his resounding vote of confidence, now has the opportunity and responsibility of dealing with them all. Considering
the seriousness of these problems, and the urgency of their
solution, he will deserve full support for all constructive policies. Such support Mr. Stanfield, with his respect for Parliament, can be counted on to give.

Mr. Trudeau should have no hindrance placed in his way. It
is far later than anyone likes to think. The government must
have every chance to succeed.

The Implicit Promise

THE PETERBOROUGH EXAMINER
June 28, 1968
EDITORIAL

Canada turned what may be the most important corner of its young life yesterday. It tossed tradition into the trash-can and took off in a new direction. Rudely almost, the nation's voters decided they wanted no part of Robert Stanfield's adequacy and thoughtful sobriety, but preferred instead to follow a virtual stranger—Pierre Elliott Trudeau—to wherever he would lead them. The mandate that had so long eluded Lester Pearson the Canadian voters gave to Prime Minister Trudeau, a man who refused to promise anything in words but whose bearing suggested, in an almost mystical sense, that this was the man they had so long awaited.

Trudeaumania did what its doubters felt it couldn't do. It translated into votes. . . .

Prime Minister Trudeau's victory, easy as it may finally have seemed, was a major political accomplishment. Twelve months ago he had scarcely been heard of. When Mr. Pearson announced his resignation, only a scattered few would have given the justice minister a chance to succeed him. . . .

Mr. Stanfield proved himself to be a good Maritimes politician—which is to say a man quite foreign to the tastes of Toronto and Winnipeg and Vancouver, and the new kind of Canadian that was coming of voting age in what was once rural Ontario. At a time when Canadians were full of Expo and wanted to take risks, he warned of not taking risks. He misunderstood the mood, misread our 1968 temperament.

Perhaps because he was an English-Canadian and Pierre Trudeau was not, Mr. Stanfield fumbled the constitutional issue. The west was lost to the Tories in large part because Mr. Trudeau emerged as the man strong and wise enough to keep the country together. The election was lost for the Conservatives when Robert Stanfield elected to force an issue on which he could not win.

Mr. Stanfield lost the election, but Mr. Trudeau very definitely won it. He came under severe criticism for his habit of avoiding specifics and falling back on a vague but refreshingly honest approach to our problems. And this apparently was what Canadians wanted. Not formulae or swift solutions; not promises of subsidy or sudden charity; but a man who recognized the problems for what they were and seemed to feel that *we*—not some government agency—were capable of solving them. . . .

The Prime Minister

THE TELEGRAM, *Toronto*
June 26, 1968
EDITORIAL

A substantial majority of Canadians has confirmed Pierre Elliott Trudeau in the office of Prime Minister and for the first time since 1958 has elected a government with an overall majority and a strong, national mandate.

While the great base of the Prime Minister's strength lies in Ontario and Quebec, only in Prince Edward Island have the Liberals been shut out. The Maritime provinces predictably held strongly for Robert Stanfield.

But across the rest of the nation Mr. Trudeau swept his party to important gains and from sections of western Canada will come Liberal representation for the first time in a decade.

In his statement to the Canadian people late last night the Prime Minister was modest and gracious in victory, and it was apparent the responsibilities of his high office are already clearly apparent to him.

Although Mr. Trudeau was meticulous last night in sharing credit for his victory with his colleagues and with Liberal organizers, the triumph was largely his alone. He owes no political debts. He faces no promises demanding fulfilment. The response from the voters was largely generated by faith in his ability to lead and grapple with the problems facing the nation.

A clear-cut choice was offered yesterday between the Prime Minister and Mr. Stanfield, and no doubt was left in the decision. The first-rate record of Mr. Stanfield's public service, his undoubted integrity, his careful listing of the issues and his precise commitments as to what he would do if elected, counted for little against the belief of the Canadian people that Pierre Elliott Trudeau was the man needed by the nation now. Not tomorrow, after further experience in Parliament, but right now.

There are testing times ahead for the Prime Minister and for the nation. He will need time to bring about the changes he undoubtedly intends for Canada. But Mr. Trudeau has earned the right to govern and the right for time and understanding while he works toward his objectives.

Canadians should give him that time and understanding. The campaign is over and differences should be forgotten.

Now it is the duty of all to put the country first and all other considerations a distant second.

The Election

THE CALGARY HERALD
June 26, 1968
EDITORIAL

One of the great gains for the nation in yesterday's election was the return of majority government to Ottawa.

Canada thus seems assured of four years of stability on the federal scene, a gratifying contrast to the unstable situation which has existed with minority administrations since 1962.

To Prime Minister Trudeau must go most of the credit for the Liberal party's victory. His brand of leadership, strangely new to the Canadian scene, but undoubtedly attuned to a time of dramatic technological and social change, brought a new vitality to sagging Liberal fortunes. It must be added that Liberal party organizers throughout the country responded to the opportunities which Mr. Trudeau's leadership offered and ran a vigorous campaign, notable for its lack of mistakes. . . .

Mr. Stanfield made a grave error at the outset of his campaign when he took on Mr. Marcel Faribault as his Quebec lieutenant in an attempt to win the French-Canadian province

over to the Conservative side. This inept act failed in its purpose and lost Mr. Stanfield a greal deal of support. It raised
party divisions, with Mr. Diefenbaker and Mr. Camp making
clear their disapproval of any seeming tie-in with Quebec proponents of two-nations and special-status policies.

The Conservative party badly mismanaged its campaign. It
was dull and uninspired compared to that staged by the Liberals.

One of the noteworthy things about the election as far as
Alberta is concerned was the great gain in popular strength
made by the Liberals in this province. Part of this undoubtedly
is due to the attractiveness of the Trudeau personality. Part
may be attributed to Mr. Stanfield's failure to respond to the
overtures of Premier Manning's social conservative philosophy
and to conservative Social Credit leanings.

Today, all Canadians will wish Prime Minister Trudeau well.
His opportunities are immense, and so is the challenge he
faces. It is now not a matter of personality but of achievement.
The coming weeks and months are sure to be most interesting
ones.

In the words of the old song, "We don't know where we're
going but we're on our way."

One Nation, Indivisible

THE SUN, *Vancouver*
June 26, 1968
EDITORIAL

In the first year of its second century Canada voted yesterday
to continue to grow as one nation indivisible, free of prejudice
and stronger in inter-racial harmony than ever before.

It rose to the tough but inspired leadership of a French-
Canadian patriot at a time of crisis which he best understood
and was most competent to solve. History may say that, without him, the victory for national unity could not have been
won. With him, the prospect of amicable settlement of ancient
grievances and misunderstandings between the two founding

races is brighter now than anxious Canadians had dared to hope. By boldly opposing the forces of disruption, Prime Minister Pierre Trudeau now bids fair to end them and to become the new father of a rededicated Confederation.

The most heartening aspect of the outcome is Quebec's repudiation of separatism in any of its forms or gradations. French-speaking Canadians said overwhelmingly that they are against the *deux nations* theory, against the whole doctrine of special status, and entirely opposed to the breakaway fringe elements. Even the surprising re-emergence of the Creditistes in major strength reflects the disgruntlement of rural areas with their economic lot rather than an outpouring of Quebec nationalism, for Mr. Caouette, for all his financial eccentricities, is a staunch one-nation man.

Into a New Era

THE VICTORIA TIMES
June 26, 1968
EDITORIAL

Yesterday's Liberal victory was much more than the reinstatement of the government with a solid majority of seats in Parliament. It marked in a most tangible way the emergence of this country from the old to the new, the acceptance by the nation of a new role in this final third of the twentieth century. It proved, excitingly and surprisingly, that Canadians could renounce their traditional image of caution, restraint and reserve, and launch out on an unprecedented political gamble. Canada has crossed a psychical watershed.

All this was done on the inspiration of one man. Pierre Elliott Trudeau caught the imagination of Canadians as it has rarely been caught before....

What now lies ahead may be one of Canada's most dramatic periods. Mr. Trudeau's party is in full command of parliament, and Mr. Trudeau is in full command of his party. That will be as stern a test of Mr. Trudeau as it will be of his program.

Canada has gambled on the result. We have broken out of the flatlands of the past and now move ahead to the promise of the unexplored but rising ground ahead.

A Vote for One Canada

THE TIMES, *London*
June 27, 1968
EDITORIAL

Mr. Pierre Elliot Trudeau has brilliantly kept faith with his party. The Liberals made him leader last April in the hope that he would give them the new impetus that would merit victory. He has not only won; he has also given Canada what most Canadians, have longed for—an end to minority governments. This is a remarkable achievement for a man who has emerged from political obscurity so recently. His qualities, however, were seen by Mr. Lester Pearson as those needed in a leader able to carry Canada safely through its crisis of unity and nationhood.

There is no question that this is Mr. Trudeau's mandate. By his discharge of it he will be judged in Canadian history. Throughout the campaign he has made it plain that he stands for a single nation made up of two cultures and two languages stretching from the Atlantic to the Pacific. He has not hedged, and at an eve of poll meeting in Montreal he overcame an angry mob of separatists because he was still saying it without compromise. His opponent. Mr. Stanfield, was prepared to be more equivocal on a special status for Quebec. The results show clearly that English-speaking Canada has voted for a French-Canadian who is coolly ready to have it out with Quebec. Ontario, where the big businessmen had predictable fears when faced with a man who has never concealed a leftist political apprenticeship, evidently felt he must be given a chance. The Liberals picked up at least ten more seats in that province. Still more impressive are the Liberal gains in all three prairie provinces, and British Columbia. Only on his own ground—the Maritimes—was Mr. Stanfield able to hold his own.

Most important for the future, however, is the response of Quebec to a new French-Canadian leader—or, perhaps it would be more accurate to say, to an emerging French-Canadian junta, for Mr. Trudeau is backed by a handful of remarkably able Quebeckers who have moved in on the federal scene. Their united efforts have comfortably held the Liberal position in Quebec. The Conservatives, in fact, lost seats to the Creditistes, who are, however, nationalist "ultras" in the rural and religious sense, rather that secessionists. Mr. Trudeau can now look the provincial Premier, Mr. Johnson, straight in the eye in the duel that is to come. Mr. Johnson can feel none too happy at his own prospects in the provincial elections. He has been out-generalled by his countryman.

Those who know Mr. Trudeau by his writings may see him as a remarkable combination of ruthless French logic and British jurisprudence. It could be a combination to find new solutions based on old truths for Canada. But Mr. Trudeau is also a North American, and knows that economics are half the battle in Quebec. He is in a unique position of authority now to insist that Canada solves its own problem in its own way.

The Promises Mr. Trudeau Coaxed from Canadians

THE VICTORIA TIMES
June 29, 1968
STAN McDOWELL

More eloquent than all the post-election analyses of the meaning of Pierre Trudeau's victory for the future of Canadian unity is one simple statistical fact: The Prime Minister's most concentrated support came from his home province. In Quebec, and only in Quebec, did he win more than 50 per cent of the popular vote. Mr. Trudeau's mandate from Quebec is the mandate he won from the rest of Canada. In this case— Quebec is a province like the others, only more so.

Multiple, confused and sometimes self-contradictory as the motivations of individual voters may be, the mandate that the

Prime Minister is entitled to claim from this election is clear and straightforward.

It was the constant message of that strange series of sermons, happenings, love-ins and beatitudes that was the Trudeau campaign: the building, for the first time in the country's history, of a single, workable, Canadian consensus.

The fundamental strategic error of Mr. Trudeau's opponents, both Conservative and NDP, was in misreading him as a man of confrontation. The error could easily have been avoided if they had gone through his writings with an eye for understanding, rather than ammunition.

Having made this mistake they left Mr. Trudeau alone without competition on the only ground where it was possible to rally a consensus congenial to east and west, French-speaking and English-speaking, rich and poor, even, to a surprising degree, undoctrinaire progressives and undoctrinaire small c conservatives.

On the crucial French-English question both Conservatives and NDP, neither of which has any broad roots in French Canada, worked on the assumption that there could not be one Canadian consensus, there would have to be two, linked by a kind of agreement to disagree.

Their view is half-justified by history. Beginning with the hanging of Louis Riel and continuing with the conscription crises of two world wars, periods of intense and shared emotion in this country have rallied Canadians into two camps, not one, and the two camps have confronted one another across the linguistic frontier.

But the same facts of history suggest that a 'policy of agreeing to disagree,' which may be livable in periods of calm, and is easier and less demanding of generosity and understanding, becomes explosive under stress and has become suicidal now that an independent Quebec is a genuine possibility.

The confrontations during the Trudeau campaign were around the borders of the consensus. Their purpose was to protect it, not to split it.

The most spectacular of them, and the one that got all the attention, was the confrontation with the handful of politicians and, especially civil servants in Quebec City who were attempting to behave as if Quebec were an independent country.

But the consensus in favour of "one nation with two official languages" had to be defended from more directions than one.

Regularly, while campaigning in English-speaking parts of Canada, Mr. Trudeau had to confront members of his own party who told him, "don't speak French here; the people aren't ready for it." Regularly he went ahead and spoke French and just as regularly the people applauded.

The applause that Mr. Trudeau won for the French language in Calgary was a basic plank in his platform in Quebec, as the applause that he won for "one nation" in Quebec was a basic plank for his platform in Calgary. . . .

Other political leaders before Mr. Trudeau have won power on the strength of the country's longing for a common Canadianism. But unlike at least one who managed for a short time to weld all Canada's regional chauvinisms into one big, coast-to-coast chauvinism, Mr. Trudeau made his campaign an effort to exorcise the local demons that have made every region of Canada feel like an "orphan", resentful of all the others.

This meant that, as he said at Fort Langley, B.C., "we must all be coassurers one of another."

Things like that have been said before. But Pierre Trudeau specified what the insurance should cover, the basic essentials for a consensus necessary to make the country workable.

The language of a third of the population must be at home and respected everywhere. Deprived regions, groups and individuals must receive from the more prosperous, "not as charity but as justice," the help they need to get on their own competitive feet. But those who can compete should compete and not look to the taxpayers for a free ride in terms of protective tariffs, subsidies or transfer payments. . . .

Much as it was a Canadian mandate Mr. Trudeau sought, his campaign was not against Quebec. To assume that it was was to forget that, until they decide otherwise, Quebeckers are still Canadians.

It was a mandate to build the basic Canadian consensus the country has never had before, a consensus in which, for the first time, French Canadians could feel they belonged.

And no matter how complex the voting motivations of voters in Quebec as in the other provinces, no matter whether by conscious approval or by the default of the other parties, it was the people of Quebec who most strongly endorsed Mr. Trudeau's appeal at the polls.

It is also the people of Quebec who have risked the most. Consciously or not they have in great measure staked the future of their culture in North America on Mr. Trudeau's ability to carry out his mandate by holding the Canadian people to the promises he charmed them into making one another during his campaign.

SATURDAY NIGHT
August, 1968
KENNETH MCNAUGHT

... The word for the new politics is "style". Like many recent trends in Canadian politics, the concept of style as a definitive factor in public life stems from the era of John F. Kennedy. It is, of course, an extremely dangerous trend. For, when you come right down to it, style means a leader's ability to persuade a majority of electors that the issues are not nearly as important as the manner in which they are approached. As Kennedy used to say: the problems of today are not the same *kind* of problems that used to create great passionate divisions of opinion and which led, often, to differences of ideology. Today, he argued, we are all pretty much agreed on the direction we should follow and on the basic assumptions of our democratic society. Thus our problems are really problems of management and attitude rather than of ideology or social purpose.

The politics of style, thus conceived, leads directly to the politics of leadership and even of faith. Such politics minimizes the importance of platforms, issues and rank-and-file candidates, and places all stress upon the managerial skill and general panache of a leader. Nothing could be more perilous in a democracy, however often democracies hanker after such solutions.

This is not to argue that M. Pierre Elliott Trudeau consciously set out to obliterate the issues in a cloudburst of style. He tried very hard to keep a real issue—the matter of the constitution—front and centre. Nevertheless, the momentum of trends previously begun was given tremendous new force by the electrical charges of his own personality. Moreover, on all matters save the constitution, he does appear to agree pretty much with the late President Kennedy (not to mention some old standard-bearers in the Liberal party) that the problems of our present society call for good management rather than different directions.

Because of the potential dangers inherent in any drift towards a leadership-oriented politics of consensus it is probable that the most important result of the campaign and election was the survival of the NDP and the Créditiste surge in Quebec. The importance of our decision to maintain a substantial "third party" on the federal level has several aspects.

The vote for the Créditiste and NDP confirms a trend in Canadian political life that began at least as long ago as 1921. That is the healthy suspicion that the two old parties are not really very different from each other and that they thus offer little real choice other than to support the establishment. Frank Underhill used to say, when he was helping establish the CCF back in the 1930's, that a two-party system only works well when there are more than two parties. By now, however, it should be apparent that our system is not just a two-party arrangement with a third party in the wings. It is, in fact, a multi-party system. Barring a great crisis it is unlikely that the system will produce in the near future majorities for any government comparable to those garnered by St. Laurent or Diefenbaker....

Trudeau: The Nehru of North America

THE DAILY TIMES, *Lagos, Nigeria*
December 14, 1968

The Canadian fascination with Prime Minister Pierre Elliott Trudeau is likely to be repeated in many parts of the world.

In its weariness with the cast of characters offered in the

presidential elections, even the American Press began to look longingly to the North.

Everyone, it seems, is looking for youth, charm and intelligence. Pierre Trudeau has youth enough to sustain his superbly managed swinging image; and he has remarkable charm and a proved intelligence.

It is difficult to think of parallels for the man. The name of John Kennedy has been widely used but the analogy is superficial.

They both make an appeal to youth and cultivate the intelligent, and both are the sons of millionaires.

But Trudeau has none of the professional (and ruthless) political background of the Kennedys.

He has developed his own convictions about the kind of country Canada ought to be and politics has been the obvious way to try them out.

It remains to be seen just how much intelligence he will attract into the business of governing Canada; but to the extent that he cultivates the clever it is because he has a brilliant mind himself; Kennedy collected intelligence because he knew he needed it to win and to govern. . . .

A closer parallel is perhaps Nehru. The gentle authority, the reaching out after the best of liberal idealism, the philosophical cast of mind, the modest bearing covering a supreme self-confidence (which has been saved so far by a strong inner life from becoming arrogance); these are the striking elements in the man.

Like Nehru, he has radiated something to an entire people of great diversity.

Yet it is not done with oratory or with moments of passion. His set speeches are, on the whole, rather dull. The key is always minor and he generates affection and respect rather than excitement.

What is different from Nehru is the wit which is effortless and continuous: and (like his whole bearing) thoroughly French.

Superb in English with an individual speech rhythm which just might be an accent; almost (they say) as masterful in French as the General himself; determined to make Canada one bilingual country.

It is not hard to see why he has won so much so easily. The style was the man and the style is hard to match anywhere.

What of the substance? Where will Trudeau take this vast wealthy country with its lonely geography and rising population? What does he really care about?

It is important to an understanding of the man that he is a French Canadian and that he belongs to a sceptical intellectual tradition with much of the style of English radicalism. . . .

He starts with the same absence of basic commitment to the outside world as the Spanish Americans or the great majority of the inhabitants of the United States. (In this respect, it is worth noting that he did not serve in the Second World War, something which would have been remarkable in an English Canadian of his background.)

He is particularly uninvolved in Europe for which he feels the admiration of a civilized man of French and English culture: but this is combined with the sort of political detachment which Americans felt until they were overwhelmed by the realities of European politics.

He has suggested that the Canadian commitment to NATO should be reviewed.

The excitement over Trudeau may pass as quickly as it has grown. Television can break, through boredom, what it builds up in fascination.

The sense of being more intelligent than those around him may degenerate into an attempt to decide everything.

He may prove to be a poor administrator or he may come to prefer flatterers. He remains in many respects an unknown quantity, not least to himself.

But the Canadian public, which is not noted for gambling, has decided to chance it. As the Commonwealth and the world get to know the man, they will undoubtedly see why.

CHAPTER 2

THE HOPE
ON THE HILL
1968-70

FEDERAL - PROVINCIAL FLIGHT NUMBER SIX, NOW BOARDING

Sept. 15, 1970.

No man could have fulfilled all the expectations raised by the popular and press enthusiasm that greeted Pierre Elliott Trudeau's first months in office, but Mr. Trudeau made a good attempt at it. To the momentum of his dazzling election victory, the Prime Minister quickly added several additional political advantages: a lively intellect, a newsworthy private life, and an apparent willingness to consider new approaches to old questions. Dams were breaking as Mr. Trudeau, to the delight of his supporters and much of the nation's press, began to move where other statesmen feared to tread: casually mentioning that diplomatic relations with communist China seemed a sensible idea, instituting a review of Canada's NATO commitment in Europe, speaking out firmly against racism in South Africa, and swiftly introducing the Official Languages Act. This last event was greeted with great hope in Québec, and accepted more calmly but still positively by the press in English Canada as confirmation that at last Canada had a Prime Minister who understood what Québec really wanted.

Time to Think

SOUTHAM NEWS SERVICES
July 6, 1968
CHARLES LYNCH

Perhaps the most remarkable thing about Prime Minister Pierre Elliott Trudeau's new cabinet is his concept that ministers should have more time for politics.

Or, as he puts it, to think about things.

Thinking ministers, comprising a cabinet genuinely at grips with the issues of the day, would be a tremendous breakthrough.

That isn't as comical as it sounds—as anybody can testify who has seen the harassment of ministers whose plates were too full and whose desks were too cluttered while they had to sit long and unproductive hours in the House of Commons.

Under these conditions, ministers who are supposed to be at the centre of things can become amazingly out of touch, not only with the country around them but with one another, and notoriously with matters inside their own departments.

Some of the howlers committed by previous cabinets can be traced to this very factor, and Mr. Trudeau will have earned the gratitudes of his ministers and of the country if his approach bears fruit.

His objective is to have ministers and parliamentary secretaries who are as much at grips with issues as are the senior levels of the Civil Service—ministers who can conceive and defend their policies without needing to be propped up by professional experts and advisers.

This is Mr. Trudeau's justification for expanding his cabinet to 29 members, making it the largest ever and posing the risk it will be unwieldy, or even unworkable.

Mr. Trudeau has set up a system of checks and balances within the cabinet in the form of committees, and also a massive direction agency in the presidency of the Privy Council, to be filled by one of his most trusted ministers, Donald Macdonald.

Instead of chaos, Mr. Trudeau is predicting order and efficiency—and only the future will tell whether or not it can be made to work.

In effect, the prime minister is saying that the ministry had to expand because there is so much more to understand and to cope with in today's society.

He seeks to upgrade the role of politicians inside the government departments, inside the House of Commons and inside the parliamentary committees.

His ideas for the committees are particularly striking, especially when taken together with plans for televising committee sessions.

It is his intention to have parliamentary secretaries on all parliamentary committees to act as spokesmen for the government—as he puts it, "to carry the government line."

These broad changes in the concept of the role of cabinet ministers may be more important than the precise changes in the ministry that he announced Friday night—though these contained no less than 17 surprises out of 29 portfolios.

Principal eyebrow-raisers were the appointments of Jean

Chretien to Indian affairs and northern development, Jean-Luc Pepin to trade and commerce, Jean Marchand to regional development, Jean-Eudes Dube to veterans' affairs, and Don Jamieson to defence production.

Despite Mr. Trudeau's eloquent praise for Mr. Pepin, the conclusion seemed inescapable that the prime minister was determined a Quebec minister should have one of the "old" senior portfolios and, with external affairs and finance not available, he gave trade to Pepin.

Mr. Trudeau spoke glowingly of Mr. Pepin's legal and economic knowledge, his ability at negotiating, and his innate astuteness. He also said that responsibility for the wheat board would remain with trade and hence would be Mr. Pepin's baby.

The switches left only two members of the cabinet in the same seats they held under Lester Pearson a scant three months ago—Paul Hellyer in transport, Leo Cadieux in defence.

With so many of the portfolios changing, it's hard to assess promotions, demotions, or even seniority in terms of the power pecking order.

Obviously, Mr. Trudeau wanted to give the impression that Mr. Macdonald was a powerhouse, though this is the first time he has ever been named to a specific portfolio.

Equally obviously, Jean Marchand has a hot hand in his new field of regional development.

But does Arthur Laing move up or down, from northern affairs to public works?

Is Allan MacEachen smaller at manpower than he was in health and welfare?

Is energy bigger than agriculture for Joe Greene?

Some promotions are easier to spot—John Turner to justice, John Munro to health and welfare, Bud Olson to agriculture, Ron Basford to consumer affairs.

We'll have to see more than window dressing to know whether Eric Kierans really has a plum in communications, or Don Jamieson in supply and services.

Mr. Trudeau makes them sound good.

But then at this stage he makes everything sound good.

Cabinet Needs Regional Voices

THE OTTAWA CITIZEN
July 9, 1968
BEN MALKIN

The arguments in favor of selecting a cabinet solely on the basis of merit are strong. But they must be reconciled with two basic circumstances: Canada's dual culture, and its regional concerns. These are more substantial than a mere attachment to tradition.

Prime Minister Trudeau has attempted the reconciliation. There are eight French-speakers in the cabinet—seven from Quebec, and one from New Brunswick. Every province is represented with the exception of Prince Edward Island.

Fortunately, Mr. Trudeau can have his cake and eat it. With good men available from every part of the country, his cabinet can represent the nation's talents as well as its regions.

But if he had to select between regionalism and intellect, he would likely have chosen regionalism, even if this meant appointing one or two men of few gifts.

No prime minister has been able to escape this choice, and as far ahead as we can see, no prime minister can.

The factor of cultural duality is an obvious consideration.

At the February constitutional conference, Mr. Trudeau emphasized that the French-speaking Quebec members in Ottawa were as much the representatives of the French community as the legislature in Quebec City. A strong Quebec voice in Parliament—and, by inference, in the cabinet—was needed both to promote national harmony, and to protect the rights of French-Canadians.

Regionalism is an equally clear consideration. Differences between the country's economic and geographic areas can most fairly be resolved if each has at least one representative in the cabinet. And these differences are very real.

The Maritimes and Western Canada favor lower tariffs, while industrial Ontario and Quebec don't. Maritimes fishermen want higher prices, paid through subsidies if necessary, but Montreal and Toronto consumers don't. Eastern farmers want lower prices for the feed they import from the West, while Western farmers would prefer to do the feeding themselves. . . .

Because of this fundamental condition of Canadian life, a small, policy-making inner cabinet is unlikely. All the regions would have to have a voice in policy-making.

The new committee system, however, will probably be workable. Routine matters can be decided in committee, without the full cabinet being bothered with them very much.

Policy can also be proposed through the committees. But each cabinet minister will have a chance to study and criticize proposals before final decisions are reached.

Thus, if a cabinet committee decides it would be a good idea to build an oil pipeline from Alberta to Montreal, with restrictions placed on cheap, imported oil to the Montreal refineries, cabinet ministers from this region could tell the committee not to be silly.

The committees will be able to come up with splendid ideas; the multitude of brains in the cabinet guarantees that. Regionalism is there to shoot them down.

Mr. Trudeau Is Right

THE SPECTATOR, *Hamilton*
August 19, 1968
EDITORIAL

A number of veteran members of Ottawa's Parliamentary Press Gallery are making no secret of the fact that they are disenchanted with Prime Minister Trudeau for insisting that all members of the Liberal cabinet adhere to a secrecy policy. Some of them have gone so far as to claim that Mr. Trudeau has placed a wall between the government (meaning the cabinet) and the electorate.

The disgruntled newsmen are mistaken. Mr. Trudeau is right in insisting that his ministers remain silent on important issues that come before them in cabinet. He is on firm ground. It makes for better government in the long run if responsible ministers can talk freely in cabinet without having to worry about "political practicalities."

The point is that the cabinet must have a free hand to formulate government policy without the public being privy to everything they say off the cuff behind closed doors. In the Pearson and Diefenbaker years, some ministers evidently felt quite free to "leak" cabinet secrets. It got so that a few important ministers were afraid to speak their minds in cabinet.

Mr. Trudeau wants his ministers to speak their minds in cabinet. He likes controversy and free-wheeling discussion. He knows that innovators and other original thinkers often are self-conscious if they can't operate in an environment free from prying eyes and ears of newshawks.

It is nonsense to even suggest that Mr. Trudeau has placed a wall between himself and the country. He has done no such thing. He holds regular and lengthy news conferences and welcomes all relevant questions. No prime minister in our history has been more available to the press. He obviously and rightly considers himself his government's chief spokesman, especially when Parliament is not in session.

What transpires behind cabinet doors is the cabinet's business. Government policy and programs must always eventually come before the Commons and at that time they become public knowledge. There is no need for policies-in-embryo to become public knowledge.

Our system makes it quite clear that when the government is ready to go ahead on a matter it must present its case to the Commons and be prepared to defend it. There is nothing which says that the public must know before Parliament does. If newsmen can get the news to the public first, all the more power to them, but they shouldn't expect the government to cooperate.

The Hope on the Hill

LA PRESSE, *Montréal*
September 12, 1968
EDITORIAL BY RENAUDE LAPOINTE

"We ask only one thing of Pierre Trudeau as he sets off: Hold firm the Canada that we have built together so that our children's children may also live here happily."

That is the message addressed to the Prime Minister upon the opening of the new session by the Toronto Telegram, a notably Conservative newspaper. Mr. Trudeau, the editorial reminds us, has surrounded himself in the cabinet and the civil service with men who wrote and fought beside him in the past to modernize Québec.

Today, these men hold the reins of power in Ottawa and once again face the "impossible, finding solutions for constitutional, linguistic and social problems, solutions which must be found if Canada is to survive as a nation.

"With the first authentically French Canadian Prime Minister in our history," the editorial continues, "our brothers from Québec will finally possess the federal power they have so long desired. The pressures upon them will be greater than on former governments, which they themselves criticized and which failed in the monumental task of creating a stable, permanent nation because they never succeeded in dealing with French Canada as an equal." Such is the substance of our Toronto colleague's reflection. They are worthy of being communicated to the population of Québec on this day when a new government, with a majority for the first time in eleven years, sets itself to work with the faith, élan and vigor of neophytes and, let us not fear admitting it, under the anxious scrutiny of the entire Canadian population, which also has the clear impression of entering a new era.

It is a young and dynamic government which really assumes office today. Let us be consistent with ourselves and with our choice of June 25 and offer it our confidence. Canada was born of an act of faith. A second act of faith may give us, we hope, a new Canada.

Mr. Trudeau's Debut

THE TIMES, *London*
September 14, 1968
EDITORIAL

The first taste of Mr. Trudeau's style as Prime Minister is shown in the omission from the speech from the throne yesterday of any reference to the Queen or the Commonwealth. It must reflect his own conviction that in his defence of the unity of Canada, he cannot afford to irritate the French Canadians by forms and titles which they regard as foreign or outdated. Many English-speaking Canadians will be shocked, but others will see it as part of their new French Canadian leader's tactics for outmanoeuvring separatism in Quebec, balancing his insistence that the new Official Languages Bill shall open the entire country to the minority and its language. If he succeeds, Canadians will probably think that taking the Queen for granted in the person of the Governor-General was worth while.

No doubt the significance of omitting any reference to the Commonwealth from the speech will emerge when the Prime Ministers' conference next January approaches. Mr. Trudeau's concern to withdraw Canada from involvements overseas while she has not solved her central problem at home permeates the speech. The review of Canada's foreign commitments has evidently been affected by the Czechoslovak crisis, on which hitherto Mr. Trudeau has remained reticent. It upsets any ideas of bringing Canada's air and ground forces back from Germany.

Mr. Trudeau is probably girding himself for his inevitable confrontation with General de Gaulle. He means to insist on respect for Ottawa. He sharply criticized the behaviour of a French official in stirring up French Canadian grievances in Manitoba a few days ago. The next skirmish may well arise over the ceremonial with which Mr. Johnson, the premier of Quebec, is received in Paris next month.

Towards a Truly Bilingual Canada

LE DEVOIR, *Montrèal*
October 21, 1968
EDITORIAL BY VINCENT PRINCE

The Trudeau project [on official languages] is at once realistic and firm. It is realistic in that it demands nothing impossible and firm in that it includes mechanisms for implementation of the reform to be implemented. The civil servants who will be required to have a knowledge of both languages will not be refused entry to or promotion within the Civil Service for the mere fact of not being bilingual. They will however have to commit themselves to becoming bilingual. The government will provide them with the means for learning a second language. Moreover, bilingualism will not be required where it is not truly essential.

A federal civil servant in a centre which is 95 percent English-speaking will not have to learn French, except in cases where this centre is within a bilingual district. (On the subject of bilingual districts, the intention of the federal government is to define them in consultation with the provinces. This will perhaps bring the provinces to act more quickly on the recommendations of the Laurendeau-Dunton report. On the other hand, if these consultations cannot take place or are inconclusive, the federal government will proceed alone.)

Since this will be a law, the courts will see to its application. If the rights it confers are not respected, the possibility of court action will be more effective than the process of grievances with which we had to be contented in the past. The creation within the law of the position of ombudsman of official languages demonstrates the government's intention to have the law work. There will be a watchdog to alert public opinion to instances of bad faith, at whatever level they may occur. The time of pious intentions is behind us. Deep-reaching reforms will occur in the face of all resistance.

We had said earlier that Mr. Trudeau has picked a ripe fruit. We do not, by this, wish to diminish the importance of his gesture. On the contrary, we believe he should be warmly congratulated for this initiative. Mr. Trudeau has also moved with much celerity. We should be thankful.

Nation-Building

THE OTTAWA JOURNAL
October 21, 1968
EDITORIAL

As Parliament begins consideration of the official languages bill it is highly desirable that everyone keeps in mind what the bill means. It is stated in the second paragraph of the bill: "The English and French languages are the official languages of Canada for all purposes of the Parliament and Government of Canada, and possess and enjoy equality of status and equal rights and privileges as to their use in all the institutions of the Parliament and Government of Canada."

This is a principle that surely had not been significantly opposed for some time now, and such opposition as there was to it was not worthy of the country it is designed to keep united.

The bill, once enacted, will be a general guideline, the carrying out of whose details will require understanding, imagination and good common sense. If it is to win those attitudes from the people of Canada it is essential that Parliament's discussion of it be conducted in the same atmosphere.

As Canadians march along the road of co-operation and team effort we must avoid allowing each step forward to seem to be another crucial hurdle of conscience that must be magnified into fearful dimensions. A policy of equal status and equal rights and privileges is a challenge not to stubbornness but nation-building.

By October of 1968 two blemishes had appeared on the Prime Minister's glowing public visage: one created by himself and the other by Claude Ryan. The first was Mr. Trudeau's flippant "Where's Biafra?" comment. The millionaire P.M.'s insensitive reaction to the plight of a country convulsed by civil war and beset by massive starvation startled and upset many. Then, the editor of the highly respected and influential Montreal daily Le Devoir, *Claude Ryan, wrote a series of articles criticizing the Prime Minister's "rigid" and centralist approach to federal-provincial relations. However, at this early point Mr. Ryan's voice was a lonely one that was soon buried by the mounds of favorable year-end press reviews Mr. Trudeau would receive. All in all, for Canada's new prime minister, 1968 was still a very good year.*

Between Opprobrium and Contagion

LA PRESSE, *Montréal*
October 31, 1968
EDITORIAL BY GUY CORMIER

Even the most fervent and faithful admirers of Prime Minister Trudeau withhold their praise when their idol talks of Biafra.

The government gives the impression that it seeks, above all, to avoid a cruel dilemma. If Canada demonstrates the least bit of sympathy towards the secessionist Biafrans it risks encouraging indirectly separatism in Québec. Within this hypothesis, it would be answerable to some Québécois who would say: "Good Lord! You encourage autonomism abroad while defending the federalist doctrine in Canada."

If, on the other hand, he openly reveals his preference for the cause of the Nigerian federalists, he is likely to attract some of the opprobrium aimed at the perpetrators of this "genocide."

But why should Canada concern itself with this distant occurence? In truth, the extent of suffering in Biafra has been made clear to all since the Pope, in July, and President Johnson, some time later, launched appeals for mercy.

Nigeria, like Canada, is part of the Commonwealth. Both countries prefer a rigid federalism. In Halifax, the Prime Minister admitted he was no more in favor of independence for the Ibos of Biafra than he was for the people of Québec. This was an inelegant and imprudent way of abandoning all reserve. Would it not be wiser for Ottawa to exert strong pressures upon its friends (most of all Great Britain) so that they will increase their efforts to serve the cause of peace in Africa?

Short of Shouldering Arms

THE GLOBE AND MAIL, *Toronto*
October 28, 1968
EDITORIAL

In the long and passionate debate about what should or should not be done to relieve the agony of the Ibo people, good many intemperate things have been said. The charge of genocide has been flung in circumstances where there has been little or no reason to believe that such an extreme is intended or would be countenanced by the Nigerian Government.

The claim has also been made despite widespread evidence of slaughter and starvation of women and children that what is happening in Biafra is purely an internal matter—none of the business of the white world, which has problems enough of its own begging for solutions.

The causes of the Biafran uprising are so complex and the results of the fighting are so tragic that extremism is probably inevitable in any discussion of that faraway war. Still, it must come as a shock to most Canadians to hear the most extreme arguments of all those heard on either side of the issue coming from their own Prime Minister. The position taken by Prime Minister Pierre Trudeau and his Government (after hesitating to acknowledge that what was going on in Nigeria was any concern of ours) is that Canada should try to aid the victims of fighting on either side but that we should do nothing that Nigerians or other Africans could possibly regard as an effort to support or put down tribal revolt against the government of an emerging nation.

"Remember Katanga," the Prime Minister said at the week-end, invoking the unhappy memory of Canada' share of the United Nations' frustration in trying to stem the blood-letting in the Congo.

Mr. Trudeau's stand is not indefensible. What cannot be justified by any yardstick are the arguments he has used to support his case and contradict his critics. Even the impertinence of youthful pickets in Halifax Friday night cannot be regarded as an excuse for the monstrous analogy Mr. Trudeau drew between Biafran defenders of the villages beyond Umuahia and German invaders of Russia in the Second World War. The Germans had been surrounded at Stalingrad, he said, asking: "Should we have gone in and said we will help the poor Nazis who are starving?"

The question is as contemptible as Mr. Trudeau's assertion that the "pious" people who feel we are not doing enough on the Biafrans' behalf are actually telling Canada to become involved in a civil war between Africans.

Pious Innocent Naive. Call them what you will. There are many Canadians (not all of them Conservatives, New Democrats, or professional do-gooders) who believe that there is a good distance this country can go, short of shouldering arms.

● Canada, as a senior partner in the Commonwealth, should bring pressure on the British Government to halt the sale of arms and supplies to Lagos. (Mr. Trudeau's answer to this is: "Sure, sure, sure. I'll tell Harold Wilson what the Canadian socialists told him: that he shouldn't ship arms. He told them to go jump in the lake." Mr. Trudeau surely doesn't believe that the Government of Canada has no more influence in the United Kingdom than a few members of an opposition party. If he does, we are indeed in a bad way in this Commonwealth of ours.)

● Canada should send a senior representative to Lagos to make sure there will be no more of the obstructionism that for two weeks prevented shipment of aid to Biafra, in clear contravention of a commitment from Dr. Okoi Arikpo, Nigerian commissioner for foreign affairs. (Mr. Trudeau acknowledged in the Commons Friday that he had that commitment, "but apparently the people on the spot are not able to operate in that direction.")

● Canada should give its support to the growing group of African states which contends that the Nigerian war should be debated by the human rights committee at the United Nations. (Mr. Trudeau says: "We do not believe that we should intervene, as one African leader [the representative of Mali] described it . . . in a way which would be determined by the imperialist press or by opportunism." Does the Prime Minister feel that Canada was yielding to the imperialist press or opportunism when it helped drive South Africa from the Commonwealth or argued against apartheid at the United Nations?)

After his recent return from Biafra, Globe and Mail correspondent Charles Taylor wrote that nothing short of the shipment of military supplies is likely to bring real relief to the beleaguered forces of Lt.-Col. Odumegwu Ojukwu. Mr. Taylor may be right, but Canada in conscience cannot turn away from this dreadful struggle until it has tried everything short of

shipping military supplies in an effort to bring the fighting to a
halt and rescue the casualties.

The Lame Policies of a "Just Society"

LE DEVOIR, *Montréal*
October 26, 1968.
EDITORIAL BY PIERGIORGIO MAZZOCCHI

As in the fable, the ass betrays himself by his actions despite
the lion skin he wears to disguise himself before society. We
have only seen the first measures of the new Liberal government but they have clearly demonstrated that the avant-garde
ideas which Mr. Trudeau used during the election campaign
were only powder cleverly thrown into the eyes of the electorate to impress and confound it. It would have been easy for
any politician to speak as Mr. Trudeau did of a "just society":
they might have done it with less elegance and panache but the
result would have been the same.

   The betterment of a society is not brought about with words,
no matter how well spoken, but through actions. The economic
policy of the new government, as revealed so far, foresees no
progress and we can even say that it represents a significant
step backwards in social development. Only two interpretations
of this phenomenon seem possible. Either Mr. Trudeau has
chosen collaborators who have not understood his idea of a
"just society" or he himself does not believe in this idea.

The Real Face of Neo-Federalism

LE DEVOIR, *Montréal*
October 30, 1968
EDITORIAL BY CLAUDE RYAN

Pierre Elliott Trudeau had the great good fortune to be elected leader of his party and was returned to power without having had to reveal to the Canadian public the true nature of his political thought. He was able to put forth during many months the worst exaggerations: in the climate of euphoria created by the arrival of the "Messiah," no criticism could seriously affect public opinion.

The prodigal son of Canadian politics was accorded full confidence: all reasonable discussion was, one might say, suspended during this period of Mr. Trudeau's apparition.

Four months after the June 25 election, things are returning to their normal dimensions. Realities must now replace words and images. Meanwhile, what we have been able to discern for some time promises nothing good for Québec. The proposals emanating from the government announce, on the contrary, the return to the kind of federalism whereby the federal government believes it has a free hand and thinks it is justified in governing as if Québec were not a reality different from the others.

We have pointed out in the last few days examples of this phenomenon in the social and economic fields.

Mr. Benson, for example, has imposed on Québécois a new "social program" tax. This tax is from two points of view, a flagrant denial of the distinctive reality of Québec. This tax is first of all a reprehensible instrument of blackmail and since in effect it tells Québécois in thinly veiled terms that they will have to pay tax for a program which they might legitimately decide they do not want to participate in. Secondly, this measure is the expression of an unacceptable constitutional theory: for it is the declaration by Ottawa of its intention to collect taxes for programs that fall obviously within the competence of the province.

Mr. Benson's budget provides two other examples of this tendency: These consist of changes in the inheritance tax and in the taxes on co-operative and fraternal life insurance corporations. In the first case, the federal government acts as if there did not exist in the Québec Civil Code precise measures which, if ignored by federal legislators, will create serious injustices for the Québec taxpayer. In the second case, the government starts with the principle that all institutions be they co-operative, fraternal or capitalistic must be treated equally within the tax laws: Through such reasoning, Ottawa risks limiting the development of the only economic sector where French Canadians have begun by their own efforts to cut themselves an impressive place. The government forgets that the principle of unlimited and unfettered competition is only meaningful for competition of nearly equal strength and that in the absence of this condition, unregulated competition can only favor those who have already taken a solid lead in the race. . . .

It is too early to draw definitive lessons from the Trudeau experience. Let us only conclude for the moment that this experience, launched on a shaky foundation, is producing the fruits that certain criticis had feared. Mr. Trudeau is unknowingly preparing the final failure of Mr. Lesage. He is also creating for Mr. Bertrand the pressing obligation to end his silence on the constitution and to address Ottawa in the only language befitting the Premier of Québec: that of proud intransigence and categorical refusal before the entry upon the political scene of sophisms we thought had died in 1960.

Good Engines Run Quietly

THE PROVINCE, *Vancouver*
January 3, 1969
EDITORIAL

Just before he left Ottawa for his Christmas-New Year's vacation, Prime Minister Trudeau offered Canadians a seemingly commonplace idea that nevertheless may be highly significant. It may well reflect his whole philosophy of administration and be a public guide to his methods and his policies.

Good government, said the prime minister, is boring. He went on to explain that successful leadership is essentially the prevention of crises before they develop.

This must come as a great disappointment to those who expected Mr. Trudeau to be a "swinger" who would create endless excitement in the capital. Now the "swinger" tells them not to expect any such thing; he thinks his job is to make government run smoothly and quietly, like an efficient engine that can hardly be heard, even at top speed.

This is a concept that Canadians may have a little difficulty in getting used to. Under Mr. Diefenbaker and Mr. Pearson there was crisis and conflict almost every month. Occasionally there was the spice of scandal. Now the effort will be to head off such fireworks.

No doubt the opposition parties will manfully endeavor to preserve an atmosphere of tension and conflict and do their parliamentary job by trying to point up the government's shortcomings.

In this they deserve public support up to a point—but only up to that point. Beyond it they run the risk of becoming repetitious and boring—the mortal offence in the political guidebook.

The parliamentary brannigan over the government's determination to plan the House's timetable is illustrative. As Michael Barkway comments in The Financial Times of Canada, "What democratic purpose can possibly be served by allowing an opposition to hold up all the work of Parliament in endless repetitive debate? It is as destructive as allowing a score of militant students to hold up all the work of a university with sit-ins."

Keeping government in even tempo is not easy. There is always the temptation to rise to a demagogue's bait and say and do intemperate things that may make news but not good government.

Mr. Trudeau says he hopes to make news in another way by quietly and lucidly explaining to Canadians what his government plans to do and why. This is his idea of participatory democracy, not giving the country ringside seats at a weekly parliamentary brawl.

There are some who no doubt will nod wisely and say that Mr. Trudeau's way is nothing more than a quiet way toward dictatorship. If this is so it will become apparent as the months go by and, ultimately, the electors will be able to pass judgment on the new technique.

In the meantime it makes sense and deserves a fair trial. There should be more power and less noise from under the hood at Ottawa.

LA TRIBUNE, *Sherbrooke*
January 14, 1969
EDITORIAL BY ALAIN GUILBERT

Eastern, Townships-area members of both Parliament and the provincial legislature ... appear to believe that 1969 will be a year of reconciliation or the breaking up of Confederation....

These two choices are not new. They have been discussed for several years....

There was much talk of reconciliation, especially during 1968. According to several politicians and a number of citizens Pierre Elliott Trudeau was to be the man who would straighten out everything. In the English-speaking Western provinces he was seen as the man who would "put Quebec in its place" and save Canada.

But the months have gone by and the problem remains as big as ever.

As for Quebec, the one who first proclaimed "equality or independence" is no more. Daniel Johnson died suddenly.... But the death of Daniel Johnson did nothing to still the demands of Quebec....

Everyone is talking about the intransigence of Pierre Elliott Trudeau, who considers Quebec "a province like the others," something the majority of Quebecers do not accept.

Reconciliation in 1969? No ... but no breaking up either. This does not mean that reconciliation or disintegration will never happen, but certainly not for several years....

However, if the situation continues to deteriorate as it has in the last few years, there will be without doubt a breakup before reconciliation.

The Trudeau Year

THE GAZETTE, *Montréal*
January 2, 1969
EDITORIAL

In Canadian political history, 1968 will be remembered as the year of the Trudeau phenomenon—the phenomenon of a man

who charged from far off stage onto the Canadian political
scene to capture the Liberal Party and win over the country, all
in five hectic months.

It was a political success story with few parallels in Canadian
or any other political history. The June election victory was
compared to John Diefenbaker's bandwagon triumph of 1958,
and John Kennedy's victory, in the United States in 1960. It
had elements of both, but there were also substantial differences.

For one, Mr. Trudeau's victory in June did not come close to
the sweep of 208 seats made by John Diefenbaker in 1958. Nor
was it as close a victory, as painstakingly charted out, as the
Kennedy one in 1960. Yet Mr. Trudeau seemed to be given a
mandate by the Canadian people much broader than that
given to Mr. Diefenbaker and he has raised expectations in this
country even higher than John Kennedy did in the United
States. Once more, six months after the victory, both the man
and his government still enjoy a high rating on the popularity
charts.

Few unpopular things have been done.

The answer is that in most major areas of domestic and
foreign policy, the new government has not had time to consider all its options and choose a course of action. This is
especially true in the foreign policy field. The government has
ordered a full review of the whole foreign policy picture, and
major decisions must await the findings of the report.

On the domestic side, reviews also have been ordered in
many major policy areas, postponing substantial changes. But
the single fact which has limited innovation in the last six
months—and must be considered in any new initiatives—is the
tight financial situation facing the federal government and all
the provincial governments.

Mr. Trudeau's government came to power after five years of
unprecedented prosperity accompanied by unprecedented government spending, but at a time when inflation was gnawing at
the prosperity and spending was getting out of hand. Despite
pledges from leading members of the cabinet that it was fully
mobilized for the fight against inflation, at year end interest
rates took another leap to still higher levels.

The state of government finances may well have wider implications. For example, it could slow progress in another important area of domestic policy—constitutional reform. The rebuff which the provinces received at the hands of Finance Minister Benson at the federal-provincial fiscal talks in mid-December may substantially affect their attitude when the federal government starts the process of constitutional renewal in February.

So, there was doubt accumulating at the end of the year about the federal government's fiscal policy, which could be the first sign that the gloss was wearing off the political bloom.

Then there was a slight hint in one other recent move by the government that the opposition parties, after months of frustrating shadow boxing with the Trudeau phenomenon, may have found an opening. This was the performance and attitude of the government in the recent controversy about rule changes for the House of Commons.

The idea of reforming the rules of the House was not new. The impetus was built up over the last six or seven years. But the Trudeau government carried through the reforms, and it, deservedly, will get the credit for the changes.

However, the attempt by the government to slide through section 16-A giving to a single minister what amounted to a "divine right" of deciding the allotment of time for any business before the House was successfully challenged by the opposition parties, and finally dropped.

But the fact that the government put forward a proposal so obviously hitting at the core of parliamentary power, plus the recent shift system adopted by Cabinet ministers in the House, has raised doubts about the government's intentions toward Parliament itself, and the seeming lack of sensitivity of its leading members to the best traditions—and the essential powers—of Parliament.

These were only hints and they came very late in the year. For the most part, the enthusiasm and excitement, the freshness of vigor, the high expectations and flush of confidence which blossomed across the country in the year of the Trudeau phenomenon, are still very much in evidence as 1969 starts. It was Pierre Elliott Trudeau's year, and future historians, no matter what happens from now on, will have to see it that way.

Pierre Trudeau's trip to attend the Commonwealth Conference in London in January of 1969 was the first chance Canadians had to show off their new prime minister. For the press, the event was seen as a test for a man who still showed more promise than performance.

Mr. Trudeau's pre-departure description of the Commonwealth as an "anachronism" unsuited to the requirements of the modern world, coupled with his casual attitude towards the British monarchy, led some to expect very little from the conference. In any event, the coverage of Mr. Trudeau's night-life overshadowed any assessments of his real contribution.

In retrospect it is clear that the loose amalgam of former colonies grouped about the British Crown was in a state of crisis. Black African members wanted a commitment to armed intervention against White Rhodesia. Trudeau was among those praised by his fellow leaders for defusing the explosive climate. An organization for which he had expressed disdain survived in part because of his mediation. This implication was lost on most reporters and was left for the columnists to ponder.

The front pages of Canadian newspapers continued to carry Trudeau gossip. The press had become accustomed to reporting the Prime Minister's encounters with lovely women. He had been photographed kissing women across the country during and after the election campaign, and, not surprisingly, the habit he had encouraged pursued him. Across London reporters interviewed his dates and followed his progress through the London nightspots. Finally, the P.M. had had enough. He accused the press of invasion of privacy and generally "crummy behavior." Reporters were surprised at the vehemence of his reaction; commentators sensed a tinge of hypocrisy. The Prime Minister, it was felt, had exploited the press' vicarious participation in his social life; such coverage had contributed to the shaping of his public image. Some reporters treated him like their creation: he owed them a good story.

His flare-up in London signaled that, for now, the show was over. It had a sobering effect on press coverage as Trudeau approached the end of his first full year in office. Close scrutiny and critical analysis began to replace gossip in the newspapers of the country.

Defence Review

THE FREE PRESS, *Winnipeg*
January 8, 1969
EDITORIAL

The North Atlantic Treaty is not one of the issues before the Commonwealth prime ministers now meeting in London; but it has been raised by Britain's Prime Minister Harold Wilson and Defence Minister Denis Healey in private talks with Prime Minister Trudeau and External Affairs Minister Mitchell Sharp. The British spokesmen clearly are still disturbed about the highly equivocal statements the Canadian prime minister has been making about NATO and Canada's future role in that organization. Their efforts were directed toward persuading Mr. Trudeau not to weaken the organization by reducing Canada's commitment to it.

Undoubtedly their anxiety stemmed from Mr. Trudeau's most recent remarks about Canadian defence policy, in which he implied that inasmuch as the United States would protect Canada in an emergency, this country did not need to worry about that aspect of defence and might well spend the money it would otherwise use for collective security in some other area. In any event, Mr. Trudeau has not budged from his stand that everything must await the outcome of the review of defence policy now going on and which, at the prime minister's request, has been speeded up.

The results of the review will be awaited with great interest not only by Canadians but by Canada's friends abroad. It is to be hoped, however, that while it is completed with all possible despatch it is sufficiently comprehensive as to leave no unanswered questions. Defence cannot be reviewed solely by itself. The implications of a drastic change in defence policy are such that any change would make itself felt in other vital areas. For example, what would happen if the government in its wisdom should decide that Canada should pull out of NATO, and divert its energies into, say, peace keeping; and Canada's friends and allies, the United States in particular, judged that by doing so this country was not pulling its weight in defence. A lack of co-operation from Canada here almost inevitably would lead to a lack of co-operation by Canada's friends and allies in other fields—in trade and economic matters in particular. This could have far-reaching effects on this country and could totally invalidate or cancel out any potential or hoped-for gains to be made from a new defence policy. Any review of defence must, therefore, go well beyond the immediate problem to consider the over-all effects on this country.

Learning to Understand Trudeau-ese ...

THE PROVINCE, *Vancouver*
January 11, 1969
EDITORIAL

Britons have joined Canadians in the sport of Trudeau-watching, seeking special insights into the sometimes cryptic public statements of the Canadian prime minister. It is becoming clear that Mr. Trudeau is experimenting with something quite new in political communication—an effort to talk with the people, not at them.

In London Mr. Trudeau has been talking about the necessity of paying attention to demonstrators, no matter how small their numbers. He said men like Gandhi and Canada's Louis Riel live on "and they obtain more perhaps by martyrdom, imprisonment or execution than they would by merely standing there."

At a time when demonstrators and "activists" are giving public leaders a headache this seems to give carte blanche to their noisiness and caused the London Standard to comment that Trudeau had delivered "as radical a homily as has ever fallen from the lips of a visiting statesman."

All this overlooked a significant qualification in the PM's statement. It was that he was sympathetic with SINCERE demonstrators. He did not say he was sympathetic to ALL demonstrators, or with those bent purely and simply on agitation for anarchy's sake. Indeed, it is difficult to imagine anyone looking back on the immense human reforms of the last 30 years and not being impressed with the efforts of sincere reformers. So nobody should go away with the impression Mr. Trudeau backs everyone who wants to throw bottles at policemen or imprison university presidents in their own offices.

And yet misunderstanding persists about this and other items in Trudeau-ese. In another talk he was reported as saying "if the social structure is a fraud, it should be torn down," an opinion that does little more than paraphrase St. Matthew's parable about the foolish man who built his house upon the sand and saw it collapse when the first storm came upon it.

One news report declared that Trudeau was ready for radical changes, that he had said "the social structure is a fraud. It should be torn down"—a completely different sentiment.

Obviously Mr. Trudeau's efforts to think out loud and enlist everyone in discussions instead of confronting them with simple and arbitrary outlooks and policies, entails risks. He probably hopes that by paying the public the compliment of assuming it is ready and anxious for more sophisticated dialogue with public leaders he will get an understanding response.

But if he is consistently misinterpreted and misunderstood in his efforts to achieve more meaningful communication and as a result finds himself in political hot water, he will no doubt be forced to retreat into the oversimplified, unassailable stances favored by politicians for the past two hundred years.

That could be a loss for Mr. Trudeau, for the public and for the whole idea of a fuller partnership between leaders and led.

The Wheel Turns

LA PRESSE, *Montréal*
January 14, 1969
EDITORIAL BY GUY CORMIER

After the Throne, the Altar. After a *tête-à-tête* with her Majesty the Queen, an audience at the Vatican. And we are told that the trip to Rome is only a prelude to the nomination of an Ambassador to the Eternal City.

The only curious element in all of this is the coupling of two seemingly disparate aims. While Mr. Trudeau's entourage was revealing that he would take a plane for Rome Thursday, the news from London stated the Prime Minister's firm resolve to recognize Communist China. The sending of ambassadors to the Vatican and Peking is only a part of the creation of a new foreign policy. Must we consider them as trial balloons? Not necessarily. But by announcing in the middle of a Commonwealth Conference in London that the visit of the Prime Minister to the Vatican can no longer be delayed, by flying over Paris on the way to Rome while thinking of Peking, Mr. Trudeau demonstrates a truly original eclecticism.

The Practical Man and Mr. Trudeau

THE MONTREAL STAR
January 14, 1969
EDITORIAL

The views of Fleet street about Mr. Trudeau are of small meaning. It is not in the United Kingdom that Mr. Trudeau must shine; it is in Canada. But here too we profess some disappointment. At intervals since his election, the Prime Minister has rewarded those who supported him by giving evidence that he is not a politican like the others. He did this when the intellectual in him triumphed over the practical man. But of late, and particularly in London, it is the latter who appears to be in charge, as when he told a gathering of Canadian students in the Westminster Theatre that the difference between the intellectual and the politician was that, while the intellectual would opt for the best solution, the politician would settle for second or third best.

We have had and will always have such practical men. In political history Walpoles have always been with us and in more recent times, von Papen in Germany and Laval in France took us to the end of this particular road. We have not lacked them in Canada and some are still close to the seats of power. Few are pretty to look at or inspiring to emulate. Their achievements, when worth recording, have been almost wholly negative.

Reaching for the stars is not now nearly so impractical a target as twenty years ago the practical men would have had us believe. They are today within reach and man has spun around a moon which once only cows jumped over. It is time, we suggest, for politicians as well as more ordinary men to opt for the best and not to settle, as Mr. Trudeau suggests we must, for something more earthbound....

The calm, cool, studied Mr. Trudeau, swaddled in the comfort of an affluent past and a secure future, is not the man who was elected to high office by Canadians. If the country had wanted that man, Mr. Stanfield was available. It was essentially the dreamer of dreams who was chosen, the intellectual for whom the second best was intolerable.

Prisoners of the Elite

THE FREE PRESS, *Winnipeg*
January 15, 1969
SHAUN HERRON

The prime minister said: "My political action, or my theory— insomuch as I can be said to have one—can be expressed very simply: create counterweights." An increasing number of people who were enthusiastic about Mr. Trudeau agree with him that there are moments that call for counterweights.

It is difficult at this point to express qualifications about the prime minister without being falsely accused of a failure of appreciation that must have some dark motive. But the fact is: Mr. Trudeau talks a good deal of meaningless nonsense; he is a practitioner of the ancient art of sleight of tongue. That is very good fun. Unhappily it may say quite serious things about him that could be expensive, in a grave public sense, in time to come, and perhaps quite soon.

One of the least serious examples of his sleight of tongue nonsense came out in London, when he talked about minorities. We should seek dialogue with demonstrators and all mi-

norities should be heard; the old idea of majority rule is not
good enough now.

This sounds sprightly, refreshing, "different," as people keep
telling us, "from the usual run of politicians." But the fact is
that "the old idea of majority rule" has never been good
enough, has not been practised without qualification and its
qualification has always been the condition on which majorities have been able to rule. His statement is a species of
intellectual den-mother pablum.

We should seek dialogue with demonstrators: But he qualified this. Demonstrators must accept the rules of society. John
Diefenbaker says the same. Everybody says the same. There is
nothing refreshing here. The tone of voice does not qualify as a
difference. But it sounds impressive; other politicians take it
for granted; Mr. Trudeau turns it into revelation, exploiting the
childish myth created about him by childish communicators.

All minorities should be heard: The record says very clearly
that in this country they always have been. **Heard**.

What does that mean? The claims, arguments, clamor of
minorities have always modified the actions of majorities; there
are practical limits to this modifying process, otherwise the
state would be fragmented out of existence. The French minority in Canada "will be heard." They will be heard to the point
of modification. But the minority of the minority will be heard
and not heeded—our French-Canadian prime minister will
deny them their separatist demands. Mr. Trudeau has said only
what is familiar and agreed.

But these are merely semantic games the prime minister is
playing. They are part of the Trudeau froth—like John Diefenbaker's righteous rages. He is playing also more serious games
with a deeper import involved in them.

The great debate on parliamentary reform was phony. The
debate itself was unimportant; it didn't enlarge the nation's—
participatory—understanding of the reform issues; it is what it
may have cleared the way for that bothers me: the domination
of governmental decision-making by an alliance of technocrats
and academics. This alliance—misalliance—is far advanced in
the United States in forms long removed from the original
initiatives of F.D.R. with his Brains Trust. It now has its own
mythology, the shape of power, its lines of communication.

It seems that Mr. Trudeau is greatly attracted by it. His favored advisors appear to be men whose chief interests are the technocratic adaptation of business administration to politics. The proper academic relationship to such a development is independent criticism—even in the ivory tower—but not, emphatically not, collaboration. The scholar has his function and it can only be served well if he preserves his independence and is not seduced by the prize that is becoming, for academics, deadlier than the love of women—power; power and the satisfactions of a kind of status almost new to scholars, the status of counsellors to power holders. One need only talk to academics who have been thus seduced to see and taste the corrupting vanity that grows in them like fungus.

I begin to see in Mr. Trudeau an intention to create a computerized processing plant where academics corrupted by power and technocrats interested in the processing of information and methodologies collaborate to replace the vital functions of the elected politician. Mr. Trudeau says he wants to give the running of the country back to Parliament. What I think he means is that he is tempted to take it away from the senior civil servants and place them also under the domination of a technocratic-academic elite of his own choosing whose theories or illusions can now be rammed down Parliament's throat.

What Mr. Trudeau meant by "participatory democracy" it is now impossible to tell. So far the opportunities for "participation" have been opportunities to give money to the Liberal party and to overhear an increasingly stupid and incredibly prolonged yak-yak about foreign policy (which is beginning to make Canada look juvenilely perverse). The fact is that foreign policy is becoming rather like some of Mr. Trudeau's other mouth-music: a kind of public game that might be called "Contemporary Mythologies." . . .

My point is that Mr. Trudeau is the prisoner of the mythologies of the kind of people he trusts, his own elite; and they are the prisoners of their own trend theories; and we are all destined to be the prisoners of the Trudeau elite, unless the politicians, and the technocrats and the academics will end their collaboration and begin to engage in independent, separate and honest social criticism.

Who Sins by Indiscretion, Trudeau or the Press?

LE DEVOIR, *Montréal*
January 15, 1969
PIERRE O'NEIL

More than any other situations which may have arisen in Canada, the trip to London by Pierre Elliott Trudeau has emphasized the problem of the border between his private and public life, of his personal attitude *vis-à-vis* this question and finally, of the behavior of journalists in this respect. The British press, at least a part of it, and the Canadian press, gave broad coverage to the Prime Minister's meeting with a certain Eva Rittinghousen and to the long session with reporters that this young woman devoted to the meeting and her friendly relationship with the Prime Minister.

The story is well known. The day after his arrival in London, Mr. Trudeau had breakfast with the young woman. He was accompanied in this case by one of his political advisors, a plainclothesman from the RCMP and another from Scotland Yard. As a *tête à tête*, we have seen better.

Mr. Trudeau offered only one public indication of his displeasure with the whole affair. He told reporters at a certain moment, that his real friends do not talk about his relationship with them. But later, he also said he was in no way embarrassed by the behavior of Miss Rittinghausen. These two statements illustrate Mr. Trudeau's ambivalent attitude in regard to his private life.

On the one hand, he insists that it be strictly respected and that reporters not pressure him during his holidays and brief trips outside of Ottawa. This was the case for his trips to Florida, Spain and more recently the coast of Yucatan.

But on the other hand, Mr. Trudeau is frequently the first to break his own rule. If, in reply to a question from a journalist, he can make a play on words about his effect on young girls, he does not hesitate to do so. It is often he who reveals to reporters that he was with a charming blonde.

The evening of his problems with Miss Rittinghausen, a

reporter asked him a haphazard question in the course of a press conference: "Who are you going out with tonight?" Answer: "I hope you won't try to find out or you'll ruin all my dates. It's a very lovely girl, and I am sure she won't tell you anything, even if you find out her name."

This kind of statement is not designed to fend off reporters and if Mr. Trudeau really wishes to have his private life respected, it is high time he became a little less talkative and less concerned with demonstrating that young women like his company.

PM's Privacy Fully Respected in Ottawa

SOUTHAM NEWS SERVICES
January 17, 1969
BRUCE PHILLIPS

Ottawa—Prime Minister Trudeau's outburst in London against reporters left the Ottawa press corps in a mixed state of amusement, indignation, but most of all astonishment.

The suggestion that his privacy has been consistently, wilfully and unjustifiably, invaded by the workmen of Canadian journalism struck reporters here as just the type of wild exaggeration against which the prime minister himself has complained.

The case for the defence, if one needs to be put, is simply that he has got his facts all wrong.

Setting aside the London episode and his famous dinner with the beauteous Mrs. Rittinghausen for a moment, the fact is that Trudeau's private life in Ottawa has been scrupulously respected by the press. The argument among pressmen here is not whether he gets too much exposure, or is subjected to undue prying, but whether the press is not failing in its duty by letting so much go by and leaving the man alone so much of the time.

When the official black Cadillac pulls away from Parliament Hill at the close of the working day, conveying Trudeau to whatever the evening holds in store for him, the press puts away its pencils, cameras and microphones.

He is never followed, his house is not watched (as is the White House in Washington and 10 Downing Street in London) and if he is observed about the town in his off hours it is entirely by accident.

When he goes off to the prime ministerial lodge maintained at Harrington Lake in the nearby Gatineau Hills, no one knows who goes with him, or makes any attempt to find out. The same is true of the modest cottage he keeps in the Laurentians.

On his last vacation, to an island in the Caribbean, no one tailed him down, although his whereabouts were known. An earlier holiday, in Fort Lauderdale, was covered by exactly one man, who made a point of keeping out of his way. On both occasions, Trudeau tried to keep his destination secret, but when the locale was discovered, there was no general stampede to follow him.

In this respect, Trudeau is being treated just about the same way his predecessors were treated. For better or for worse, it has been a tradition in Ottawa that the private lives of public men were pretty well left out of the news columns, at least as far as the men themselves would allow it to be overlooked.

Trudeau, despite his oft-proclaimed feelings on the subject, hardly helps himself in his quest for privacy. He appears frequently in public here, at movies, at parties where newsmen are present, on dates. Although the papers have carried brief reports of these excursions, sometimes naming his companions, coverage has not extended beyond these simple facts. Considering the fact he is rich, a bachelor, with a most un-prime ministerial way of doing things, has kissed hundreds of women in public, slid down banisters, engaged in foot races with his fans, the kind of coverage described above strikes newsmen as the least they owe to their duty as recorders of facts of general public interest.

Examine one or two of his complaints in detail: There was the diving exhibition in Stratford during the election campaign, televising of which provoked his ire. The fact is, one of his own aides informed the TV reporter when and where it would take place, and who is to say that such a spectacle (a) is not good news, or (b) did not help him win an election. Or take the complaint that the press won't let him have a quiet holiday by himself: Various news organizations here have made strenuous efforts to work out agreeable arrangements with the prime minister so that his holidays can be spent out of sight and sound of the press but good enough that the press would not be completely in the lurch in the event of some sudden problem arising when, just conceivably, he might want to say something to the Canadian people. Trudeau would have none of this, insisting that his whereabouts be clothed in mystery, challenging every reporter in the capital to find out where he had gone. In the upshot, his whereabouts were discovered, but he was left undistrubed.

That is the situation in Ottawa. Come now to the London experiences of the last few days. Every reporter here knew Trudeau was about to undergo a style of journalistic scrutiny practically unheard of in Canada. The British popular press doesn't give two-bits for anybody's privacy, and it was the British press that pursued Mrs. Rittinghausen to her flat and obtained the interviews to which he took such strong exception. The Canadian reporters, many of whom stifled their own inclination and better judgment in not following up the story, felt they had no choice in the circumstances but to publish what the British papers were saying about the incident.

After that, according to the CBC's Tom Earle in a broadcast from London, Mrs. Rittinghausen was only too anxious to get access to Canadian reporters to correct what she claimed were misquotations in the British papers, and perhaps mollify her indignant escort of two days before, the Canadian prime minister.

This account sets forth the accepted practice in Ottawa among the capital's newsmen, whom Trudeau described as lousy, and ungentlemanly.

As for his other suggestion, that the police should be set to work building files on the private lives of newsmen, the general reaction among the rank and file here is that the spies would be in for some dull reading.

The Education of a Prime Minister

THE GAZETTE, *Montréal*
January 16, 1969
EDITORIAL

Prime Minister Trudeau flies back to Canada tomorrow after two weeks abroad, most of it spent at the Commonwealth conference in London. The first question to be asked is: what did the trip accomplish and what effect is it likely to have on the Prime Minister's, and ultimately, his Government's thinking?

It should be said first that Mr. Trudeau went to London two weeks ago under unusual circumstances. First, it was his first official trip outside the country as prime minister. He was not only a "new boy" at the Commonwealth conference, but he was "new boy" in the larger game of international diplomacy.

Second, the circumstances were unusual because the Canadian Government is still in the process of reviewing its foreign and defence policy. In other words, he went as head of a government uncommitted on any future policy, including a future Canadian posture on the Commonwealth itself. In fact, he went further when he suggested the Commonwealth's days might be numbered. At least, this is the implication of a remark he made that the Commonwealth was "probably an anachronism."

All this, plus the interest stirred abroad in his election last June, guaranteed that he would be a central figure at the conference. He was.

Much is expected of Canadian prime ministers at these meetings, not only because Canada is a senior Commonwealth country after Britain in this association of "equals," but because of Canada's position in the world as a rich, small power; and also because of the disproportionate influence Canada has had on world affairs in the last 25 years.

Mr. Trudeau was obviously aware of all this. He served notice before he left that he would do more listening than talking at the meeting. He was deliberately setting out to take a back seat—to be a student rather than a teacher.

Under the circumstances it was a good, if safe, position to take because if the conference had failed to make headway (the Commonwealth conferences don't decide anything) on the more pressing problems facing its members—Rhodesia and the Nigerian civil war, to name two—then there would be little disappointment. This, of course, is exactly how it turned out.

What, then, could possibly have been learned?

There was much comment about Mr. Trudeau's speech at the end of the conference in which he seemed to commit Canada firmly to the Commonwealth. In fact, he committed the country only to the Commonwealth principle and then he went on to add: "The Commonwealth is an organism, not an institution, and this fact gives promise not only of continued growth and vitality, but of flexibility as well."

This may appear to be an about-face after the declaration he made before he went that the Commonwealth was probably an anachronism. In fact, it leaves the Government free to suggest many changes in the Commonwealth—even including one which Mr. Trudeau has made in the past of expanding it to include French-speaking countries, embracing La Franco-phonie.

What can be gathered from this, then, is that Mr. Trudeau liked the idea of the Commonwealth meeting; the atmosphere which allows free exchange of ideas. This is one firm impression he evidently took away from the meeting.

But another impression which came out clearly from the meetings—and perhaps the most important one—was that there is a great deal of impatience with the length of time it is taking the Government to formulate a new foreign and defence policy with the British becoming especially anxious.

This is nothing new, of course, because other countries, outside the Commonwealth, have been politely prodding the Government for the last few months on its review.

The message is, of course, that Canada cannot simply retreat behind a curtain for 10 months (the time the review has been underway) expecting every other country which deals with us to keep the ball in the air, while the Government decides how the game will be played—even whether it will be played at all!

Mr. Trudeau has said again and again that many options are open to Canada in foreign and defence policy. It is stimulating exercise working through the various options, but as the Commonwealth conference showed, Canada's friends abroad are getting impatient. It could be that when Mr. Trudeau gets back from his trip tomorrow, he will find that Canadians are getting impatient, too.

Trudeau's Role in London

THE FREE PRESS, *Winnipeg*
February 13, 1969
TIM TRAYNOR

London—Here, for the record, are a few final observations on Prime Minister Trudeau and the Commonwealth prime ministers' conference. Now that the dust has had time to settle, it is apparent that everything was grotesquely overblown.

The advance billing was too heroic, the fanfare on arrival too loud, the dalliances overdramatized. Attention was diverted from the prime minister's considerable contribution to the conference, and he made things worse by going overboard in his lecture to the "crummy" press.

The ultimate vindictiveness of his British critics was as inflated as had been their advance expectations—whether relative to his personality or his offering to the conference. Back in Ottawa, the parliamentary opposition worked itself up into a hopelessly exaggerated fit of indignation.

It was a sorry affair, all in all, but there are a few things that should be remembered. Among knowledgeable and impartial observers here there is considerable admiration for Mr. Trudeau's performance at the conference. The fact that he disappointed a segment of the British Establishment is considered less important than that he effectively brought to bear a subtle blend of moderation and provocativeness. Despite the lack of Canadian initiatives, it is by no means clear that the Canadian contribution to the conference compares badly with earlier performances. It is quite probable that there was no occasion for anything more dramatic than what took place.

The prime ministers met in circumstances much different from those obtaining at earlier conferences. Old certainties had collapsed, new sources of disruption had been exposed. The pattern was worldwide, but the Commonwealth was particularly deeply affected by it.

Nigeria was in bloody turmoil, British racial toleration had been corroded, economic crises had weakened defence and trading links. Paradoxically, Commonwealth ties had been eroded by positive developments as well. The old imperial trading preferences had been further reduced by international tariff cuts agreed on in the Kennedy Round negotiations.

The impressive thing about the conference was that the leaders reacted to the new situation sensitively and on the whole constructively. Though they might deplore actions taken by fellow-members, they were mostly ready to recognize the part played in such actions by larger forces only partly controllable by individual governments.

It would have been easy to overstate the damage done to the Commonwealth, but the tendency was rather to try to come to terms with the forces at work.

The departure from precedent cannot be overemphasized. In the past the conferences have concerned themselves with working out a framework for the transformation of the Empire into a grouping of independent states.

Members were sufficiently confident of the framework to use it as a platform for all-out struggles on issues such as Rhodesia. But with the removal of the decolonization rationale, there is no longer a simple focus, and this has perhaps led to a greater appreciation of the limitations of the Commonwealth's power to chart its own course in isolation from broader realities.

At any rate, when the leaders met this time there was a positive revulsion from the past clamor for bold initiatives and instant remedies.

There was, rather, a premium on unpretentiousness, pragmatism and sensitivity to the contemporary world movements to which the Commonwealth must adjust. Distractions aside, Mr. Trudeau's style was well suited to the circumstances. He has been criticized in Canada for seeking to look beyond the problems of the moment, but many of the leaders would have endorsed what he said.

His speeches both inside and out of the conference chamber were not despised for being quizzical and inconclusive, or at least such a reaction was not discernible. As in Canada, he talked about the challenges of diversity and youthful frustration, and he succeeded in conveying a sense of fresh perspective and open-mindedness.

His remarks to protesters outside the conference could easily be written off, but they are liable to stick in the minds of the many who valued his alertness and unorthodoxy.

It may be said that Canada could have taken specific initiatives to develop the Commonwealth infra-structure, but it should be pointed out that several ideas which had been put forward by the secretariat were vetoed by other major member countries. It is not clear that the lack of Canadian initiatives was a blow to the group, as was suggested in Parliament.

But what decisively takes the wind out of the critics' sails is Mr. Trudeau's contribution in avoiding a confrontation over Rhodesia. It deserves closer scrutiny than it has had.

Ottawa residents have learned to live with two recurring and not particularly productive occurrences: the Ottawa winter and federal-provincial constitutional conferences. Agreement on repatriating the constitution or on other significant constitutional issues such as language rights or special status for Québec eluded federal governments before Mr. Trudeau, including the Pearson government. This did not deter Trudeau, however, from making a serious attempt to forge a new constitutional consensus on the sensitive issue of language rights at the federal-provincial conference from February 10-12, 1969.

The stage was set for the Prime Minister's first domestic political confrontation as his intention to press for constitutional guarantees of bilingualism was opposed by the three western premiers before the conference began. They wanted instead to talk about money, and the implication was clear that their part of the country was not interested in Mr. Trudeau's language policy.

Canada's new knight in federal armor set out hopefully to tilt at provincial windmills, and returned with the usual results.

The Constitutional Conference

LE DEVOIR, *Montréal*
February 5, 1969
PIERRE O'NEIL

The events of the last few days and the concern that has arisen about the results of next week's constitutional conference bring us back to a few months ago and the great ambiguity of the results of the June general election.

During that electoral campaign, millions of Canadians came to believe that Pierre Elliott Trudeau would save the country by making life hard for Québec.

People tended to forget that the Prime Minister had made his bilingualism policy an essential element of his party's platform and a condition for solving the crisis in national unity. Some will say that the Prime Minister himself contributed to the decline in emphasis on this part of his campaign, and will accuse him of having preferred to take advantage of the backlash against Québec that was manifested in the West.

The fact is nonetheless that bilingualism was an important part of Liberal policy. It seems that many Canadians forgot this on the way to the polls. They are now becoming aware that they too must pay a price and it is truly a small price, to ensure Canada's survival. Their disillusionment comes a little late. One would have wished it would have occurred earlier. For, as a colleague said yesterday, we would have been spared this sudden fluctuation in the stock market of national values which will, in the short term, compromise next week's constitutional conference and risk compromising the progress that could be made in the months to come.

Language Rights

THE FREE PRESS, *Winnipeg*
February 10, 1969
EDITORIAL

The constitutional conference which opened today in Ottawa

did so under less than auspicious omens. Position tables, made public in advance by the federal and provincial governments, showed a clear-cut diversion of views on some of the most basic questions to be discussed. The rift was particularly deep between Ottawa and the governments of the three Prairie provinces. Not only did the latter question Ottawa's priorities at the meeting but they questioned the validity of the federal government's top item of business—the proposed entrenchment of language rights.

The Prairie premiers have been insistent that before constitutional changes can be made there must be an acceptable settlement of financial matters, so that the provinces will know in advance that they can carry out their constitutional responsibilities. They argue that by insisting on putting language and human rights changes before anything else, Prime Minister Trudeau is putting the cart before the horse, that the meeting would have a greater chance of success if it were preceded by a financial agreement.

Mr. Trudeau has taken the opposite tack. To him, financial matters, though important, are less important than the entrenchment of language and other rights.

"It would be an act of irresponsibility if we assumed, in the face of the steadily mounting evidence to the contrary in our society, that the individual human being needs no protection of his basic rights against the inroads of governments and the bureaucratic institutions which governments spawn. It would be an act of irresponsibility if we accepted the simplistic argument that there is nothing wrong with Canada that a revision of revenue sharing would not correct."

Nobody, of course, claims that a resharing of tax revenue would correct all that is wrong in this country today. Here it seems to be Mr. Trudeau who is employing the simplistic argument. But certainly economic and financial inequalities are responsible for much of the unrest in parts of Canada, Quebec included.

If Mr. Trudeau has his way and presses his language changes, he will run into opposition from provinces calling into question the constitutionality of his proposed official languages bill. This, among other things, calls for courts, in bilingual

districts, to be able to operate in English or French; and for
the civil service in such areas also to conduct itself bilingually.

Oppostion to these changes seems to vary directly with the
distance of the province concerned from Quebec; and also with
the number of French-speaking inhabitants. Thus Ontario,
Quebec's neighbor, of whose population 8 per cent speak
French and English, 1.5 per cent French only, is in favor of the
bill. "The concept of a bilingual Canada must include the
recognition that all citizens should be able to deal in either of
the two official languages with the various levels of government with which they come into contact."

In Alberta, however, where 4.3 per cent speak English and
French, .4 per cent French only, the recommendations are
considered—by the provincial government—"objectionable and
unacceptable." Saskatchewan, with about the same percen-
tages, wants, with Alberta and Manitoba, to have the constitutionality of the bill tested.

Manitoba, where 7.4 per cent speak both languages, .9 per
cent French only, takes a milder approach. The Manitoba
government is not opposed to bilingualism where it is needed
and desirable. It does object to bilingualism being legislated.
"Drastic extension of language privileges by legislation must
fail in its objective and divide rather than unify the nation.
More effective is the extension of those privileges by a process
of gradualism, which is occurring as witnessed by the amend-
ment to the Manitoba Public Schools Act permitting the use of
the French language as a language of instruction.... Such
process has the advantage of acceptance by the people of all
provinces and a substantially reduced cost of implementation."

Which is very true. And, ideally this approach has much to
commend it. Certainly it is an improvement over the heels-
digging-in approach of the Alberta government. Mr. Trudeau
is seeking to unify the country by legislating language rights.
He could, as Manitoba warns, divide it even further if opposition to his legislation were to take deep root. On the other
hand, many French-speaking people would, with reason, question whether under a process of voluntary gradualism they
would ever have the right to conduct government business in
their mother tongue. They want action now, not at some inde-
finable time in the future. On the bright side it must be noted

that in the past few years there has been a great desire on the part of many English-speaking people to see that French-speaking Canadians achieve their language rights and a sympathy on the part of these people for French Canadian aspirations. The question is whether this desire and sympathy will be diminished and eroded if language rights are forced on Canada by legislation.

Unique Spectator Sport ... and It's All Canadian

SOUTHAM NEWS SERVICES
February 12, 1969
CHARLES LYNCH

Ottawa—It's not clear just what we have been watching here this week, but it seems quite clear what we haven't been watching. We haven't been watching a constitutional conference, or even the beginnings of one. Whatever format may be arrived at for drawing up a new constitution, it's unlikely to resemble a federal-provincial summit conference.

Not that the conferences are a dead loss. Like the Grey Cup, and the Stanley Cup, and the Calgary Stampede, they have become national institutions. Canadian content is 100 per cent. No other country has anything to rival these conferences as a spectator sport. . . .

The wonderful thing about it all is that it doesn't seem to matter much. Nobody, apart from Mr. Trudeau, seems all that anxious to have a new constitution, perhaps because the country seems to run reasonably well without one.

The government's language bill is important, but we don't need a new constitution to get that through Parliament.

The division of taxing and spending powers is important, but that's what federal-provincial conferences are all about. Since federal-provincial conferences are here to stay, they must have something to discuss.

Human rights and fundamental freedoms are important, but

we have them in such abundance it is almost embarrassing, when you look at less fortunate countries.

The truth is that the lack of a new constitution does not weigh heavily upon the Canadian people.

As one Quebecker put it to me: "We are too happy a country. Happy people don't write constitutions." Quebeckers, he assured me, really are very happy, even if they don't laugh as much as they used to.

He added that federal-provincial conferences were really a quest for unhappiness, as witness the determination of most of the premiers to use the conference chamber as a wailing wall. But induced unhappiness is seldom convincing.

To get a constitution out of it, the unhappiness has to be real —in fact, people have to be at one another's throats. That condition is hard to achieve in the second most prosperous and perhaps the most democratically governed land on earth....

The Conference Ends

THE EVENING TELEGRAM, *St. John's*
February 14, 1969
EDITORIAL

Trying to find the thread that binds Canada is like trying to get hold of an eel in a barrel of cod liver oil. Even if you think you have it, it slips away before you can pin it down. For three days the 10 provinces and the federal government endured the blazing heat of many television lamps so that the whole of Canada could see them in action in glorious technicolor. They created real drama as they ran the whole gamut of emotions from tragedy to comedy, anger to impassioned pleading.

At times it was good television, other times it was dull and repetitious and the cliches piled up in mounds as the spotlight moved from one performer to the next. It might have been a good week for television producers but it is doubtful if it is the way to work out the salvation of a country....

Was the three day conference a success? There are probably two million opinions on that but it at least showed that all the participants were still talking to each other as it ended. No one walked out, few decisions of any importance were reached, the important items were referred to committees, and the Quebeckers got in an eleventh hour outburst of intransigence to show they are as toughminded as ever on their own brand of cultural and lingual nationalism. One thing the conference did was to perpetuate itself and to move from an annual show to a quarterly one. Whether the people are going to be able to absorb that amount of participatory democracy is another matter.

Too much haggling in public over the rights of Quebec may add to the anti-French feeling among English-speaking Canadians. And the constant whining complaints of the Atlantic premiers are becoming embarrassing and unnecessary. They remind one of the emaciated cripples who sit in public places in Eastern countries with their begging bowls moaning out their ills and needs. They behave like people lacking in pride, dignity or the courage to challenge the future themselves.

It Was Interesting

THE CALGARY HERALD
February 13, 1969
EDITORIAL

The second constitutional conference in the current series ended yesterday on the expected inconclusive note.

If past experience is any guide, little more about constitutional change will be heard until the next conference comes along, perhaps a year from now.

On the other hand, Mr. Trudeau gives the impression of being a man in a hurry. He may be so determined to provide Canada with a new constitution that he will keep the premiers at it until one is forthcoming much sooner than most people think. He cannot be expected to give up easily his ambition to make Canada a truly bilingual nation.

He was thrown somewhat off course in this respect by so many provincial premiers insisting on conference priority being accorded fiscal and tax issues related to division of constitu-

tional powers between federal and provincial levels of government. But he never let the delegates lose sight of the fact that
linguistic rights stand foremost in his mind as the most urgent
business of the nation.

This week's conference once again, through being fully open
to the public by means of press, television and radio, provided
an opportunity for Canadians to become thoroughly informed
on the major national issues of the day. Another unique opportunity was afforded Canadians to become acquainted with the
leading personalities on the national political stage. Undoubtedly, provincial premiers took advantage of a chance to turn in
the best possible performance for the folks back home. But, at
the same time, they summed up in three days the essence of
varying shades of provincial, regional and sectional thought
across the nation. This represents a highly useful exercise.

Now the problems which were discussed at large will be
placed in the hands of committees of federal and provincial
ministers and top-level civil servants for continuing analysis in
detail. So many fundamental disagreements exist on constitutional changes which might be made that it is difficult to see
what positive results can possibly emerge by the time the next
conference convenes.

One thing seems sure, however, and that is that the nation
will continue on its way quite unhampered by the fact it still
operates under the most flexible, durable and benign of all
national charters, the good old British North America Act.

*The "Quiet Revolution" which had transformed Québec society
through the sixties was coming to maturity in 1969. The power of
the clergy had been broken, institutions transformed, and the
ragged agitation of fringe groups like the Ralliement pour l'Indép-
endance Nationale had given way to the more respectable Parti
Québécois. Even the prospect of separatism was coming of age.*

*There was pride among Quebeckers that the transition from
the despotism of Duplessis to the open society of the sixties had
been accomplished without significant violence. Of course, there
had been the requisite scribbling of revolutionary grafitti, a few*

mail boxes had been destroyed, and Wolfe's monument in Québec, a favorite target in times of upheaval, fell for the fifth time.

But the bomb that exploded in mid-February at the opening of the Montreal Stock Exchange marked a sharp escalation in these tactics. It was, as some of the more perceptive writers saw, a clear warning. The people of Québec, having recently freed themselves from subservience to their own institutions, were beginning to fight for control of federal institutions in their province. Some, including René Lévesque, would fight at the polls. But others who were alienated from the political process would opt increasingly for bombs and other forcible measures. Political violence in Québec and Canada had come of age.

The Endangered City

LE DEVOIR, *Montréal*
February 15, 1969
EDITORIAL BY CLAUDE RYAN

The bomb which exploded at the Montreal stock market Thursday came from an unknown hand. It may be a bomb made and delivered by a team pursuing political objectives. It may have come from a citizen gone mad. It may also be a crime for more sordid reasons. It may seem naive to appeal at this moment to those who have, anonymously, the dubious honour of having captured the headlines of papers across the country. But the act they have committed seems to derive from motives so different from those that govern criminal acts that we feel obligated to appeal, despite any feeling of vindictiveness, to the sense of humanity which they no doubt still feel in order to ask them in all sincerity: "Why have you done this? Why do you consent to plans which must necessarily place many innocent lives in danger?"

One can understand, if not necessarily agree with, the motives which have in different eras inspired numerous revolutionaries. These people, having concluded that the classic pattern of liberal reform leads nowhere, opted at a certain moment, in the name of a greater justice, for the destruction of the established order. And it sometimes happens that history, though it may condemn them and ignore them at the time, will later honour them and raise monuments to them. There exists in the actions of true revolutionaries, a profound love for their people, a pre-eminent concern for the ordinary citizen which induces them to safeguard the lives and security of ordinary people. Guevara, hidden in the mountains of Bolivia, retained a profound respect for the peasants he met along his way, even if he deplored their lack of understanding. It would never have occurred to him to destroy them. One does not find this sense of compassion for the common man in the act of those who caused a bomb to explode in the centre of the stock market before closing time.

The authors of the first bombings committed here were at least concerned with preserving the lives of common people. They attacked objects, visible symbols of a power they wished to destroy. They guarded themselves from any thoughts of destroying persons, particularly innocent ones. For the good of the very people they wish to "liberate" we dare beseech those responsible for the bombings of the past year to return to other methods. They will have seen for themselves, if they still walk the streets of Montréal between crimes, that ordinary citizens, those who have no privileges to defend, strongly reject their methods.

How could they be so blind as to ignore that their actions can only end in disaster for themselves and for the city?

Some will mock this appeal. But it arises from a situation where the editorial writer, rendered powerless like everyone else, must bare his soul in public. In this particular case he wishes to make it clear that even if he is, like everyone else, tempted to become angry, he wants to reach not only the guilty sought by public opinion, but beyond that, the men who remain, despite our differences, his brothers.

The explosion at the stock market has justly aroused a general sentiment of horror and condemnation. One must not forget, however, that this act was aimed at an institution which represents, for thousands of citizens concerned about justice, certain serious inequalities in our kind of society. We must, faced with such acts, act immediately to defend the city. But we must also remember that behind the opulence of a place like the stock market, there hide within the city grave injustices and that it is largely from this reality that emerges the violence that we condemn today.

A City Aroused by Violence

THE GLOBE AND MAIL, *Toronto*
February 17, 1969
EDITORIAL

The stock exchange bombing in Montreal last Thursday was a dramatic and shocking incident in itself. But what makes it even more chilling is that it sustains the pattern of violence with which Montreal has had to contend for several years, and has led people to refer to the "climate of violence" in that city.

The Montrealer's sense of security has been shaken by dynamite explosions on an average of once a week during the past year. During 1968 there were at least 75 killings in the city area —an increase of nearly 50 per cent over the previous year. Huge sums of money were taken in the 2,000 armed holdups of 1968, and there was strong evidence of highly organized underworld activity.

It appears, however, that the stock exchange bombing, with its injury to 27 persons, has had a galvanizing effect on the people of Quebec. Editorial opinions ... are infused with a determination to take vigorous contermeasures against those whose aim seems to be to plunge the province into anarchy.

La Presse bristled at what it called "deplorable apathy in high places," and demanded energetic action before it is too late to ward off "a mortal threat held over the whole population." The Montreal Gazette called upon Premier Jean-Jacques Bertrand to take the lead in the mobilization of the law-enforcement agencies.

The sense of anguish, frustration, and alarm must have deepened at the weekend when news came from Montreal that an unknown assailant had thrown acid in the faces of a father and his son and caused minor burns to the mother. Again, the mind is repelled by the cowardice and brutality of the act. Hard on the heels of this came another horrifying episode in which an accountant, being held hostage in an attempted bank holdup, was shot during a gun battle.

Perhaps now that the public has been thoroughly aroused, the potential for mounting a strong attack on crime is at its greatest. One heartening indication is found in the co-operative activity of three police forces—the Royal Canadian Mounted Police, the Quebec Provincial Police and Montreal Police Department. This, together with the large rewards that have been offered, may give Montreal its best chance of striking back at those who make life miserable for decent citizens.

Bomb Madness

THE CALGARY HERALD
February 15, 1969
EDITORIAL

A sane motive for the bomb explosion in the Montreal Stock Exchange is hard to imagine.

It is shocking to think that people may be exposed to sudden painful death or injury at any time and in any place in Canada's largest city.

That knowledge is bound to have a frightening effect on the people of Montreal and on those who go there for business or other purposes.

Mercifully, no one was killed in the Thursday blast, although twenty-seven people were injured. The slaughter might have been terrible since there were about 350 people in the exchange when the bomb went off.

Rewards now totalling $51,000 offer some hope of eliciting information leading to a solution of the crime. But rewards were posted to no avail last year during which fifty bombs were planted in Montreal. There have been eight bombings already this year.

No apparent pattern exists for the bombings. They may be planted anywhere. If the bombs are placed by separatists or other dissidents, it might be expected that the person or persons responsible would want to declare their cause in some way and thereby demonstrate its power and invincibility. But nothing so rational has occurred.

Most of the bombs have exploded until now in places where damage to life or limb would likely be minimal. The latest explosion in a downtown skyscraper gives rise to fears that the terrorism is being raised to a new and far more dangerous level.

Montreal police have little or nothing to go on. The ingredients for bombs are easy to obtain. The factors for conditioning people capable of using them are all too prevalent in today's society. Irresistible forces for change produce tremendous social pressures. Orderly processes for resolving differences are being destroyed or ignored. Chaotic outbursts can have dangerous repercussions.

Following the inconclusive ending of the federal-provincial conference, Mr. Trudeau turned his attentions south with a visit to his colleague Richard Nixon. Mr. Trudeau has been Canada's most widely travelled Prime Minister (see Appendix A), and has consistently received positive press coverage during his foreign travels, where his intellectual capabilities and social finesse have been a source of general pride back home.

Miracles All Over

SOUTHAM NEWS SERVICES
March 25, 1969
CHARLES LYNCH

Politics makes strange bedfellows, and you have to cast your mind back a bit to see just how strange is the match between Richard Nixon and Pierre Elliott Trudeau.

They are meeting in Washington as equals—or as close to equals as the president of a super-power and the prime minister of a middle power can be.

It is fashionable to refer to the president as the "New Nixon" since he has left the old tooth-and-claw school of politics and assumed the mantle of statesmanship.

It would be equally accurate to refer to the prime minister as the "New Trudeau" since he, too, has been forced by the pressures of office to change his ways and his public attitudes.

As a consequence, the meetings now being held in Washington are taking place on quite different ground than would have been the case had the old Nixon met the old Trudeau.

It was the awful prospect of such a meeting that led some of us to speculate last year, before either the Canadian or the American elections were held, that the worst possible combination would be Trudeau and Nixon.

What we could not foresee was the moderating influence that power would have on the two men.

Earlier in their respective careers, it is doubtful that either would have wanted to meet the other, or that they would have had much to say to one another if they had.

During the years when Nixon was a red-baiting member of the United States Congress, he would have had little use for what Trudeau was doing.

What Trudeau was doing, it will be recalled, was bumming about the world, visiting places like Moscow and Peking, shunning active involvement but acquiring sufficient of a pinko tinge for his credentials to be called into question.

They were called into question by Paul-Emile Cardinal Leger in Montreal, who barred his appointment to the faculty of the University of Montreal.

And, by Trudeau's own statement (although official confirmation is hard to obtain), they were called into question by the U.S. government, which put his name on its border blacklist . . .

The career lines of the two men, having diverged so widely, did not begin to parallel one another until last year when, for vastly different reasons, Nixon and Trudeau emerged as natural candidates for the leadership of their respective countries.

Both looked like rank outsiders—Trudeau because of his lack of practical political experience, and Nixon because he had been around so long he was regarded as a spent force.

Both men won astonishing victories.

Trudeau, the intensely private man, became the object of public adulation because of his fresh approach to Canadian problems.

Nixon, by retreading his public image and running on a platform of moderation in all things, won the presidency because a majority of U.S. voters were fed up with Lyndon Johnson and the Democrats....

(Most Canadians were fed up with Lester Pearson and the Liberals, too, but Trudeau managed to close the door on all that.)

Both emerged as miracle men, and if you had said two years ago that President Richard Nixon would be sitting down with Prime Minister Pierre Elliott Trudeau, you would have been certified bonkers.

And yet, there they are, discussing a wide range of common interests on a basis of mutual respect and understanding....

Mr. Trudeau's Visit

THE WASHINGTON POST
March 25, 1969
EDITORIAL

The chief significance of Prime Minister Pierre Elliott Trudeau's visit to Washington may well be that it has given some Americans a first-hand acquaintance with a dashing new figure in Canadian public life.

In the past, visits across the border have often been notable for an exchange of friendly gestures in public and of gripes in private. But Mr. Trudeau has made a specialty of breaking with tradition. The least that can be said is that his unique style and his unorthodox methods have spurred interest in his country, whether or not he succeeds in solving its formidable problems.

In Ottawa, Mr. Trudeau has demonstrated that he has courage and imagination. There is much evidence too that he understands both of the sharply divided factions in Canada and the underlying dream of the great majority for more effective nationhood. As a French Canadian, he has vehemently resisted the separatist movement in Quebec and sought to save the Canadian federation from the paralysis of excessive provincial autonomy.

We surmise that the manner in which Mr. Trudeau deals with these basic problems will be far more important in the end than the present controversy over the anti-ballistic missile system or any of the other specifics which are said to have been the staples of the Prime Minister's discussion with President Nixon. Canada is demonstrating its independence and vitality by reaching out for new international relations, including diplomatic contacts with Communist China. Yet its stickiest problems remain at home, and these can be resolved only by the Canadians themselves.

It was no minor event, therefore, which brought to the highest office in the land a new figure with a direct appeal to the people. It has not yet been demonstrated that he is the catalyst who can bring to Canada the reforms essential to virile nationhood. But the millions on this side of the border who watch Canadian progress with the interest of friends and neighbors will wish him well in a truly great undertaking.

An Exercise in Bafflement

THE FREE PRESS, *Winnipeg*
March 26, 1969
RICHARD PURSER

Washington—Mr. Trudeau made a good surface impression in Washington. He was a hit with the press club and he got along affably with Mr. Nixon. Good "channels of communication" were opened, as the diplomatic lingo goes.

Now, with that out of the way, it has to be said that he treated American officialdom to the same exercise in bafflement over his approach to foreign policy that has bedevilled the Canadian public for months. Mr. Nixon may have a few more clues to Canada's revised attitudes toward Atlantic and

North American defence than the rest of us have, but even that is painfully uncertain.

Some passages from his speech on Tuesday to the Washington press corps suggest that Americans have some right to wonder just what is going on:

"I hope that we Canadians do not have an exaggerated view of our own importance," he said. "We prefer to think that our place in the world is such that we can occasionally experiment with good ideas without risking a complete upset of the whole international order. We are as pleased as is any country when our views are sought or our assistance requested.

"But we may be excused, I hope, if we fail to take too seriously the suggestion of some of our friends from time to time that our acts or our failure to act this or that way will have profound international consequences or will lead to wide-scale undesirable results."

It would surely not be amiss to take this as a thinly veiled reference to the fears raised over the future of NATO if Canada should withdraw. Especially since one reasonably knowledgeable Canadian involved in the talks here was overheard heatedly attacking the view that NATO would collapse if Canada quit. It would be weakened, he admitted, but it wouldn't collapse. The same person then argued that such a negative line of argument was irrelevant. What was needed if Canada was to stay in NATO were positive arguments as to what it had to gain from doing so.

If this attitude reaches high up, then the horrible truth could be that those very Canadians who are making the big decisions are oblivious to the meaning of the Western defence alliance. . . .

Mr. Trudeau in Washington

THE GAZETTE, *Montréal*
April 3, 1969
EDITORIAL

There has been little criticism but much praise from below the border following Prime Minister Trudeau's visit to Washington last week. This is a measure of the Prime Minister's remarkably successful mission there, for Mr. Trudeau said a lot of things during his visit about issues on which Americans are very touchy and on which Canada disagrees almost completely with the popular U.S. view. . . .

How did Mr. Trudeau manage to handle so many delicate matters in a manner which caused a minimum of friction? The answer lies both in the content of his statements as well as in the style. Mr. Trudeau's responses to questions had been well-studied and well-thought out. They were delivered in the quiet, scholarly manner to which Canadians are now accustomed— but not Americans. Americans found themselves applauding opinions they have violently opposed.

Perhaps the simplest explanation is that Mr. Trudeau was practising the Nixon belief in "lowering our voices" long before the new President proclaimed it. Mr. Trudeau brought a calm approach, sensible, logical and reassuring, to questions which have caused excited, sometimes over-excited debate.

Mr. Trudeau's argument for Canadian policy toward Cuba, for instance, was a firm rejection of Washington policy. In content, it might have been interpreted as a lesson for Americans to learn. The quiet manner in which it was presented made it more a bit of thoughtful advice given to a friend, and only because the friend asked for an opinion. This is, ideally, the way it should be.

Mr. Trudeau's calm approach has been of immense value, not only to Canada, but to the whole continent. By the time he arrived in Washington, the ABM controversy had deeply excited debate in the legislatures of both countries.

Since he refused to make violent statements about it, the debate has become quieter—and more useful. Both countries can thank Mr. Trudeau for putting the matter back into proper perspective.

On this and other subjects he illustrated how valuable Canada's independent views can be to the United States. Mr. Nixon's cordiality proves he appreciates this fully.

Prime Minister Trudeau's first "tour" in Washington was an unqualified success.

Justice Minister Pierre Elliott Trudeau cheers on his supporters just before the fourth and final ballot of the 1968 Liberal leadership convention. *(CP Photo)*

A greeting for Opposition Leader Robert Stanfield before the Christmas recess, December 19, 1969. *(CP Photo)*

Posing with John Lennon and Yoko Ono in December 1969. *(Public Archives Canada—PA110805)*

Left: On the way to present the trophy to the winners of the 1970 Grey Cup Game in Toronto. *(CP Photo)*

Below: Talking to reporters following the release of James Cross in December 1970. *(Public Archives Canada— PA110806)*

The Nixons and the Trudeaus at the National Arts Centre in Ottawa, April 14, 1972. *(CP Photo)*

Dancing with Margaret at the RCMP centennial ball, May 23, 1973. *(CP Photo)*

The Canadian press may be easily pleased with generalist speeches by a prime minister in Washington and photos of P.M. and President shaking hands, but it is less pleased with substantive policy changes that may signal a reassessment of Canada's close military ties with the Western bloc. On April 3, the Prime Minister announced that Canada would be reducing its troop-strength in NATO. Two days later the flak began to fly.

Token Defence

THE CALGARY HERALD
April 5, 1969
EDITORIAL

Prime Minister Trudeau has committed this country to a change in foreign policy which may well have serious consequences.

In deciding to make phased and planned reductions in the already very modest Canadian air and ground contingents in NATO's European forces, he has rejected a heavy counter-weight of opinion.

The advice of Canada's allies, of a parliamentary committee which just completed a European fact-finding tour, of the Canadian ministers of defence and external affairs and a number of other cabinet ministers, has been that Canada should continue to play a responsible military role in the Western mutual security alliance for some time to come.

While Mr. Trudeau has decided to defy what it seems fair to say is the overwhelming weight of Canadian public opinion, he has not given out the details as yet of the extent and manner of the Canadian phase-out after this year. But it has to be assumed that the reduction of Canadian military strength in Europe will be much more than a token one. Otherwise there would be little point in Mr. Trudeau making his announcement.

Judging from proposals which have been given close study in recent weeks, it is distinctly possible that a reduction of manpower in the Canadian NATO forces in Europe will be accompanied by a diminished weapons role. This may involve token ground forces consisting purely of infantrymen, with back-up infantry units in Canada transportable by air to the site of a future emergency situation. A diminished air contingent may be divested of nuclear capability and serve purely reconnaissance or interceptor functions.

Prime Minister Trudeau displayed a lack of respect for Parliament in saving his important policy announcement for the day after MPs had gone home for the Easter recess. His disregard for parliamentary niceties is anything but reassuring, just as it was totally unnecessary.

Mr. Trudeau displays little understanding of military logic in holding that this nation's defence posture can be strengthened at the same time its forward line in Europe is being weakened. When he speaks of Canada protecting its own sovereignty he sounds like a pale reflection of France's President de Gaulle. The bitter experience of this country, if it has proved anything, is that isolationism and nationalism not only don't pay, they are downright dangerous. Mutual security, inter-dependence and the pooling of some levels of sovereignty, on the other hand, yield great rewards, as the history of the past twenty-five years has made clear to anyone who is not blinded by emotional idealism.

This country will be making a grave mistake if it thinks it can enjoy the best of all possible worlds, letting other countries carry its burdens while it grows fat and affluent, hiding its shame behind the mask of dispensing food and aid to backward countries who show little disposition to do much for themselves.

Mr. Trudeau has blundered politically. It remains to be seen if his political opponents have the ability to turn it to good account.

Canada has a prime minister who nurses an intellectual disdain for and abhorrence of all things military. It is doubtful if a great and technologically-advanced nation like ours can afford such a luxury at this particular time.

Keeping Faith with Friends

THE SUN, *Vancouver*
April 5, 1969
EDITORIAL

Canada's defence policy remains basically unchanged. The Great Debate stirred up by Prime Minister Pierre Trudeau produced little or nothing of practical consequence. It merely alarmed Canada's allies unnecessarily, divided the federal cabinet and aroused vain hopes among the dormant isolationists and professional anti-Americans.

At his press conference on Thursday Mr. Trudeau announced that Canada will remain in the North Atlantic Treaty Organization. It will, however, bring about phased reductions in the strength of its 10,000-man NATO contingent in consultation with its allies and beginning next year. There's nothing new about that.

Decision to cut the six-squadron air division by 20 per cent had been made, too trustingly as it turned out, before Russia invaded Czechoslovakia last August. This reduction was quickly cancelled. So can any other reductions planned for 1970 or any other year if new circumstances dictate otherwise.

"We have rejected the solutions of absolute pacificism," Mr. Trudeau announced. "We cannot be neutralist; we must be aligned." Presumably the cabinet took about as much time to reach that conclusion as it would have devoted to a proposal that Canada seek a pact of mutual defence with the Soviet Union.

Mr. Trudeau had other gems. "To the extent that it is feasible," he said, "we shall endeavor to have those activities within Canada which are essential to North American defence performed by Canadian forces." But not, apparently, to the extent that it wouldn't be feasible.

The prime minister gave first priority for Canada's armed forces to the preservation of Canada's sovereignty including "surveillance of our own territory and coastlines." This could

have been deduced fairly readily from the fact that about 90
per cent of the forces' establishment is already being retained
in this country.

Second in Mr. Trudeau's list comes the defence of North
America, which makes good sense geographically. It also happens to be the reverse of the prime minister's own coin about
Canada knowing "darn well" that the United States is bound
to defend her northern neighbor.

Then comes the NATO commitment, and finally the peace-
keeping roles which Canada may accept "from time to time."

All of this is very neat. But is it new in any essential particular? Or is it mostly window-dressing intended to mask the fact
that the whole exercise in defence review had at best a negative value? . . .

NATO Policy—a Re-examination Is in Order

THE OTTAWA JOURNAL
May 30, 1969
EDITORIAL

Twenty years ago Louis St. Laurent and Lester Pearson were
hailed as strong men of NATO. Canada was a key nation in
forming the great Atlantic partnership. NATO has been one of
the great successes of the post-war world.

What a difference we have today! Defence Minister Cadieux
returns from the Brussels meeting of the NATO Defence Planning Committee stigmatized by Canada's allies as an architect
of NATO's destruction. One delegate reported that the attitude
of the meeting to this country's proposed cuts in its NATO
forces was "absolutely unanimous, spontaneous and really hostile."

Prime Minister Trudeau and the other proponents of the
withdrawal of Canadian forces from Europe could hardly have
expected any benediction.

But the intensity of the disapproval is a matter of disquiet for Canadians who still haven't been told how many troops are coming home.

It is now clear that the withdrawals which were talked about were substantial. The reaction of the Nato ministers otherwise would not be so severe. American officials say the projected restrictions would cut the numbers of troops by two-thirds and their combat capability by 80 per cent.

The irony is that Defence Minister Cadieux, a NATO supporter, had to present a case in which he obviously had no heart. But his heart should be in reporting to Trudeau and the rest of the Cabinet the profound anxiety and resentment he encountered in Brussels.

The British Defence Minister, Denis Healey, was reported as saying that Canada was "trying to pass the buck to its allies." That is harsh language among friends. But on the face of the Canada-first attitude of the Government, it is understandable.

However Trudeau might want to pass off Canada's NATO policy as essentially a domestic matter, that is now no longer possible; probably never was. Canada's action has become a central issue in the defence policy of the West because of its political impact.

The extraordinary thing is that while debate rages on the proposed Canadian withdrawal of forces, the Canadian people have not been informed what they are. When the defence minister appears in the House on Monday he should tell the taxpayers what allies in NATO have been told about what Canada proposes.

The Government should re-examine its NATO policy in the cold light of what was said to Cadieux. This country does not want to be a parasite living off someone else's defence budget or turn to a narrow isolationism which we have historically deplored.

Canada's Role in Nato

LE DEVOIR, *Montréal*
April 6, 1969
EDITORIAL BY PAUL SAURIOL

The decision of the Canadian government, announced by Mr. Trudeau Thursday, to reduce our military participation in NATO is not surprising since it was the opinion he expressed during last year's election campaign. It seems that this decision could have been announced last fall had not Soviet troops invaded Czechoslovakia. The emotions aroused by that event made even a partial withdrawal more difficult. Mr. Trudeau made much of the fact that the situation in Europe has changed dramatically over the past twenty years, especially from an economic point of view. Canada's military effort in Europe has become too much to carry, given the immense size of its own territory and the considerable resources which the allied countries of Europe possess. But we are only "revising" our commitments in Europe. Mr. Trudeau has said that Canada will continue to "co-operate closely with the United States within NORAD and, under other forms, with defense agreements." These "other forms" probably refer to the future anti-missile missiles which will be installed near the Canadian border.

If Canada wishes to have its sovereignty respected and exercise a peaceful influence, particularly within the international peacekeeping forces created by the United Nations, we must try to limit as much as possible our military servitude towards the United States, especially in regards to atomic and nuclear armaments.

Canada Steps Backwards

THE TIMES, *London*
April 9, 1969
LEONARD BEATON

The Canadian Government's decision to cut back its forces in Europe was clearly a personal one made by the Prime Minister, Mr. Pierre Trudeau. From his earliest statements on foreign affairs, Mr. Trudeau has made it clear that he regards continental defence as a high priority but places little importance on Canada's links with Europe. This basic attitude has now shaped itself into a policy. Apart from the benefits to the Canadian dollar (and equivalent losses to the Deutsche Mark), a few thousand fewer Canadian troops in Germany will make little difference. But the assumptions on which this decision are based are important and fundamental. If (as is possible) they are applied to Canada's whole outlook on the world they could leave the country very much poorer.

The northernmost people of the western hemisphere have been almost alone in rejecting the notion that the Atlantic Ocean divides two worlds. Like a conservative province resisting a revolutionary ideology, they have never been anxious to cut themselves off from their European roots. Alone of the Americans, they neither proclaimed a republic in majestic language nor found it necessary to sustain it with tear gas or police brutality. Unlike the English and Spanish to the south, they found it unnecessary to invent a myth about having escaped from European tyranny into a freedom unknown to the Old World. Indeed, they alone of the Americans were prepared to face the appalling costs of war in Europe to prevent the Hitler tyranny.

Like most great conservative achievements, this Canadian outlook was based on instinct rather than convincing argument.

The makers of this Canada were plain men who felt no need to explain to themselves or to others the assumptions on which they were building their country. With a Prime Minister who is a master of definition the defenders of this old order are unlikely to acquit themselves convincingly. No doubt the bitter Cabinet debates about the Nato decision showed this only too clearly.

It may prove a tragedy but it is certainly not a paradox that the most civilized of the Canadian Prime Ministers is probably the least European in his links. Like the dominant families in English and Spanish America, the French Canadians are now several centuries away from their European origins. Unshared revolutions widen the gap even more. While the Atlantic may look narrow from a Black Watch drill hall, it is very broad from a *Collège classique*.

Mr. Trudeau's natural instinct is clearly to think in national and continental terms and to be concerned to concentrate resources on the vast problems of enriching a continent. It is a familiar and indeed almost inevitable outlook in new countries, even when they are not as new as they imagine. But in conserving resources to develop the country Mr. Trudeau may cut off much of what is needed. Radical reformers in France or China can pretend they are destroying an old order while in fact retaining their own character and their own history. But when Americans do the same thing they run the risk of ending up with a barren continent. Some might say that that has been the chosen fate of much of the United States.

The decision about Canadian forces in Europe is, of course, only a small part of this issue. For Britain to have kept forces in Germany all these years is comprehensible for a country which in 1940 contemplated the real possibility of invasion from the Continent. For the Americans it is equally comprehensible as the foundation of American leadership of western Europe.

For the Canadians, Nato was undoubtedly exciting and important at a time when they felt they were one of its inventors. Canada still saw it as her business to educate the Americans about the realities of the great world beyond. But as time went on these emotions wore out and there is nothing obvious to replace them.

In recent years, both the Americans and the Europeans have also become more openly dedicated to continentalism. Herr Brandt and Dr. Kissinger are showing distress at the Canadian decision. They seem not to have noticed that they have proclaimed their destiny to be a united Europe and have thrown their energies in recent years into the creation of a discriminatory grouping which, while sponsored by the United States, has predictably alienated other potential friends. The reason why a non-European power should spend money for European defence in these circumstances is too subtle for any public to be likely to understand. When the Prime Minister sees it the way the public does, the case is lost.

The direct results of this decision will not be spectacular. It is a Canadian illusion that the Canadian example has an important impact in the United States. The forces will be missed but so are a large number of other needed Nato forces which have never been provided.

What is regrettable is the growing incomprehension in Canada of a central truth: that the Atlantic is a narrow sea and that only in the unity of western Europe and north America can either be prosperous, Europe secure or the common inheritance sustained. More than any Europeans, the British understood this. More than any Americans the Canadians understood this. The close unity of the two countries reinforced these convictions. Now Canada, like Britain, is grasping at a narrow continentalism at a time when it is most obviously dangerous.

The tragedy is that it should come at a time when France has at last discovered French Canada and begun to lay the foundations for something of the rich relationship which Britain and Canada have enjoyed.

The PM and the Press

THE FREE PRESS, *Winnipeg*
June 11, 1969
EDITORIAL

The prime minister, in an address to the International Press Institute, has held the newspapers responsible in part for the government's failure to communicate with many Canadians in the matter of the official languages bill.

As evidence, Mr. Trudeau points to the experience of Mr. Pelletier, the secretary of state, who has made many speeches attempting to explain "institutional bilingualism." To quote the prime minister: "As far as I was able to find out, his speeches were not very well reported, and not very well editorialized on."

This is both puzzling and disturbing. It is puzzling because Mr. Trudeau has brought a general indictment on the basis of very limited study. He made an exception of one western paper; which had, he said, done a magnificent job. But he was not able to answer a question about the Globe and Mail—a newspaper widely read in Ottawa—because he does not read the press that closely.

Either the prime minister has been remarkably selective in

his research or else he is relying upon an impression formed by someone else.

Even more disquieting, however, is the breadth of Mr. Trudeau's indictment, which goes beyond reporting to deal also with the adequacy of editorial comment and the apparent assumption that the press is in some way responsible to government for the role it plays.

No such pretensions can possibly be accepted by newspapers with any respect for their independence.

It is doubtless true, as Mr. Trudeau says, that the government has failed to communicate. But it does not follow that the newspapers are at fault. Surprisingly, the indictment comes from a prime minister who has relied more than any of his predecessors on electronic journalism.

If television is the all-pervasive influence which the government seems to assume, why kick the newspapers when things go wrong? It may be true that some papers failed to hang on every word uttered by Mr. Pelletier, but it is also rather generally accepted that a message propounded over and over again ceases to be news.

If Mr. Pelletier failed to make the desired impact, is it not possible that the fault was his own? And if the secretary of state was unsuccessful in stimulating understanding and arousing enthusiasm in Western Canada, why did not Mr. Trudeau make an effort himself?

It is odd, and possibly unprecedented, that the prime minister did less to overcome opposition to the bill than Mr. Stanfield, his leading critic in Parliament.

Mr. Trudeau argues, as he is fully entitled to do, that this is a measure of exceptional importance because it is related to the issue of national unity. The argument has been repeatedly made in the columns of The Free Press. But it is the right of any newspaper to agree or disagree with the prime minister's estimate of its importance, with his priorities, with the urgency he attaches to the measure or with any particular aspect of the bill.

Newspaper readers are affected by many actions and policies of government and it is not for government to direct how much space or attention shall be devoted to one issue on an editorial page and how much to another.

In fact, the Trudeau government has not failed to communicate on language alone: A recent poll showed heavy Liberal opposition to the government's NATO policies and it cannot possibly be argued that newspapers have failed to discuss those in the degree to which they have been revealed. Or, to suggest another example, are the newspapers to blame because Prairie farmers appear less than satisfied with present policies relating to agriculture?

It is a common observation that the admission of error comes hard to ministers. Policy cannot be wrong; the error must lie in public understanding. Either the government has been so busy with good works that it has not devoted sufficient time and effort to the business of communication (which may be true in this instance) or else the newspapers are at fault and must be publicly reprimanded.

If there is a difference in the present case, it is that Mr. Trudeau has worried, in a general way, about communications ever since he assumed office. Evidently he has now narrowed his concern to the newspapers, finding that, with one or two meritorious exceptions, they have failed in their duty. They are admittedly imperfect, often insensitive to official guidance, and no more omniscient in their judgments than Mr. Trudeau was in his own writing days.

But it is surprising that so busy a prime minister can find time to perform the role of newspaper guardian and critic; after all, the government must still deal with many other difficult problems and unfinished business for which Mr. Trudeau certainly has a much clearer mandate.

On Monday evening, July 7, 1969, the House of Commons gave final reading to one of the most important pieces of legislation introduced by any of the Trudeau governments: The Official Languages Act. This was followed in December by a related, if less important development, the publication of the final volume of the Report of the Royal Commission on Bilingualism and Biculturalism established some years earlier by Prime Minister Pearson.

Canada in the Making

LE SOLEIL, *Québec*
July 9, 1969
EDITORIAL

The final adoption in the Commons of the Official Languages
Act is representative of the present evolution of our country
towards the realization of its greatness. The adoption of a flag
and of a national anthem are part of the affirmation of an
authentic Canadianism. The present extension of the French
fact around the country through the Official Languages Act
inscribes Canada's linguistic and cultural dualism in the heart
of our national existence.

Canadians Grow Up

LA PRESSE, *Montréal*
July 9, 1969
EDITORIAL BY RENAUDE LAPOINTE

By unanimously adopting Bill C-120, which makes of French
and English the two official languages for all areas of federal
administration, the House of Commons realized on the evening
of Monday, July 7—henceforth an historic date—one of the few
promises Mr. Trudeau made during his election campaign,
which was to bring to the building of a just society the essential
element of linguistic equality. This first step in the audacious
plan to transform Canada, and even more important, the attitude of Canadians, has, happily, been taken. And if we judge
from editorials in English-language newspapers across the
country, public opinion is much less hostile to these changes
than we would have expected from the reaction to publication
of the first part of the Laurendeau-Dunton Report.

For those of us who have for so long demanded the official
equality of the two languages at the federal level, this victory
has a great significance. We owe it to our representatives in

Ottawa who have in this case given stunning proof of their sincerity, their *savoir-faire* and of their prestige.

Languages Bill and the Future

THE GAZETTE, *Montréal*
July 10, 1969
EDITORIAL

The Official Languages Bill has passed the House of Commons after much debate there and in the country. The spirit in which it is applied will be the important thing.

All this implies change, upheaval and upset to many people. In fact, the Official Languages Bill, except in some details, is only the legal statement of a policy which successive governments have been working towards since the early sixties. The creation of the Royal Commission on Bilingualism and Biculturalism in 1963, in a sense, anticipated this legislation by the very fact that it was set up. Its reports since then have set out clearly the need for the bill. The B & B Commission did much to stir public debate, even public acceptance, of such a bill.

In 1965 Prime Minister Lester Pearson announced a government policy on bilingualism in the public service. The underlying principle in that statement—that all persons seeking promotion and, in some cases jobs, in the government must be willing to learn the second language—is also the underlying principle of the Official Languages Bill.

It should be remembered that the law applies only to federal government services. The provinces can still do as they wish, although more and more of the predominantly English-speaking provinces are providing services in French to French-speaking citizens. New Brunswick is now an officially bilingual province.

The federal bill raises the question: Will the evolution continue in the English-speaking provinces? Only with the wider use of French by the provincial governments will the two languages, in fact, enjoy something approaching equality across the country.

The key service provided by the provinces, of course, is education. This is where the crux of bilingualism lies. Again in this area the provinces—particularly Ontario—have moved in the last few years. What good are French-language government services to a French-speaking Canadian moving to Edmonton, if there is no publicly-supported school where his children can be educated in French?

The provision of French-language public schools in the major English-speaking provinces would do more to promote the equality of the languages than a bilingual External Affairs Department, although obviously the importance of a bilingual External Affairs Department is considerable.

If there is concern about educational facilities for French-speaking Canadians outside Quebec and New Brunswick, there is also concern about the educational facilities for English-speaking Canadians coming to Quebec. Despite official pro-nouncements about the status of English-language schools in the province, the St. Léonard school crisis of last year raised some fundamental questions which have not been totally re-solved.

Publicly-supported English-language education is more than 100 years old in Quebec. These were 100 years when other parts of Canada were adopting legal measures against French-language public education. Now that the wheel is turning to-ward full circle in other parts of Canada, the anxious question being asked in Quebec and outside is: will Quebec turn back the clock?

All the ground work laid by the B & B Commission and federal political leaders will be in vain if the passage of the Official Languages Bill lulls the predominantly English-speak-ing provinces into a feeling that language equality is now a reality, and no more reforms are necessary; or equally as im-portant, if the Bill is followed by moves in Quebec towards official unilingualism.

The Official Languages Bill, as a law, is a big step forward for Canada. But the most important part of it, like any law, is the spirit. If the spirit is allowed to die, or is killed, the law is dead.

This is why the Official Languages Bill, really, is only a beginning.

Sorry Performance

THE CALGARY HERALD
July 9, 1969
EDITORIAL

The official languages bill has been passed by the Commons.

The final step had been expected for some time.

Members of Parliament didn't cover themselves with glory in taking it. This wasn't because they all approved a bill about which there are misgivings in many part of the country. It was because they didn't seem to take it seriously enough.

Fewer than half the 264 MPs were in the Commons when the bill came up for third and last reading. The chamber should have been full for such a fundamentally important piece of legislation. The only excuse for missing third reading should have been illness. Furthermore, there should have been a recorded vote on third reading rather than a voice vote which tells electors nothing about how their representatives voted. Even the seventeen Conservatives who voted against the bill on second reading weren't present for the final vote. Apparently they didn't want to embarrass their leader.

It's not the first time that MPs didn't fulfil their duty to be present and counted on an important issue. The voting record on medicare, for example, is a sorry one. Many people are awakening only now to the full implications of the medicare legislation. Unfortunately, it is too late.

There may be a similar awakening when the effects of the languages bill hit home.

The government says, for example, that candidates for civil service jobs won't have to be bilingual. That may be true in many cases. But for the more rewarding career jobs, bilingualism is being made a practical necessity by the bill.

The federal civil service is now a bilingual service. It must be expected that anyone who wants to get anywhere in the service should be bilingual too. The government says bilingualism will be only one of the merit factors to be considered in filling civil service jobs. But no one has said that it won't be the main factor.

There is another element which also makes the MPs' performance particularly sorry. It involves the legal basis for the bill. There have been suggestions that the languages bill contravenes Sections 91 and 133 of the British North America Act. The MPs haven't given the impression that they cared very much one way or the other.

They've done very little to inspire public confidence in the languages bill.

The week after the passage of the Official Languages Act, the Prime Minister set out on a political tour of the Western provinces. He neither mended fences nor found greener pastures, and in fact received one of the most hostile public receptions of his career. The vehemence of the wheat farmers who confronted Trudeau surprised the press both East and West.

The Pampered West

LE DROIT, *Ottawa*
July 10, 1969
EDITORIAL

The Manitoba election had not yet taken place when already Prime Minister Trudeau was being blamed for the humiliating defeat of the Manitoba Liberals.

Mr. Trudeau is inclined too much toward Quebec, it was said. He laughs at our Westerners' problems. The prime minister, it is true, once committed the indiscretion of saying what a number of Eastern voters—from Ontario to the Maritimes—were thinking: The sale of wheat is the problem of Western farmers.

Always given privileged treatment by governments, some more co-operative than others, the Western farmers depend on Ottawa to sell their produce or not to sell it. When their harvest is abundant they depend on Ottawa to sell it and blame the federal government if the Canadian Wheat Board does not happen to dispose of the entire harvest, as if it could fill foreign granaries by force. When the harvest is poor or even non-existent they seek subsidies in compensation.

On the other hand, rare have been the occasions when the farmers of Ontario or Quebec or the fishermen of the Maritimes have been the object of the same treatment. When Mr. Trudeau says producing, selling or not selling grain is exactly like producing, selling or not selling maple sugar, vegetables or fish, he is criticized. They call him "Quebec-oriented" and vote against the Manitoba Liberals. . . .

Oddly enough, at the same time that Mr. Trudeau is being judged as too inclined toward Quebec, some people in *la belle province* are calling him a traitor to Quebec and blame him, even in his absence, for the difficulties of the Montreal celebrations of St. Jean Baptiste Day.

Count the Fences

THE CALGARY HERALD
July 15, 1969
EDITORIAL

As Prime Minister Trudeau sweeps across the Western provinces on his stated mission of mending broken fences, it would be wise if the people didn't hold their breaths too long.

Actually, the most that can be expected of the prime minister is that he make serious count of the fences that have been sent sprawling, not only by his year-long administration but by the Liberal administration before him which, also, was proved to be no mean hand at bowling Western fences.

To our mind his first fence to be mended would be the one known as Attitude. That is, instead of trying to warm up with his storied charisma, his vaunted mentality—which long since have been cooled by his intellectual aloofness towards matters which mean so much to us simple folk in this neck of the woods—he should move among us with open mind and heart. If he does this it is not impossible that he will learn from us.

Someone also should advise the prime minister that fence-mending is best performed with the sleeves rolled up. That way there is no cuff and, hence, no speaking from the cuff which, assuredly must have done more than its share to alienate many of his former Western admirers.

Such remarks as, "Why should we sell your wheat," and (at Calgary when he spoke on NATO rather than on a hoped-for pronouncement on a national oil policy) "I like to disappoint people sometimes," are especially galling when there have been near-disastrous harvesting conditions, when export sales of wheat are nowhere near up to expectations and Canadian oil is faced with an Alaskan find of, as yet, unspecified size.

Let there be no mistake about the fact that the prime minister is in deep trouble in the West. And he knows the truth of that or he would not be on his fence-mending trip. Certainly his minister of agriculture knows. Only on Saturday Mr. H. A. Olson said in Ottawa while on a tv panel show that, "There's a feeling . . . that the government is far more concerned with what happens in Ontario and Quebec—and always has been—than with the West."

Actually, Mr. Trudeau's fences are not only in Western Canada. They are, in fact, to be found, for one reason or another, almost all over Canada, not least of all in the Commons. There his contemptuous dismissal of the Opposition's stand on what amounts to the government seeking the rights of closure shook many more of his former friends, not only from the ranks of the Opposition but from his own Liberal supporters as well.

Trudeau Begins to See the Light

THE STAR-PHOENIX, *Saskatoon*
July 18, 1969
EDITORIAL

Prime Minister Trudeau seems to be getting the message about the farmers' plight. In Saskatoon Thursday, his attitude appeared to be changed from a somewhat stiff-necked posture in Regina the previous day.

Then, too, when he addressed the Saskatchewan Farmers' Union delegates, the Prime Minister acknowledged that the threat to the prairie wheat economy was a problem of national importance, and therefore it called for federal government aid in solving it.

Mr. Trudeau said what made the problem so difficult was how to cope with it in two of its main phases: aiding the farmer with capital but without cash; and trying to remove the poverty pockets where farmers have neither capital nor cash.

When account is taken of the uncomplimentary wording on the slogans carried by delegates, and on their tractors, it was surprising that the crowd listened so attentively, and cheered and applauded the Prime Minister.

Much of this friendly reception was due to the leadership shown by Roy Atkinson, president of the SFU and the National Farmers Union. The audience responded to his request that they give the Prime Minister a fair hearing.

So, it may be that Saskatoon is the turning point insofar as Mr. Trudeau is concerned, not only in his more positive response to farmers' woes, but also in the beginning of a rapport between himself and the farm organizations. But maintenance of this good will depends on speedy follow up of plans and programs. If it is long delayed, Mr. Trudeau will lose the ear of the farmer which he gained yesterday.

Abuse of Trudeau Disgrace to Canada

THE EDMONTON JOURNAL
July 18, 1969
EDITORIAL

Prime Minister Trudeau was entirely justified in telling Prairie farmers that if they want to see him again they had better not carry signs that are defamatory and grossly insulting.

The conduct of some farmers in Saskatchewan and Alberta will be resented by all decent people. Such signs as "Trudeau is a pig" and "He hustles women", and a mock scaffold with a noose labelled "Where is Trudeau?" are a disgrace to Canada.

Western farmers have legitimate grievances. The West as a whole has good reasons for feeling it has been neglected and victimized by Ottawa in favor of the central provinces and the Maritimes. Mr. Trudeau's dislike of subsidies rings strangely on the ears of Westerners who have long been victimized by being forced to pay subsidies in the form of tariffs to protect Eastern industries.

But none of this justifies tactics of intimidation against the prime minister and his office. Intelligent and courageous men are not impressed by them, a fact that often is overlooked by militant students, belligerent trades unionists, angry farmers and others. The best advice for all of them is to cool it.

Nothing Is Served by Rudeness

LA PRESSE, *Montréal*
July 19, 1969
EDITORIAL BY ROGER CHAMPOUX

In Ottawa a few days ago Mr. Jean-Luc Pépin signed an agreement to sell 7.5 million bushels of wheat to Peru. Signing for the Peruvian government was the Minister of Finance, General Francisco Morales y Bermudez, who agreed to a cash downpayment of 10 percent. The balance will be paid over the next five years and will include an interest charge of 4⅜ percent. It must be remembered that this is second quality wheat that sells for $1.84½ per bushel. This, keeping in mind the present state of the world wheat market, would seem to be an extremely interesting transaction. But the Western farmers are not satisfied!

It is true that these farmers, and it must be underlined that they are not poor, have in the past received up to $2.15 a bushel for prime quality wheat that is now selling for $1.95. This price does not satisfy them and they took the occasion of Mr. Trudeau's visit to demonstrate their dissatisfaction in the most grotesque and impolite manner. Some will say that the people of Québec have given bad examples of similar behavior and we have to agree that this is true. We thought however that Westerners had better judgment than this small band of agitators. Obviously not. Their rudeness towards a man who sought to examine with them the problems of their milieu surpasses all acceptable limits.

By throwing rotten wheat in Mr. Trudeau's face, by surrounding him with insulting placards and by hanging him in effigy and by revealing themselves incapable of a civilized dialogue these people have demonstrated how anger can push individuals to extremes of degradation. Mr. Trudeau twice walked out of halls and he was right in doing so. There is nothing more normal than to disagree with a head of state. To act abominably towards him is unforgiveable. "I didn't enter politics to be insulted and I will never accept insults from people I am addressing," replied Mr. Trudeau, who, by retaining his composure and self-control provided a lesson in manners to people who have none.

Who's a Pig?

THE SUN, *Vancouver*
July 19, 1969
EDITORIAL

A bad year for wheat sales seems to have coincided with a poor crop of manners in some sections of the Prairies visited this week by Prime Minister Pierre Trudeau.

Organizers of the demonstrations in Regina, Queen City of the West, have probably apologized to him by now for the boorishness of some of their ignorant zealots. Western hospitality is famous, and justifiably so. It must be a source of public and private shame to most westerners that Canada's head of government should be greeted with insulting placards and pelted with wheat, especially when his mission was motivated by a spirit of sympathy and helpfulness.

Mr. Trudeau was human enough to protest publicly against such treatment. But it must go almost without saying that he is also big enough not to let it influence his judgment about federal aid to the cash-short farmers.

"I realize you need dough," he said in Humboldt, Saskatche-wan. How much dough and how it is to be apportioned is a question that may await announcement before a special debate on the problem in the Commons next week. About all that the prime minister has said so far is that there will be no indiscriminate handouts. The federal government will do what may be necessary to prevent a collapse of the Prairie economy and to assist cases of real hardship.

Such a policy will be welcomed by Canadians of all regions on grounds of simple humanitarianism. The extent of the aid to be given is bound to be less than enough to satisfy all of the distressed recipients. But, as Mr. Trudeau has already learned, the outlook of a minority of them is hardly predisposed toward plain courtesy, let alone gratitude.

From 1967 to 1968 Canadians had been carried from one height of euphoria to another, starting with the Centennial celebrations and Expo 67 and concluding with the Trudeau phenomenon. Such a sustained outpouring of emotion and enthusiasm was uncharacteristic of Canadians; by late 1969 the inevitable return to earth had taken place, bringing with it a more realistic assessment of the Liberal government and its leader.

The Dominant Figures of a Troubled Political Year

LE DEVOIR, *Montréal*
December 31, 1969
EDITORIAL BY CLAUDE RYAN

The year that is ending has not been particularly creative on the political level. There have been no notable achievements on the great questions that concern the French Canadian people, or on the search for a more democratic social, political and economic order.

Pierre Elliott Trudeau continued during 1969 to dominate the federal political scene. The Trudeau myth does not have the magical quality it had in 1968. The charismatic quality that so seduced the anglophones at the beginning has gradually given way to technocratic elements.

Those who expected miracles of Mr. Trudeau have been deceived. Mr. Trudeau appeared on the political scene a year and a half ago almost like a legendary personage. The last year has brought him back to a more human and truer measure.

Such a demystification might have destroyed a lesser man than Mr. Trudeau. In his case, it was not enough to usurp his position in the forefront of federal politics. For nearly a year, Mr. Trudeau has been the uncontested master of the federal scene: by the strength of his intelligence and of a will much stronger than we imagined, by the fact that political events have continued to run in his favor, although they may be preparing him for bitter deceptions in the future. Mr. Trudeau enjoys, at the end of this year, an exceptional power as much *vis-à-vis* his cabinet as with his party, parliament and Canadian public opinion. Both within and beyond his government and party, there are those who find Mr. Trudeau at times overly authoritarian, too rigid and aristocratic. In Québec, he is accused of being too much of a centralizer. In English Canada, people speak all too easily of the Prime Minister and his team as "French Canadian power."

Despite all of this, Mr. Trudeau still seems indispensable and unique no matter what angle he is viewed from.

French Canadians are proud of this man who represents them with elegance and vigor. English language Canadians continue to believe that he possesses the extraordinary qualities necessary to solve the problem of national unity.

Even his political adversaries admit in private that no one in the opposition parties can compare with the Liberal leader on the level of talent and vitality.

Mr. Trudeau used his strength in 1969 to have the Official Languages Act adopted and to launch a war against inflation. He has, however, worked in vain to advance his conception of federalism. At the end of 1969, Québec and Ottawa are further apart than ever before. And there seems to be no possibility of rapprochement unless Ottawa returns to more conciliatory attitudes, which Mr. Trudeau himself considered, not long ago, as being heretical.

At the economic level, Mr. Trudeau has given the impression of rowing counter to the inflationary current. He has provided no clear sign of economic direction.

In sum, Mr. Trudeau has dominated the federal scene thanks to his exceptional personality. But his policies have been less successful. And the men around him, especially on the anglophone side, have often seemed to be spectators rather than the committed members of a party in which only the band leader and a few close associates seem to be in control of all the facts.

A Second Diefenbaker?

THE CANADIAN FORUM
October, 1969
D. J. DOOLEY

Can the question be meant seriously?

They don't look alike, their weights are different, their styles of oratory and conduct could not be farther apart. What I am suggesting, however, is that two examples may indicate the existence of a pattern or syndrome: the Canadian electorate, every ten years or so, chooses as prime minister, by an over-whelming majority, a man who has not demonstrated that he possesses the qualifications for the job, and the man then proceeds to show conclusively that he does not have the neces-sary talents. Trudeau threatens to rival Diefenbaker as the greatest disappointment in Canadian politics.

In the two landslide elections, ten years apart, it was the man who was chosen, not the party. Recall Alister Grossart's amusing account of how he deliberately de-emphasized the Progressive Conservative Party; remember the enormous pic-tures of that wavy-haired, good-humoured head, the introduc-tion of Joe Nobody as Your Diefenbaker Candidate in Lower Yorkville, and the mention of the Party which paid for the advertisement in the smallest size of type which could be used without its being insulting? Recall the famous campaign speech, which lit fire in the heather, established Diefenbaker as a man of vision, and made people from coast to coast enquire of one another, "I think he's sincere, don't you?" A few newspaper reporters made guarded suggestion that if you tried to analyse the substance of the speech, you found that it didn't say very much. But that didn't matter; in the wave of popular enthusiasm, there was very little criticism of Mr. Diefenbaker, even by the Liberals. If some took his advice and went north, and found it cold, that was later on; for the time being, his image imposed itself on almost all Canadians except the "intellectuals." ...

In almost every situation in which he [Trudeau] has been involved, however, the new manner has produced misgivings. When he called Parliament together only to dissolve it for an election, he could have taken a few more minutes of the House's time to pay tribute to Lester Pearson, who would have been five years in office on that very day: both political sensitivity and common politeness should have told him that. Perhaps he had reasons for taking U Thant's line on Vietnam when the two of them received honorary degrees from the University of Alberta—but it was slightly awkward for him to criticise American policy just at the start of the peace negotiations in Paris. And he perhaps had reason for taking an independent line on NATO—but again, it seemed stupid of him to take the attitude he did just after Czechoslovakia. At the Commonwealth Prime Ministers' Conference, he was perhaps sensible to sit back and watch, but his show of irritation when he was asked about Anthony Grey, the English journalist under house arrest in China, was unwarranted. Like Mr. Diefenbaker, he seems to pursue certain policies with stubborn implacability. Like Mr. Diefenbaker, he has had trouble with his Cabinet: one strong contender for the Liberal leadership, Mr. Hellyer, has departed, and another, Mr. Sharp, has been turned into a trained seal. And his participatory democracy has come to mean the process by which he goes over the heads of Parliament to explain his decisions to television audiences. ...

After declaring on his western trip that he was not going to discuss matters with people who appeared before him carrying placards telling him to hustle wheat not women, it ill behoved him to call the opposition a bunch of nobodies. Patrick Nichol-

son commented, "I have never seen a prime minister vociferously and widely booed on the floor of the House before." So
much for the "tough, disciplined application of power" to
which Peter C. Newman refers; it seems to be only the worst
sort of demagoguery.

As a comparatively young man, Mr. Trudeau can be expected to have greater flexibility and greater potential for
change than Mr. Diefenbaker had. If he remains set in his
ways, we may well find ourselves wondering, "Is this the political leader of the 70's? Will it take us till 1980 to get rid of
him?"

Trudeau: Not a Superman

THE BEACON HERALD, *Stratford*
January 30, 1970
EDITORIAL

Have you noticed that few people use the word "Trudeaumania" these days? It seems only a short time ago that the
capabilities of this man were being discussed by everybody.
Not only was he potentially a great politician who would lead
Canada out of the wilderness into just the right blend of bilingualism, biculturalism and the "Just Society," but here was a
man who had color. He was good at the sports he enjoyed. He
was single and thus gave many a mother the thrilling thought
that perhaps someday her daughter might be first lady of the
land.

Mr. Trudeau was almost too good to be true. He seemed to
possess, if some of the glowing press reports were to be believed, all of the virtues of our former prime ministers and
none of their vices. To some people he was the answer to all of
Canada's dreams, to others who were somewhat more cynical,
or where they were just being realistic, he was the product of
some over-zealous public relations men. The fact is that he
caught the imagination of the Canadian people in time to get
him elected. In addition he became a favorite topic of conver-

sation for many people in other countries, all of which added to his charisma or mystique.

Today many Canadians, even many staunch Liberals, will admit that all this just isn't so. The "Just Society" is still little more than political wishful thinking. For wheat farmers, frustrated French Canadians and middle-class taxpayers society may seem more unjust than just. Mr. Trudeau has not been able to lead us out of the political wilderness. He has alienated many people by his stand on NATO, he has already had one senior cabinet minister resign, our postal system is still the laughing stock of the nation and, as we pointed out the other day, he has the once prestigious Department of External Affairs in a state of demoralization. In fact, he has people concentrating on his shortcomings instead of on all his qualities.

We do not mean to condemn Mr. Trudeau and his policies, but only to attempt to point out that he never was the man that so many people believed him to be, or wanted to believe him to be. He is a well-educated, intellectual colorful politician with strong convictions.

So far he has had his share of successes and failures in Parliament, but has yet to really prove himself.

It is, at least, a healthy sign that Canadians have ceased to consider him as some Wunderkind, and have come to accept the problems that Canada faces are tough nuts to crack, for Mr. Trudeau or for anybody else.

CHAPTER 3

THE OCTOBER CRISIS AND AFTERMATH 1970-72

A black taxi drew up before a comfortable house on Mount Royal's Redpath Crescent shortly before 8 A.M., Monday October 5, 1970. Two men stepped out, hurried up the steps to the door, forced their way inside, and announced themselves as the Front for the Liberation of Québec. British Trade Commissioner James Cross was about to be kidnapped.

Until that October morning the FLQ had been known primarily for bombings. From 1963 to 1967 they planted some 35 bombs, and then escalated their activities with a further 25 between 1968 and 1970. By the time James Cross was abducted, FLQ terrorism had killed seven people and injured 42, but a political kidnapping in Canada was an unprecedented escalation of terror that brought a shocked and outraged reaction from public and press.

On October 6, the principal demands of the FLQ were made public. They demanded payment of a "voluntary tax" of $500,000 in gold bars, release of 23 political prisoners, publication in full of an FLQ manifesto (this was later done) and the unveiling of a police informer.

A Shocking Crime

THE GAZETTE, *Montréal*
October 6, 1970
EDITORIAL

The sympathy of every citizen goes out to the family of James Richard Cross, the British trade commissioner who has become the victim of a shocking and violent abduction.

It is a crime that fills the community with helpless rage. There is nothing that the community as a whole can do about it at this point, and private individuals, however well-meaning, should not try to intervene. The skills of the police and the good sense and judgment of the responsible authorities have to be trusted.

The problem that confronts the authorities is to free the victim of this kidnapping without encouraging this type of crime and treating convicted members of the FLQ as political prisoners.

When the perpetrators of the crime are arrested, as they must be, they should be punished with the utmost severity that the law will permit.

Terrorist Criminals

THE OTTAWA JOURNAL
October 6, 1970
EDITORIAL

Cruel as well as criminal is the kidnap of Britain's Trade Commissioner in Montreal. The man's life is threatened and his health is not robust; his family is in great distress. Yet in reward for that crime the criminals demand release of dangerous, convicted terrorists, half a million dollars, publicity for separatism and a plane ride to Cuba.

The public is aghast, angry and momentarily helpless. Yet, to vent its rage by refusing to pay ransom, if the police are unable today to track down these criminals, seems to us a temptation both selfish and unwise. It could mean death of an innocent public servant.

The argument is heard that to ransom such a victim would just encourage repeated offences, whereas to let them murder the witness to their crime would frustrate them and shame all separatist extremists into gentler ways.

We think the latter conclusion unrealistic. The real extremist, the terrorist with bombs and guns, has no sense, no conscience. He will not refrain from murder if it suits his twisted mind.

The defence against terrorism is a long-term battle. The country must cease the permissive trend of law enforcement and greatly increase the measure of punishment it hands out to convicted criminals of the terrorist type.

Society, we suggest, has lost the case involving Mr. James Cross—we should not also lose his life. There will be tomorrow and tomorrow to catch the criminals and strengthen all our defences against their diseased machinations.

But—the event should reduce to nil the soft-minded tolerance some politicians and citizens have held towards French-Canadian terrorism in any form. Not all French Canadians are separatists, not all separatists are terrorists—but all French Canadians and all Canadians should denounce all terrorists and fight to outlaw them from our midst.

Terrorism

LA PRESSE, *Montréal*
October 6, 1970
EDITORIAL BY JEAN-PAUL DESBIENS

Everyone is now aware that a British trade representative has been kidnapped by four men claiming to belong to the Front de Libération du Québec (FLQ). The FLQ has stated its conditions for liberation of the diplomat: publication of its manifesto in the newspapers, payment of a $500,000 ransom; rehiring of the Lapalme workers; freeing of 12 so-called political prisoners; the naming of the person who made possible the dismantling of an FLQ cell.

We can foresee any variety of other demands: The list is open. We can also imagine that anyone else can become a victim.

A young girl would do just fine to upset sensitive stomachs. That is why it is clear that the municipal government, the Québec government or the federal government must all refuse to give in to such blackmail. They may give the appearance of flexibility, but only if they are certain of apprehending the kidnappers. They must in no way give up on fundamentals. We have said it before, in connection with the bombs of the 30 and 31 of May: there is only one thing viler than being a blackmailer, and that is to give in to blackmail. Some will argue that a man's life hangs in the balance. We must answer that the accounting of terrorists is not concerned with men's lives and that to give in now will only mean having to pay a dearer price later: the lives of thousands of men and the very existence of the society we live in.

I'm not particularly in love with this society; more precisely, I am not particularly in love with this civilization; but neither am I its elected guardian. The elected guardians of this society cannot make concessions to terrorism.

If they have the taste for concessions, it would be better that they immediately turn their power over to the FLQ. We know very well that they will not. We cannot imagine the FLQ being able to assume power. The choice of the guardians of society is therefore clear: they must uphold society and administer. May the best side win!

The terrorists demand that newspapers publish their manifesto. All the newspapers have received it. As far as we know only one paper has printed it, a paper which prefers to run stories with blood on page one and whose reporters are non-unionized.

One can guess what "freedom of information" would exist under the rule of the FLQ: publish or do not publish this or that or else we kill.

I admit that I still prefer classic bandits to this gang of outlaws ready to use any means to achieve their end, which is to exercise their lawless rule on some corner of this planet. The thing is that terrorists are educated and can therefore envelop their crimes in ideological jargon. This accords them, *vis-à-vis* a certain abstract and irresponsible line of thought, a kind of respectability.

It is in the name of this respectability that they dare submit men to their will. It is important above all to remain calm. No one can overcome a people against its will. The strength of the terrorists lies in co-operation from the population. That co-operation does not exist here. There will be other acts of terrorism but terrorism is not rooted in our population. It remains a marginal phenomenon.

When they are apprehended, the terrorists will be tried according to laws that govern us. They will spend so long before the courts that they will come to seem like victims and will appear like heroes even in a paper as capitalistic as La Presse. Lawyers will eat away the funds collected by a group of good souls. The society the terrorists wish to destroy is soft enough and generous enough to pay itself the luxury of judging carefully and at length.

In Cuba, such men would be shot on sight. The little guys don't, in fact, risk very much. Even when found they will only serve a few years in prison. I know some, from the first wave, who were freed before their time was up, and who have worked faithfully for the government of Québec. Others pursue their studies in France.

Don't Blame Quebec

THE CALGARY HERALD
October 6, 1970
EDITORIAL

The abduction of James R. Cross, senior British trade commissioner, from his Montreal home is the demoniacal work of persons with no more respect for human dignity than might be expected from Middle East or Latin American terrorist groups.

Although the Front de Liberation Quebecois, a Quebec underground terrorist group, has been linked with, but not positively identified as, the perpetrators of this unspeakable act of political kidnapping, most Canadians might be left with the impression this is further evidence of the instability of Quebec.

Evidence that behavior such as this has spread to Canada has frightening implications, but to categorize this event as typical of Quebec would be grossly unfair.

In view of countless events of recent history, English-speaking Canada can take some justification in being displeased with the general tone of the French Canadian stance, but 5.5 million Quebecers cannot be held responsible for the deplorable behavior of a handful of fanatical and dangerous terrorists.

If in fact the FLQ is guilty of this dastardly political crime, one must consider the indications that certain members of this group acquired their rebellious habits in Algeria.

It would be more to the point at this stage to take every precaution possible to safeguard the life of Mr. Cross, and to follow it up with a relentless campaign to rid Canada of people responsible for his abduction.

The Terrible Decision

THE SUN, *Vancouver*
October 7, 1970
EDITORIAL

The spread to Canada of the diplomatic kidnapping outrage brought the governments in Ottawa and Quebec City to grips with one of the most perplexing dilemmas of our time. As in Latin America and North Africa before it, the seizing of James Richard Cross in Montreal demanded the making of a terrible decision. When does the price for one man, or a dozen men, or even 300, become too high to be tolerable?

It would be a simpler question to answer were not the politically-motivated holding of a hostage for ransom so diabolically ingenious. The success of this cruel crime—and it has been stunningly successful—devolves not just from the compassion of the government blackmailed, but, increasingly, the selection of a representative of a foreign country as the pawn. This brings heavy external, as well as internal, pressure to comply upon the host country, simply because it is that, a host, bearing all the grave responsibilities of international hospitality.

Surrender to terrorism, predictably, has proven a poor expedient, and as is so often the case in straight kidnapping-for-profit the pawn may be forfeited anyway. The criminals are encouraged to multiply, and make bigger and bolder demands. The end, which is rule by gangster, cannot lie very far ahead that way....

Although it is but a minority of minorities, the Quebec terrorist movement, like such movements everywhere, must have some popular base to exist, some tolerance, if not support and concealment. In abducting the British trade commissioner in Montreal, has the manic fringe of the separatist movement at last gone too far? Is this what its sympathizers really want and, if not, what are they going to do about it?

But that is a decision for tomorrow. Today's decision has been made. It is the right decision....

An Outrage Without Excuse or Meaning

THE TIMES, *London*
October 8, 1970
EDITORIAL

The kidnapping of Mr. James Cross demonstrates the complete political and intellectual sterility of the Front de Libération du Québec. They are at once the advocates of the most extreme chauvinism and of extreme communism, producing a preposterous blend of Maurras and Mao. To threaten to kill a perfectly innocent man, not Canadian but British, unless a number of postmen are given their jobs back and prisoners are set free is as stupid politically as it is indefensible morally. To demand a ransom at the same time is to reduce the cause of the French Canadians to the level of gangsterism.

The F.L.Q. is, of course, anti-democratic and it is therefore unreasonable in its own context to expect it to play the parliamentary game. If the people of Quebec want to secede from Canada, they have only to vote the Parti Québécois into power (it won 24 per cent at the last provincial elections). The F.L.Q. wants a Maoist socialist republic and reckons that violence is the only way of obtaining it. This is not necessarily a bad technique when the revolutionaries accept the rules of the game. When the I.R.A. occupied the centre of Dublin in 1916, and held it for a week against the British Army, they offered their own lives in the cause of Irish independence. In due course they had their reward. The F.L.Q. prefers midnight assault and anonymous telephone calls.

There is a tradition of violence in Montreal. A year ago there were serious riots when French Canadians demonstrated against the exercise by Montreal residents of Italian or English origin of the civic rights which French Canadians most vociferously demanded for themselves in other provinces, including the right to have their children taught in the language of their choice. The non-French speaking Montréalais wanted their children taught in English and the Quebec Government and Quebec hoodlums alike opposed them.

Quebec has been quiet since then. The elections last April, at which the moderate parties won a thumping victory seemed to herald a period during which the Québécois and other Canadians could work out their problems calmly and peacefully. It is possible the F.L.Q. wanted to disturb this calm, to revive agitation, in the fear that otherwise the cause of separation would die of inanition. More likely it was inspired by kidnappings in Brazil and Uruguay and hijackings by Palestinians.

The difference between the Canadian situation and that in the Middle East and Latin America is that, however wrong the tactics may be both morally and tactically, the South Americans and Palestinians have a real grievance. The F.L.Q. is playing heroics. What is quite indefensible with all these groups is their menace to the lives of entirely innocent men and women who are in no way concerned in their disputes. It becomes a universal crime like piracy and hijacking.

Creating Himself Through Political Acts

THE TORONTO STAR
October 10, 1970
PETER C. NEWMAN

Ottawa—As Parliament begins its third session under Pierre Trudeau's leadership, the enormity of the differences between him and his 15 predecessors is coming into focus.

Trudeau has deliberately upset the apple carts of all those interest groups who have shared for generations the political power that counts, rendering the formerly smug impotent with one cold gaze, or one colder action. In his treatment of his cabinet, his caucus, his party organization and even his own office staff, he has remained within the mould he's cast for himself—and outside the traditional behavior patterns of prime ministers. He governs the country like the headmaster of a rigorously administered private school, ruling by fear and keeping all those nearest him—not excluding the electorate—permanently insecure.

The effect on Ottawa has been to cool the noisy crisis atmosphere of the past decade. All of the great confrontations between provincial governments, with the parliamentary opposition and among party leadership challengers now seem outdated and irrelevant. Cabinet authority has been dispersed into so many committees and the decision-making process so fragmented that no minister except Trudeau himself has much influence on over-all government policy.

With the possible exceptions of Don Jamieson, Bryce Mackasey and John Turner all of Trudeau's ministers could disappear as quickly as Paul Hellyer did last year, leaving behind them hardly a ripple to show they had ever existed.

The power of the backroom boys within the Liberal party has evaporated, simply because Trudeau chooses to ignore them. He refuses to attend most party functions or to dip deeply into the porkbarrel to find rewards for the faithful. Last week's astonishing, enlightened Senate appointments must have shattered a thousand Liberals' happy dreams. By undercutting the influence of most of the traditional party power brokers, Trudeau has retained only one indispensable man—himself.

When Keith Davey was the Liberals' chief organizer during the Pearson years, the whole country knew of his exploits. But who has ever even heard the name of Torrance Wylie, the man who now has Davey's job? Trudeau's relationship with John Nichol, the bright young Senator from B.C. who managed his 1968 election campaign, is now described by a close acquaintance, as "non-existent."

Another source of Trudeau's strength is that unlike most prime ministers, who gather around themselves a kitchen cabinet of political cronies, he functions as his own brains trust. It is a cliche in Ottawa these days that he relies exclusively for advice on what insiders call his "French chapel"—Regional Development Minister Jean Marchand, Secretary of State Gerard Pelletier and Principal Secretary Marc Lalonde. But the fact is (and these three men admit it) that nobody, but nobody, tells Trudeau what to do.

Trudeau even limits his contacts with his personal staff, all people he has carefully selected himself. This year, for instance, he has attended only two of the regular Wednesday afternoon conferences held by members of the prime minister's staff. On one of these occasions he spent most of the time poking fun at a survey published in Maclean's Magazine purporting to show that Robert Stanfield could beat him in the next election campaign.

Almost without any of us becoming aware of it, Trudeau has turned himself into a presidential figure with a hold on power undreamed of in the U.S. Constitution.

Nearly all Canadian prime ministers have tried to create a "concurrent majority" at the summit of political power by sharing their powers with a senior politician from the other basic culture. Laurier had Sifton and Fielding; Mackenzie King had Ernest Lapointe; Louis St. Laurent had C. D. Howe. Not all of Trudeau's predecessors succeeded in finding a suitable pro-consul, but at least they tried. Diefenbaker and Pearson had to make up in quantity what they lacked in quality in their Quebec lieutenants, and together went through nine candidates for the job.

But Trudeau doesn't even pretend to be searching for a senior English-Canadian politician to become his partner in power. The recent cabinet shuffle, an ideal opportunity to designate an English lieutenant, somehow managed to demote everybody involved.

It is a paradox of the Trudeau method that despite his refusal to share personal power, the process of government policy formation has been opened up. Building on precedent, like the good lawyer he is, Trudeau has used white papers, parliamentary committees and his party apparatus to involve special interest groups in the essential policy decisions.

Trudeau has maintained such a grip on power because he has so far been more successful than any of his predecessors in achieving the ideal state of Canadian political grace—he has demonstrated his ability to occupy the political centre, while moving simultaneously both to the left and to the right.

"Our job in the past two years," he said during one of his recent tours into the political hinterland, "has been trying to kill expectations and, as you know, we brought in the first balanced or surplus budget in 13 years. People who thought I was a Communist said, 'My God, this guy's a pretty conservative prime minister,' which I suppose I am. But it is because we balanced our budget that the Canadian dollar is worth more and that the Canadian economy is a better place for people to invest in."

To tag Trudeau with any recognizable ideology, you have to move into the existentialism of the French philosopher Jean-Paul Sartre, who claims that each individual is what he makes of himself—that "man invents himself through exercising his freedom of choices." This is what Pierre Trudeau is all about—a man creating himself, through authentic political acts.

His ideas are formed by what he sees and feels as he travels the country he is charged with governing. He can only be comprehended in action, and just dimly even then. His self-imposed mission is to reveal the character of this nation to itself, and despite his flaws we probably should be glad, at this crucial moment in our history, to have as prime minister a man who can evoke genuine reactions between us and the mystical entity we call Canada.

As the week wore on the story of the Cross kidnapping gradually dropped from the front pages of the nation's newspapers. Then, at 6 P.M. on Saturday October 10, Pierre Laporte, Québec's Minister of Labor and Immigration and the acknowledged number two man in the government, was kidnapped at gunpoint in a park in front of his home in the Montréal suburb of St. Lambert.

All Quebec Held for Ransom

THE GAZETTE, *Montréal*
October 12, 1970
EDITORIAL

All of the people of this province are being held for ransom by Le Front de Liberation du Quebec. Let there be no misunderstanding about that. Every democratic institution is endangered, every civilized tradition compromised, by the resort to organized terror as the instrument for social and political change.

The FLQ has placed itself beyond all limits of tolerance. It must be destroyed. The government should not hesitate to assume whatever powers it requires to accomplish this. Those powers will be, of necessity, arbitrary. They will be repugnant to a free society. But they will be far less repugnant than to continue defenceless against those who would destroy the democratic institutions which now shelter them.

The FLQ has declared war on all Quebecers, whatever their tongue or the color of their political beliefs. No one can assume he is safe from being snatched from his home by armed thugs. No one can assume he is safe from dynamite blasts in the night. All Quebecers have a common duty to assist the police to track down the terrorists and bring them to trial. The courts must not be lenient as they have sometimes been in the past.

Terror inevitably invites counter-terror. This must be avoided at all costs. Much loose talk of individual retaliation is being heard. No one, whatever the provocation, has the right to take the law into his own hands. It is now clear the government is taking all possible measures to root out the cancerous FLQ cells from the body politic. The government and, through the government, the police are the only proper agencies for restoring the rule of law.

It should now be clear, too, that the FLQ is totally rejected by the vast majority of Quebecers on whose behalf it pretends to act. The ideology of the FLQ is as foreign to Quebec as the tactics it employs to advance its cause. No Quebecer need have the slightest qualm in giving every assistance in bringing its members to trial.

The FLQ has violated every precept of a free and civilized society. It has challenged, equally, duly elected authority and every decent human impulse. Let us rid ourselves of it as quickly as we can. It has no place in Quebec.

Nation in Shock

THE CALGARY HERALD
October 13, 1970
EDITORIAL

Canadians today are confronted by the appalling fact that their capital city of Ottawa is in a state of siege and their largest city, Montreal, clothed in an atmosphere of fear and tension. . . .

Two kidnap victims, British diplomat James Cross, and Quebec Labor Minister Pierre Laporte, remain in the hands of FLQ terrorists under threat of imminent execution if their abductors' wildly extravagant demands are not met. . . .

The two governments concerned have taken firm stands against yielding to the kidnappers' attempts at blackmail. There is every indication that the public approves this position. Blackmail cannot be allowed to pay off. Society's integrity cannot be traded away to criminals. Let the FLQ win this dastardly round, and it will lose little time in embarking on further rounds of extortion.

Canadians can only hope today that the two kidnapped men will be spared in the end by their captors and allowed to return unharmed to their families and that normal Canadian standards of safety and decency will be restored without delay.

The Dice Are Tossed, But Loaded Favoring Anarchism

LA PRESSE, *Montréal*
October 13, 1970
EDITORIAL BY JEAN-PAUL DESBIENS

Whatever the final result of the current crisis, things will never be the same. The functioning and even the existence of democratic authority have been questioned and, as a result, the population as a whole is menaced. Everyone must clearly realize this fact.

Two reasons account for the frightening efficiency of the terrorist methods.

1) Society is becoming more complex and hence more vulnerable. Only 50 years ago, the events of the past week could not have happened. This is obvious, but it is vital that everyone reflect on the fact that the perfection of a society's organization is fragile and depends upon the care each individual takes of it.

2) The two powers in conflict are brute force of machineguns on the one side and the power of the state on the other. These two do not operate by the same rules. The dice are loaded, and the state—that is the citizens—is on the weak end. Nothing can remain alive in a society in which a small group imposes its own law. For, if there was one such group there would soon be another. In such a ruleless game, brute force would win out.

The short-term risk of erratic behaviour such as that of the FLQ is to force the government, with the backing of the population, to reduce most of the liberties which we all enjoy.

Many citizens are already wondering if these freedoms are not a luxury which we are not mature enough to deserve. We must comment on this at more length one of these days. It is too early to pick out the reasons which have brought us to the point where the state has, out of human compassion, had to agree to negotiate with men who have no mandate but their own. Under the circumstances, the government had hardly any choice.

Without being able to say precisely what has brought us to the current situation, it may be suggested that complete freedom from rules is showing its true face. Such liberty destroys itself. Revolutions always are carried out in the name of human rights, and they always begin by suppressing them.

It is suicide to allow complete freedom from restrictions without thought of the population as a whole. This type of freedom is like a cancer where a cell develops as if in anarchy outside the control of the governing mechanism of the body.

If special interest groups, the press and finally each citizen reject the unity which helps them exist, they would in effect be doing the same thing to the unity which is called Quebec.

The events of these past days present us for the first time with a choice: anarchy or democracy. Anarchy means the law of the jungle. The strongest wins out. Democracy tries to ensure that law and reason triumph. Between the weak and the strong, only the law is the true liberator. Only the law protects the weak. For example, is it the weak or the strong who are against medicare legislation?

It will always be said that democracy is imperfect, and that will always be right. But imperfect democracy is still democracy. To argue that absence of democracy is preferable to imperfect democracy is specious.

In a time of crisis, positions must be clear—there is no room for doubt or hesitation. In such a basic matter there should be no fear of repeating that the only choice is between law and order and a reign of terror.

Consolidation of democratic authority is the immediate task. Democracy can only exist if every citizen believes in it and protects it. It should be added that the elected guardians of democracy must first show proof that they respect it. The people's dissatisfaction always stems from the cynicism of those in charge.

Quebec cannot afford to suffer through many more adventures such as these.

To believe in ourselves and to get others to believe in us, we must accept the discipline of reality—our reality.

Two Can Play That Game

THE WHITEHORSE STAR
October 13, 1970
EDITORIAL

When dealing with kidnappers and extortionists, as the Canadian and Quebec governments are this week, it is no time for kid gloves.

We would have handled things a bit differently. In the first place, it has long been our belief that such groups as the FLQ would wither on the vine if every publication in Canada (together with radio and television stations) agreed to avoid mentioning them. Such a conspiracy of silence is the very opposite to what those people want; this week they have garnered a wonderful harvest of publicity on all sides which is simply stoking the fires of revolution.

Secondly, when their demand for $500,000 for release of the kidnapped British trade commissioner was received, we would have bounced the ball back into their court by putting a price of $500,000 on the heads of the kidnappers, which would be removed only if the kidnapped man was returned unharmed.

And finally, being a WASP, we cannot help but note that the British Government and their trade representative stood firm and made no suggestion that the FLQ demands be met; it was the Quebec Minister of Labour, second to be snatched, who pleaded that the ransom be paid—if the notes received by government officials are authentic.

We are sorry for the families of the two kidnapped men, they are doing the real suffering. It's time to call in Mission Impossible.

" . . . Go On and Bleed"

THE GUARDIAN, *Charlottetown*
October 15, 1970
EDITORIAL

Prime Minister Trudeau laid it on the line when he said . . . "only weak-kneed bleeding hearts" would be afraid to go the limit to stop people trying to run the country by kidnapping and blackmail.

Asked by a reporter to defend the use of troops in Ottawa to guard high-ranking persons such as cabinet ministers and ambassadors, Mr. Trudeau said "there are a lot of bleeding hearts around that just don't like to see people with helmets and guns. All I can say is go on and bleed. It's more important to keep law and order in society than to be worried about weak-kneed people who don't like the looks of an army."

And echoing this strong line of determination is Ontario's Premier Robarts who said the Quebec terrorist situation has evolved into "total war" and the time has come "to stand and fight." He went on to say that the federal and Quebec governments must stop protecting the rights of the minorities at the expense of the majority—a situation that would be produced in any compromise with Montreal terrorists. The terrorists, said Mr. Robarts, will try the same thing again if they have any success this time.

Possibly Premier Robarts may seem a little harsh when he advocates "total war" but he is certainly correct when he says the time has come "to stand and fight." Stand and resist, at least, meeting force with force. The security of Canada should not be bargained away on criminals' terms.

No citizen of Canada likes to see armed guards patrolling the streets of two of the nation's largest cities; no Canadian wants to see the "total war" Premier Robarts speaks off; and no Canadian will argue with the Prime Minister's statement that it's more important to keep law and order in society than to be worried about weak-kneed people who don't like the looks of an army.

The time for firmness is now. Otherwise, in view of the latest FLQ threats, broadcast in Europe, many more Canadian cities will witness the spectacle of their prominent persons being shadowed by armed guards.

Bleeding hearts to the contrary.

A brief and welcome diversion from the grim events of the October Crisis came with the October 14 announcement of the establishment of diplomatic relations between Ottawa and Peking. The first major foreign policy initiative of the Trudeau government since the decision to cut back Canada's NATO troop commitment was greeted with favorable press reaction in Canada and China.

Canada-China Recognition: World Lesson in Realism

THE GLOBE AND MAIL, *Toronto*
October 14, 1970
EDITORIAL

The long negotiations between Canada and the People's Republic of China have at last been concluded successfully; the fiction that the Formosan government of Chiang Kai-shek controls the destiny of China's 700 million people is no longer part of this country's foreign policy.

This recognition of reality, made official yesterday by the establishment of diplomatic relations between Canada and China, should be a source of satisfaction to all Canadians and especially to Prime Minister Pierre Trudeau, who personally decided on the approach to Peking before the last federal election.

His decision could have a far-reaching effect on international politics.

In the United Nations, for instance, Canada will join the ranks of Western countries—Great Britain, France and the Scandinavian nations—who have been pressing for China's admission to the world body. This move may well cause some member states, particularly those who retreated from the issue during the confusion of the Cultural Revolution, to support or at least abstain from voting on the question of China's entry.

It is imperative, of course, that China take its rightful place not only in the UN General Assembly but also on the Security Council, where its position is now occupied by Nationalist China—mostly because of the persuasive influence of the United States.

Few important international problems can be resolved today without the participation of China. This is especially true in the Far East, as was tacitly admitted last week by President Richard Nixon when he called for a new Indochina peace conference which his aides said could include Peking. To have suggested that Nationalist China should join such a conference would have been patently absurd.

Official U.S. reaction to Sino-Canadian diplomatic recognition has been low key. Publicly, Washington can hardly be expected to be enthusiastic, but privately White House officials probably see it as a help in their own attempts to achieve a meaningful dialogue with China.

Certainly, Canada's recognition of China has provided a blueprint for other nations who wish to take the same step. This includes Italy and Belgium, who have been waiting in the wings for 20 months while Peking and Ottawa threshed out a Formosa formula.

That this has been done—Canada takes note of China's claim to Formosa without approval or rejection—clears the way for the swift establishment of diplomatic relations between China and other countries.

While the international implications of yesterday's announcement are important—perhaps in the long run even more significant to the world than to Canada—there is also the question of what it will mean to Canadians. . . .

An enhanced cultural, academic, trade and political relationship with China will not blossom overnight. But at least a beginning can now be made, and the Government of Mr. Trudeau should be commended for making it possible.

Welcome the Establishment of Sino-Canadian Diplomatic Relations

THE PEOPLE'S DAILY, *Peking*
October 15, 1970
EDITORIAL

Our government and the Canadian government have now decided to extend mutual diplomatic recognition and establish diplomatic relations on the basis of the principles of mutual respect for sovereignty and territorial integrity, mutual non-agression, non-interference in each other's internal affairs, equality and mutual benefit. We welcome this significant development in Sino-Canadian relations.

The people of China and Canada have traditional friendship. During the War of Resistence, Dr. Norman Bethune, a friend of the Chinese people, sacrificed his own life for the cause of Chinese revolution. In recent years, contacts between our two countries have greatly increased. China and Canada have now decided to establish formal diplomatic relations. It reflects the common wishes of the people of our two countries, and also conforms to the interest of the people.

Our great leader Chairman Mao has pointed out: "We reso-
lutely stand for the implementation by all nations of the well-
known five principles of mutual respect for sovereignty and
territorial integrity, mutual non-aggression, non-interference in
each other's international affairs, equality and mutual benefit."
In the past 20 years, our country has acted according to the five
principles of peaceful co-existence, and has established diplomatic relations with many countries with different social systems. Our country has already developed friendly co-operation
and friendship with many countries on the basis of five principles of peaceful co-existence. We do not encroach upon the
sovereignty and territorial integrity of other countries, we will
never tolerate encroachment by any other countries upon our
sovereignty and territorial integrity. We do not interfere in
others' internal affairs, we will never tolerate any interference
in our internal affairs by any other countries. Practices have
proven that the five principles of peaceful co-existence are the
accurate principles for dealing with relationship among nations
with different social systems. . . .

Canada is a big nation on the American continent. The
Canadian government published in June this year a White
Paper on foreign policy. It reflects the will on the part of the
Canadian government to carry out its own independent policy.
This means that the scheme of the super powers to control
other countries can no longer be carried out.

The Chinese people welcome the establishment of Sino-Canadian relations. We wish that the friendship between the
people of China and Canada will continue to develop and that
the relations between our two countries will continue to flourish.

*The October Crisis returned with a jolt in the small hours of
October 16, as the government enacted the War Measures Act.
Almost immediately police cars emerged from the underground
parking lot of Montreal's Parthenais Street headquarters, fan-
ning out across the sleeping city in their search for "subversives."
Officers were soon pounding on the doors of over 400 teachers,
trade unionists, students, journalists, social workers, writers, and*

singers, who would be hustled off to detention, usually without explanation. No one would be allowed to contact them. They had disappeared. This was one reality the press saw little of in the first few days after the Act was invoked. While a few would voice serious objections to the government's actions at this point, many writers sensed a need for more information than they were being given by the government.

This Is a State of Emergency

LE SOLEIL, *Québec*
October 16, 1970
EDITORIAL BY RAYMOND DUBE

For great ailments, great remedies.

To end a state of emergency the Canadian government, at the request of the Quebec government and the mayor of Montreal, has decided to invoke the War Measures Act. It has been in force since 4 A.M. this morning and has, since its coming into force, resulted in numerous raids by police and interrogations to put an end to the subversive acts of radical elements which are inevitably leading us to an insurrection and probably even the start of a civil war; at least temporarily, for the crisis will be averted.

The population will be accorded the protection it has a right to and order will be maintained. How long will this state of emergency last? No one can foresee. All will depend upon the effectiveness of the measures adopted by the Canadian government.

We will know later today the rules that will apply through this crisis period. For the moment, it suffices to know that if the authorities chose to resort to such extreme measures it is because they had good reasons to imagine the worst. The population owes it to itself to remain calm and to not excite itself unnecessarily.

Under the circumstances this is the best support it can provide the authorities. The decisions taken last night cannot surprise us. It was foreseeable as of yesterday, when the Quebec government sought the help of the army and when the Canadian government called on troops to protect Ottawa and the rest of the country.

It was necessary, before imposing the emergency law, to take measures necessary to maintain order. Any delay in taking vigorous action could have been fatal. There exists a state of emergency across Canada and particularly in Quebec. The temporary loss of our civil liberties is a sacrifice that we must accept serenely.

The alternative is the permanent loss of liberties, the disappearance of our democratic institutions and a period of anarchy, the consequences of which could only be disastrous for all citizens of the Canadian community.

Emergency Action Was Inevitable

THE MONTREAL STAR
October 16, 1970
EDITORIAL

The first violators of civil liberties in the current wave of trouble in this province were those who resorted to bombs as a means of social protest; the second were those who turned peaceful demonstrations into acts of increasing violence; the third were those who resorted to the taking of hostages and threats of murder. The end was inevitable—a determined social reaction by governments at all levels. The result is that for an unknown length of time we are faced in Canada with the suspension of civil liberties, involving those protections generally provided for us covering search, arrest and detention, plus almost anything else the government wishes to do.

It is to state the obvious to say that this is a sad day for Quebec and for Canada, and indeed for any civilized community. But let it be emphasized where the responsibility lies. It is not with those who react but with those who acted; it is not with those who suspend liberties but with those who violate them.

Meanwhile, we must keep the action of the government—

government in its finest sense, for Ottawa and Quebec are working in concert—in perspective. Its behavior all along has been balanced and humane, and if it has invoked the Police Act and the War Measures Act it has done so on the basis of knowledge which it has accumulated and which no one outside government is yet in a position to challenge.

The point is that fundamental structures are not violated. Soldiers are on sentry duty in Quebec and Montreal to relieve overworked police, to allow them to pursue their normal duties —in this instance aggravated by around-the-clock searches for abductors. The War Measures Act itself is subject to scrutiny by Parliament and presents no long-range threat to individual rights. Our response now is in large measure a vote of confidence in legal government.

War Measures

THE EDMONTON JOURNAL
October 16, 1970
EDITORIAL

It seems totally unreal on a beautiful fall morning to find that Canada has been put on a semi-wartime footing in the wake of the FLQ kidnappings.

The federal government has swiftly escalated its response to the FLQ threat, massing troops in Ottawa and Montreal and proclaiming the War Measures Act which gives the authorities wide powers to suspend normal civil rights.

Proclamation of the act has been followed by a wave of arrests in Quebec cities.

Many Canadians may be worried that the federal government is over-reacting by treating the kidnapping of two officials as a state of anticipated insurrection.

But we do not have the information available to the government. The federal and provincial authorities deserve the support of Canadians in their refusal to meet the terms demanded by the kidnappers.

We can only take on faith, for the time being, that the
further measures taken have been necessary for the peace,
order and good government of Canada. Members of the federal cabinet know as well as other Canadians that the powers
now invoked are tolerable only in times of genuine national
emergency.

Canada Needs the Facts

THE GLOBE AND MAIL, *Toronto*
October 17, 1970
EDITORIAL

The imposition of the War Measures Act places in the Government's hands the power to restrict freedom of the press at a
time when the country has much need of unfettered reporting.

Defense Minister Donald Macdonald has said that the news
media will be affected only "to the extent that a person—a
broadcaster—who is a representative of the FLQ uses this as
some means of transmitting messages. But it doesn't prevent
news reports of the situation or genuine reports and commentary on what is happening . . . The only way in which the news
media will be affected is if the individual in question is a
representative of the FLQ or a similar organization."

This is not very comforting, on a day when the police have
been empowered to arrest and detain without bail for up to 90
days persons who are merely suspected of belonging to the
Front de Liberation du Québec, or of speaking on behalf of
the FLQ. It is not difficult to identify political pamphlets for
what they are, or so-called newspapers devised to carry nothing
but propaganda advocating the violent means of the FLQ; but
beyond that lies a large and dangerous grey area. Will the
authorities find it possible to slip over to the point where they
decide that any news which describes the FLQ supports its
cause?

CBC president George Davidson, scrambling in panic to
keep his organization pure and ordering restraints to ensure it,

delivered himself of this fatuous comment, "I think the fact that it (the insurrection) is happening here alters the whole perspective of the thing. I think we have to show a different sense of responsibility when it happens here than we do when it happens in Guatemala, Uruguay or Brazil."

The responsibility of an ostrich, Mr. Davidson?

Prime Minister Pierre Trudeau is also a man who has objected on many an occasion to the facts being in the press. Concerning present events he said to a CBC reporter, "The main thing that the FLQ is trying to gain from this is a hell of a lot of publicity for the movement... and I am suggesting that the more recognition you give to them, the greater the victory is, and I'm not interested in giving them a victory." ...

Canada needs the facts as never before, and if the press oversteps there are the laws of libel, contempt and sedition by which to punish it. Canada cannot now afford the inhibitions which the War Measures Act could impose.

That being said, it must also be said that the press must discipline itself. If the country needs a free, unfettered press, it also needs a responsible press. The country is more important than the headlines.

A Choice Between Evils

THE SUN, *Vancouver*
October 17, 1970
EDITORIAL

Mr. Trudeau has promised the Canadian people to use only as much of the emergency regulations as the "apprehended insurrection" requires and to withdraw them as fast as circumstances permit.

He has further undertaken to canvass, with other political leaders, the desirability of bringing down new legislation "of a less comprehensive nature" than the War Measures Act.

His record in defence of civil liberties is the guarantee of his sincerity. Public reaction indicates that the majority of Canadians who listened to his eloquent address on television are

willing to believe that the temporary suspension of some of
those liberties is as repugnant to him as it is to them. They also
accept that he acted in good faith in response to urgent pleas
from the authorities in Quebec and Montreal best able to
assess the risks of anarchy.

Neither the Conservatives nor the New Democratic Party,
had either been in office, would have responded so promptly.
Their leaders, Robert Stanfield and T. C. Douglas, made a
special point in the Commons to say that they had withheld
their consent when consulted by Mr. Trudeau in advance of
the action. Mr. Douglas, in particular, would have waited until
Parliament could have been presented with, debated, and presumably passed a special act designed to restrain only so much
subersive violence as could be foreseen and to limit liberties as
little as possible.

For these stands, both Opposition leaders have been denounced by Creditiste leader Real Caouette. As a French-
Canadian, Mr. Caouette may be presumed to have a deeper
insight into the turmoil in Quebec and the threats to security
posed by Le Front de Liberation du Quebec. He had no hesitation in accusing Mr. Stanfield and Mr. Douglas of "playing
politics."

Mr. Caouette's reasoning here seemed to be that the Liberal
government had shouldered a most distasteful responsibility
for which it would get whatever credit might be earned for
averting violence. The other two national parties, by appearing
to deplore the use of an omnibus statute, could escape any
backlash without seeming to condone illegal activities. Furthermore, if the use of sections of the War Measures Act proved
effective, nobody could say later that they were parties to
insurrection. They could and do have the best of both possible
political worlds.

What good this may do them will depend on what credence
the public places in the ability of the premier of Quebec, the
mayor of Montreal and the chief of the Montreal police force
to assess an imminent crisis. It will be remembered that these
men had stalled, temporized and even sought to bargain for
eleven days with skilled, and obviously well dug-in, blackmail-
ing, terrorists holding the lives of innocent men to ransom. A
climate of violence was deepening by the hour. Was this a time

to ask Parliament to begin clause-by-clause debate of remedial measures, perhaps too little and almost certainly too late, while the terrorists governed their actions accordingly?

Mr. Trudeau has spoken of his "deep regret and grave concern" that revolutionary events should require the proclamation in peacetime of powers ordinarily reserved for threats from abroad. These are powers abhorrent in a democracy, but no others were available on the statute books. Yet, in the words of Premier Robert Bourassa of Quebec, they represented the only choice "if we were not to betray the mandate of a democratically-elected government."

In choosing between evils in those dark hours of Thursday night and Friday morning Mr. Trudeau must have been savagely torn between his ideals and the bloody reality. . . .

A Season of Mourning for Our Open Society

THE TORONTO STAR
October 17, 1970
PETER C. NEWMAN

Caught between the violent demands of fanatical men and the repressive responses forced on our leaders, we have arrived at one of those rare junctures in Canadian history when we can sense the continuity of an age being cut. What comes now will be very different from what came before.

The politics of terror have changed the inner climate of our society forever. We have had to declare a state of war in a time of peace. And suddenly we recognize the fragility—and the value—of all the freedoms we have taken for granted.

Our Prime Minister rides in a bullet-proof car. Troops occupy the country's largest city and the nation's capital. The two-year-old son of our justice minister plays in his Rockcliffe garden under the shadow of submachine-guns. No politician who values his hide can venture into a crowd; future election campaigns may have to be conducted in guarded television studios.

We have undergone a change that should be marked by a season of mourning for the open society we so recently enjoyed.

The chilling drama that has been playing itself out in Montreal, and Pierre Trudeau's invoking of the War Measures Act, challenge the very essence of our democratic society, which is based on a reciprocal social contract: That the state will grant protection to all men within its confines, and in turn exact obedience to its laws. When these laws are obeyed, citizens have a right to claim the protection of the state.

But when, as has happened during the current rampage of the Front de Liberation du Quebec, the state is no longer able to protect the citizen and when it abrogates its laws, the social contract is weakened. Some future prime minister, possessed of a less scrupulous regard for the law than Pierre Trudeau, could use this precedent to accomplish ends we can't yet imagine.

We have been cast, overnight it seems, into a revolutionary situation in which historical pace and perspective have been drastically compressed. Events now determine ideologies; the age of political dynasties is finished.

For generations, the superstructure of Canadian politics remained undisturbed. Social classes were roughly balanced in the gains they might expect from political participation. But performance somehow never equalled expectations, and now the centre will not hold.

The FLQ is modelled on the revolutionary tactics of Mao Tse-tung, Fidel Castro and Che Guevara, who have acted on the assumption that violence can by itself create a revolutionary situation. In their lexicon, the politics of the deed take precedence over social reforms and political programs. Violent acts such as kidnapping of public men become an effective means for changing the relation of forces between revolution and reaction, because they enable a small group of rootless guerrillas to resist a stronger and better armed legitimate government by splitting its ranks and gradually whittling down its authority with the people.

The FLQ's prime target is the barbarization of our society. They seek deliberately to deprive us of law and order and to create the kind of right-wing backlash which will alienate the younger generation from renewing our institutions and paralyze our progress toward constructive solutions.

Many young Quebeckers—psychologically alienated and disoriented from their fathers' traditional society, contemptuous of what they perceive to be the excessive patience and half measures of the older intellectual groups, disillusioned by democratic politics which gave the separatists only 7 per cent of the seats in the last provincial election (even though they got 24 per cent of the votes)—have opted out of their society, tacitly or actively supporting the FLQ's objectives.

The grievances of Quebec will not be redeemed by crushing the FLQ. They can only be resolved by transforming the lives of the alienated young French Canadians. The way to deal with those who feel they have nothing to lose is to give them something to conserve.

Meanwhile, the Trudeau and Bourassa governments have no choice but to react with force against the FLQ. Democracy has no hope without order. In the end, the only ultimate protection against violence is the enforcement of justice.

From being merely a great and wonderful hunk of geography, Canada has fallen at last into the grip of history and all of its associated terrors. Dark and violent discontents are tunnelling under the ramparts of our society, disclosing turbulent new perceptions of our future. The peaceful old ideologies that served us for more than a hundred years suddenly seem exhausted, museum pieces in a world that alters as we walk in it.

Confrontation in Quebec

THE NEW YORK TIMES
October 17, 1970
EDITORIAL

Were he not of French Canadian origin himself, it is unlikely that Prime Minister Trudeau would have dared take the energetic and unprecedented measures he put into effect against Quebec separatist extremists.

Assuming emergency powers never before employed in peacetime, Mr. Trudeau outlawed the Quebec Liberation Front, moved troops in to supplement police forces and had hundreds of suspects arrested. By these moves Canada's Prime Minister escalated what had begun as a pair of political kidnappings on the Latin-American model into a direct confrontation between the Canadian Government and a terrorist group which seeks a separate and socialist Quebec.

The viability of a united Canada could well hinge on the outcome of the Prime Minister's dramatic intervention into Quebec's affairs. The specter which Mr. Trudeau seeks to exorcise is, in his words, "the emergence of a parallel power which defies the elected power in this country." Understandably he fears that, if the Front won capitulation to its blackmail demands as the price of saving the lives of its two prisoners, it would secure a prestige and status rivaling the Quebec regime itself.

Successful use of such a tactic in this initial effort would, of course, encourage similar future kidnappings to exert pressure for other even more extreme political demands. Mr. Trudeau's fears cannot have been lessened by the wavering attitude of the Quebec provincial government, whose willingness to make concessions and to negotiate has enhanced terrorist standing.

Mr. Trudeau's assumption of extraordinary powers is bound to stir criticism from Canadians of many political identifications. He himself has acknowledged that his Government may be falling into a trap set by the Front. The separatists may well want to provoke extremely repressive measures as a means of radicalizing and winning over more moderate French Canadians.

Nevertheless, now that Mr. Trudeau has chosen his course, most Canadians and most citizens of this country will hope he achieves quick success in freeing the prisoners and turning back the Front's challenge. Canada is not alone among countries where, in the Prime Minister's words, "a new and terrifying" type of person has arisen who seeks to destroy the present organization of society through violence. The outcome of this confrontation in Quebec will have repercussions far outside that province, and outside Canada as well.

*The press and public were still trying to absorb the significance
of the state of emergency delcared by the government. The War
Measures Act had been in force for fewer than 24 hours when the
dead body of Pierre Laporte was discovered in the trunk of a car
parked at St. Bruno Airport.*

We Mourn Our Civilization

MONTREAL MATIN
October 19, 1970
EDITORIAL BY PAUL GROS D'AILLON

We are all seized with horror. We are overcome with indignation and fury. At the mortal wounding of a man who has
suffered the worst kind of moral agony for days and days
before being dispatched coldly and bestially, we can do nothing but weep and clench our fists.

That such an atrocity was committed on our soil, at our very
doorsteps, by men who speak our language, who were brought
up among us, who breathe the same air as we, seems simply
unimaginable. At no time, save in the darkest days of the
barbarism of primitive tribes, can we find such an example of
savagery and cruelty.

We are in mourning for Pierre Laporte. We are in mourning
for civilization, our civilization.

Pierre Laporte, must we repeat it, was a courageous man of
rare intelligence and rare will. Like all other parliamentary
correspondents of the last decade, I had the occasion to know
him and walk beside him. He knew that in many circumstances
we did not agree, but even at the height of the issue, he
remained simple, likeable and open to discussion.

It has been about three weeks since I had the occasion to
talk with him for an hour before the cameras of private television. We dealt with one of the most sensitive issues in Quebec
today, namely immigration. Pierre Laporte brought to the conversation the reason of cold logic but also a warm conviction.
He told us on the one hand of his determination to assure the
survival and grandeur of his people but on the other hand his

repugnance of the method of coercion. Pierre Laporte believed in active persuasion. He did not believe in the success of violence and force.

It is paradoxical that he himself has become the victim of terror and intolerance. Fate has once again defied logic and intelligence.

We mourn Pierre Laporte, but we also mourn for civilization. Quebec can never forget what has happened. What we all believe to be impossible here has come to pass. We intimately and profoundly feel the fading of some of the values we believed steadfast—the kindness of our people, their understanding, and respect for human life, and their tolerance. Yes, it takes only a few dehumanized persons among us to commit such crimes, but it troubles us to the very base of our souls and each among us recognizes his responsibility and feels implicated.

At the same time we must guard against floundering into another form of extremism, one which stems from the same mistakes as the first. The "vendetta" is not a solution. Terror does not repair terror. We will not prove ourselves an adult nation or a civilized people if we fall to the opposite extreme. After so much freedom, how can we breath the air of slavery, any slavery? We must defend ourselves, but we must not oppress unjustly. We need all our calm to unite and be truly strong to overcome this outrage.

To the family of Pierre Laporte, the family which hour by hour has lived through nothing but agony and chagrin for eight days only to be faced now by a tremendous emptiness, we wish immense courage. To his brave wife who has again shown her force of character in these tragic hours, to his daughter and young Jean Laporte, his son, we can do nothing but extend the hand of friendship and proclaim our understanding and our sadness. Quebec, shaken and shocked, weeps with them and demands justice.

The Darkness of a Tragic Night

LE DEVOIR, *Montréal*
October 19, 1970
EDITORIAL BY CLAUDE RYAN

Two weeks after the act that opened the Cross-Laporte drama, the confusion that has surrounded this tragic story, far from being dissipated, has only grown more profound. The kidnappings had at first seemed like an unusual drama that we persisted in believing would end well. Since the terrible nights of Saturday and Sunday, there can be no doubt about the seriousness of these events. The first acts of the drama assailed us as never before. All of that was nothing. The cruel assassination of Pierre Laporte has struck us like a blade, cutting without pity into what we hold most sacred, with a cold-bloodedness that arouses revulsion and horror.

The most serious aspect of the assassination of Pierre Laporte is not that he fell beneath the blows of his aggressors. In the United States, for example, more than one public figure has fallen to aggressors. But whereas the assassination of Mr. Kennedy was based, from all appearances, on obscure personal motives, that of Mr. Laporte was political. Its authors give it not only an ethical justification, but they threaten to repeat it. And it seems they can rely, towards this end, on a greater support, be it partial or indistinct, than we would have suspected.

The exclusive recourse to protective measures and manhunts will settle nothing in the long run. For every citizen we may find guilty of a crime, we risk creating, if discretionary powers are badly used, two, three, five citizens irritated by having had their rights denied. This could, if we are not careful, increase a certain climate of desperation which is not unusual in the emergence of a phenomenon such as the FLQ. The grave times through which Québec is living bring into question whether we wish it or not, the political system and the socio-economic structural order which we have lived in in the past decade. Problems this serious (and this widespread) do not spring up spontaneously. They grow in appropriate soil. It is more important than ever during this crisis that citizens give full support to the reasonable decisions of their legitimate political leaders and that they even accord the benefit of the doubt in instances when complete explorations cannot be immediately provided. But it is equally important that political leaders become humbly aware of the fragility of their leadership and act without delay to consolidate their leadership by associating with it those, from various milieux, whose social influence and moral authority are of another form, not less vital but often disdained by political powers, of democratic leadership. At this moment, it is not the prestige or authority of any individual but democracy in Québec that must be safeguarded. That is the goal to which we must hold through the difficulties of this unprecedented night of darkness through which Québec is living.

To the family of Pierre Laporte, in particular to his courageous wife, to the colleagues and collaborators of the assassinated minister, we express our painful consternation and our deepest sympathy. May this trial, rather than destroying Québec, serve us all as a purification on the way to a true renewal.

By Law or Terror? The Answer Is Given

THE GAZETTE, *Montréal*
October 19, 1970
EDITORIAL

"Those who gain power through terror rule through terror," Prime Minister Trudeau told the nation in his televised statement on Friday night. "The government is acting, therefore, to protect your life and your country."

Canadians can be thankful for the resolute leadership the prime minister is providing at this sad and difficult hour. His dedication to individual liberties should be fully obvious to all those who listened to him speak. The War Measures Act will not be abused in his hands.

Premier Bourassa similarly has shown great courage and firmness in the worst trial that any leader of a Quebec government has ever been called upon to endure. He, too, deserves the gratitude of citizens who value a free and civilized society.

The nation is clearly united in its determination to hold together under the rule of law. Amid the grief and shock over Mr. Laporte's murder, a new and heartening sense of solidarity is emerging.

The rule of law is gravely menaced by unseen and ruthless enemies who are prepared to go to any extreme to spread fear and undermine confidence in legitimate government. If all Canadians, French-speaking and English-speaking, who value their lives and freedom stand together, this crisis can be surmounted without fatal damage to our society.

They are standing together, if one can judge by the attitudes expressed by MPs from all parts of the country since Mr. Laporte's death. It is recognized that grief and outrage are deeply felt by an overwhelming majority of the people in Quebec, including a majority of those who want an independent Quebec and have worked towards that goal. There is a difference between Quebec nationalism and the kind of thinking and feeling exemplified by the FLQ, and level-headed persons have not lost sight of the difference.

It should be apparent to all by now that society faces a determined and fanatical enemy. The problem is more than that of dealing with criminals who have limited objectives and only a limited will to pursue them. Until Sunday at least, however, some responsible spokesmen seemed to think otherwise.

Some consolation is to be found in the evident fact that MP's of all parties now realize the seriousness of the situation and will support the federal government in its enforcement of the War Measures Act.

The act has been put into force at the request of the Quebec government and the Montreal administration. All three levels of government are determined to put an end to terrorism. What would be the chances now of restoring a reasonable sense of peace and security, if they were not so determined?

Although the War Measures Act is in force, it must be remembered that the government remains answerable to Parliament and the people for its actions. It cannot abolish Parliament. It cannot abolish elections. Successful terrorists can abolish both Parliament and elections.

This, then, is the only issue: Is the country to be governed by law or by terror? The answer has been resoundingly given by the freely chosen governments of Canada and Quebec. We will be governed by law.

An Appeal to Québécois

LA PRESSE, *Montréal*
October 19, 1970
EDITORIAL BY JEAN PELLERIN

A fanatic pressed the trigger and a man passed into history. Mad dogs raise a clamor and a deep anguish seizes the orginary citizen: How can we rid ourselves of the frightful hatred that seems to lie everywhere in ambush? How can we bring the extremists back to reason?

Violence has a new, tragic feather to its cap. Good men freely vent their indignation: they accuse governments of not having been flexible enough. They say it would have been better to give in to the blackmailers. This thesis is debatable but it is no less so than the belief that by giving in on one point the State would embark upon a slope that would lead to a complete surrender.

Prime Minister Trudeau posed the anguished question the other night: at what moment should we resist blackmail, after the first, the fifth or the hundredth risk of assassination?

Others, equally well intentioned, wonder if the government is not employing unacceptably radical measures to destroy terrorism. It is certain that recourse to the War Measures Act—even with a softening of its provisions—could lead to dire consequences if power in Ottawa, Québec or Montréal was in the hand of a Hitler or a Stalin. That is clearly not the case. The entire country—and not only Montréal and Québec—is threatened.

There has been an escalation of provocation and sedition since 1963. In seven years, the terrorists of the FLQ have killed seven people and placed 250 bombs. The last bomb attempt could have, according to a specialist, destroyed a number of buildings in the heart of the city. According to Jean Marchand, the FLQ has thousands of handguns, rifles and machine guns as well as at least 2,000 pounds of dynamite. The RCMP assures us that there are 22 FLQ cells with 130 active members and 2,000 sympathizers.

There is no doubt about their strategy: after the bombings they pass to a phase of selective assassinations. Ottawa believes this is the moment to halt the escalation and for the ordinary citizen the moment has come to choose between the FLQ and the government. The moment has come for each individual to ask himself if it is preferable to let the FLQ continuously assault our civil rights or accept that the government should suspend their rights temporarily. There is much said about the trap being laid by the terrorists. But the government says it is quite aware of these traps. Prime Minister Trudeau himself has reminded us that revolutionary groups seek to provoke authorities into hard-line positions in order to justify their own violence. To prove that it has not fallen into that trap, the government must ensure that the emergency measures will only be applied for a short period. It cannot be denied that the present measures are a threat to civil liberties. We cannot, on the other hand, forget that these measures were not imposed by a repressive government but were rendered necessary by the acts of extremists.

Madness Gone Rampant

LE SOLEIL, *Québec*
October 19, 1970
EDITORIAL BY GILLES BOYER

It is a foul murder that the FLQ has committed. Something was needed to awaken the population of Québec to the grave danger that hovers over it in the form of systematic violence and organized assassination. The FLQ has made that danger clear. A martyr was needed to demonstrate to an entire society that efforts are being made to lead it down an evil route through the use of violence, hatred and fanaticism. The FLQ has given us that martyr. His name is Pierre Laporte.

He had profoundly identified himself to French Canada as a journalist, as a Member and as a Minister. The FLQ could not have chosen a better target to turn the entire population against a terrorist organization which will henceforth be branded with the hot iron of shame and infamy.

The entire world is witness to the outrageous humiliation of

Québec by the attempt of some of its own sons to destroy their society by an abuse of the freedom that exists here.

The entire world supports our indignation.

A great deal of courage is needed in these times to assume public office. Pierre Laporte died at his work. Others must live at their task. They must be inspired by the example of one of the best-known among them and continue to indomitably work against the conspirators and terrorists who seek to undermine society from within.

Prime Minister Trudeau, in a speech which marks a page in the history of our nation, gave an example on Friday night of that courage and determination.

Northerners Agree

THE WHITEHORSE STAR
October 19, 1970
EDITORIAL

It is a wonderful thing to live in a part of Canada where the words Yukon securities mean shares in mining stocks, not armed troops. In order to keep it that way, Yukoners might export some of their calm belief in the Canadian way of life and the necessity for upholding law and order to more troubled parts of our land.

As reaction to the FLQ murder of the Quebec cabinet minister spread throughout Whitehorse over the weekend, we heard not a single murmur against the invoking of the powers normally used in wartime. To those of us who have worn a Canadian uniform, there is nothing to fear in such measures.

It was interesting also, the number of American citizens who took the opportunity to urge us to stamp out such movements now and not wait until it is too late. We appreciate their concern and agree that the burden on our federal officials is becoming intolerable; how long can the public expect a cabinet minister, for example, to expose himself and his family to the threat of kidnapping and murder? And if top government officials resign in the face of such threats, we face chaos.

We are glad that the Canadian government has chosen to act firmly and fast, rather than wait for further provocation and we are sure Canadians from coast to coast will stand firmly behind that action.

Death Knell of Separatism

THE FREE PRESS, *Winnipeg*
October 19, 1970
EDITORIAL

The sympathy of the whole nation goes out today to the family of Pierre Laporte, whose murder at the hands of the Front de Liberation du Quebec came to light on Saturday night. It goes out equally to the family of British diplomat James A. Cross, still in the fanatics' hands but still apparently alive.

But what good is sympathy at a time like this, no matter how deeply it may be felt? There are no words to express the feelings of Canadians at the senseless murder of Mr. Laporte that have not been used. Grief, sorrow, shock, anger; but anger which many people have been reluctant to express for fear that it might be misinterpreted—so delicate are the sensitivities involved in the present situation.

It is, however, indicative that Quebecers are the most grieved by the latest cold-blooded crime of the FLQ; and in the Commons it has been Quebec members of Parliament, of all parties, who have been most solid in their support of the government in its invocation of the War Measures Act—in sharp contrast to the shabby display of politics put on by some members of opposition parties, when the crying need was for a show of national unity and solidarity.

The War Measures Act has spelled the death of the FLQ. The murder of Mr. Laporte should, if there is any justice, sound the death knell of the hopes of the separatist movement in Quebec. If it does, his death, tragic as it has been, will not have been in vain.

The Inspiring Tone of a Prime Minister

THE MONTREAL STAR
October 20, 1970
EDITORIAL

In its finest sense, the prime ministership of this country found itself in capable and sensitive hands at a moment of crisis. No one can have envied the position of Mr. Trudeau during the past fortnight of abduction, tension and decision. He rose to the occasion, and aroused even greater confidence, when he faced the public on television Sunday evening to deliver a message filled with dignity, compassion and feeling. In what should prove a memorable statement, he said:

"In this moment of shock and grief, I know that all Canadians are deeply conscious of the benefits that flow from a tolerant, compassionate and free society. We recognize that if we permit hatred and violence to grow and spread, these benefits will disappear."

The tone spread through Parliament itself, as we saw yesterday when the government, in an unusual demonstration of solidarity, won support from all members—except 16 of the New Democratic Party—for its decision to invoke the War Measures Act. Mr. Douglas, in questioning the harshness of the government's decision, chose to ignore a salient point: Ottawa had no alternative but to accede to the request from a provincial government. Quebec, under the forthright leadership of Premier Bourassa, saw an emergency and took the course it thought proper by appealing to Ottawa.

To have disregarded such an appeal would have shattered the foundation of confederation. Ideally, debate might have been preferable, but the inevitable loss of time would have denied authorities the speed and element of surprise they needed in their hunt for the abductors and safeguarding of security.

The Criminal Code itself was not sufficient to cope with the circumstances; this left only the War Measures Act. As Mr. Trudeau has emphasized, the latter is too wide in scope for peacetime needs and some half-way measures will be introduced to deal with future civil crises. One might even question the severity of powers enabling police to hold a man or woman as long as three weeks before appearance before a judge.

But here is where faith in government itself must be the key. No nation, even with the most generous laws, can feel secure if its leaders choose to twist the laws or resort to evasive actions. Conversely, no nation needs to fear the implementation of emergency regulations in the hands of men it can trust. What some of us have forgotten in the controversy over the invocation of the War Measures Act is that Pierre Elliott Trudeau, with his record as a civil libertarian, must have done a great deal of soul-searching and analyzing before consenting to the long detention without bail, among other details. While FLQ terrorists were still school children, Mr. Trudeau was fighting the fight for civil liberties under the truly oppressive regime of Maurice Duplessis. Some of the men closest to him now—Jean Marchand, Gérard Pelletier, for example—knew that fight as well.

Mr. Trudeau does not require an apologist to keep the record straight. His own actions, his obvious awareness, his delicate appreciation of Canadian sensitivities, indicated especially in the last few troublesome days, will long be appreciated by men and women across this country.

Murder, Not Bravado

THE GUARDIAN, *Manchester*
October 19, 1970
EDITORIAL

The murder of M. Pierre Laporte in Canada is a miserable, brutal, but not unexpected act. It was always a strong danger that the Canadian Government's decision to turn to a tough policy at the end of last week would lead to the deaths of the two hostages. None the less the news of M. Laporte's murder comes as a shock. It must be hoped that Mr. Cross may still be saved. It must be hoped also that the shock of the assassination will undermine support for the Quebec Liberation Front's methods in Canada. People who thought the kidnappers were romantic and their actions bravado now know that they have proceeded to murder.

Mr. Trudeau's Cabinet chose the tough way out of the blackmail dilemma. It is too early to say whether it will work. If the aftermath of the present kidnappings and the Canadian Government's policy of mass arrests brings a decline in violent activity by the FLQ it will have succeeded. But no one can be sure yet. In Brazil and Uruguay the tough and gentle policies have both been tried. Neither has been conspicuously successful.

But those are countries where political violence by Government as well as insurgents is deep-seated. That is not the case in Canada; hence the Canadian Government's dilemma. It was faced with a new problem. It knew too that there is no permanent solution to kidnapping. The best means of prevention will never stop the assassin's bullet. Thwarted kidnappers may try assassination. The best remedies remain mundane and complex. Security on public officials has to be tightened. Every step must be taken to see that genuine economic and social grievances are met. Only then will kidnappers be isolated.

A Fateful Hour for Canada — and the U.S.

THE WASHINGTON POST
October 20, 1970
EDITORIAL

The murder of Quebec Labor Minister Pierre Laporte confirms not only the despicable character of his killers, the Quebec Liberation Front (FLQ), but the necessity of the extraordinary steps Canada has taken to pursue them. Even before Mr. Laporte's bloody and bound body was discovered on Sunday, Prime Minister Trudeau had suspended civil liberties and committed his government to a relentless police-army campaign against the FLQ's "insurrection." Parliamentary and public support for his unprecedented decision had been assured; it will be more widely and deeply forthcoming now. For there appears to be nearly universal agreement that the FLQ poses a head-on challenge to the integrity of the Canadian government and to Canadian democracy alike, and that the two must be defended with all the resources that the free people of Canada can muster. This feeling is all the stronger for Prime Minister Trudeau's own unquestioned devotion to Canada's libertarian traditions, and for the evident fact that Quebec separatism in its nonviolent form was *already* being treated politically, legally and culturally within the system. Indeed, one wonders whether the FLQ's desperation did not arise from the perception that the system was working too well: nothing is so dangerous as a fanatic who believes his cause is being peacefully resolved.

The question of the moment is, of course, whether the government with its new emergency powers will be able to catch the murderers and their accomplices, who still hold a second hostage, British diplomat James Cross. At this point, one can only reply that if the government fails, more than its own prestige, and more than the life of Mr. Cross, may be lost. For it is the terrorists' purpose, as Mr. Trudeau well understands, to provoke the government into repressive measures that will enrage or alarm its ordinary citizens. This is why, by the way, we would be extremely surprised if the kidnappers took up Mr. Trudeau's offer to release Mr. Cross in return for safe conduct to Cuba for themselves and five of their jailed mates whose prison sentences are nearly expired. To accept amnesty would be to relieve the government of by far the greater part of the pressure whose application was the point of the FLQ exercise in the first place. In this regard, we wonder if Mr. Laporte's murder was committed out of the FLQ's panic at being pursued by the police, or out of a decision to tighten up its credibility, which had sagged during its week of unsuccessful negotiations with the government.

Americans can scarcely look across the border at Canada's travails—and at our own ferment—without asking themselves whether a similar dilemma, growing out of similar acts of terrorism, might come to pass here.

At the very least, one conclusion is immediately clear: so

important are atmosphere and example in nourishing the minds of those who commit such acts, that the United States has a large stake in how Canada emerges from its current agony. Whatever may be the possibility of political kidnappings in this country, unquestionably it would be a larger threat if Canada had caved in to the FLQ. For that much, we have much to be grateful for in Canada's example. However, if Canada loses its struggle against the FLQ, by ultimate capitulation to the terrorists or by a demonstrated inability to deal with them effectively, then a major defeat will have been sustained by democratic forces, and not just in Canada alone. . . .

Two weeks after the first kidnapping and the beginning of the October Crisis, more detailed overall editorial assessments of the Prime Minister's handling of the crisis began to appear. They would continue long after December, when Laporte's kidnappers were apprehended and the Cross abductors negotiated a Cuban exile. Opinion was then, and remains now, divided. With the possible exception of his management of the Canadian economy, no single issue has created so much adverse press reaction for Pierre Elliott Trudeau.

New Kind of Hero

SOUTHAM NEWS SERVICES
October 21, 1970
CHARLES LYNCH

The wave of national unity that has resulted from the terror crisis has been derided by some, who say it cannot last.

What is uniting the nation at this moment seems to have two components—revulsion against the kidnap-murder tactics of the FLQ, and admiration for the way the governments of Quebec, Montreal and Canada have reacted against the terrorists.

Never have there been such manifestations of popular confidence in political leaders as are being heard in Quebec and across the land, addressed to Robert Bourassa, Jean Drapeau and Pierre Elliott Trudeau.

In Mr. Trudeau's case, the outpourings of support amount virtually to a new wave of Trudeaumania—based this time on performance under pressure, rather than on superficialities as was the case when he first emerged into national prominence in 1968.

Misgivings have been expressed in the House of Commons and elsewhere that English-speaking Canada is solidly behind Trudeau for the wrong reasons, feeling that his strong actions are designed to put Quebec "in its place."

According to all the evidence I have been able to gather, from Newfoundland to British Columbia, this is a grave error in assessment—good will toward Quebec has never run so high, and sympathy for Quebec and her people has never been so deeply felt.

As to Mr. Trudeau, suspicions have been voiced in Quebec that English-speaking Canada is running him, and that his strong actions represent some sort of Anglo plot against Quebec aspirations.

This, too, is a grave error in assessment.

The fact is that Mr. Trudeau, in the exercise of the sweeping powers he has assumed, is running the country, carrying the vast majority of Canadians along with him in support of his policies.

The last time there was such widespread support for a political leader in Canada was in 1958 with John Diefenbaker, when Quebec joined the rest of Canada in giving him the most powerful mandate in Canadian history.

It is conceivable, in fact, that we may be in the presence of a political giant—a skilful activist laying at rest the old legend that Canada could only be governed by compromise and caution.

The sides of Mr. Trudeau that have been most in evidence in recent days are coolness, steadfastness and courage—he has met the professional terrorists eyeball to eyeball, and stared them down.

Throughout his brief public life, he has refused to discuss his courage or lack of it, in the face of snide remarks. It is clear,

now, that he has great sources of inner strength, and that he is
capable of communicating these to the populace.

Those who have said Trudeau does not understand Quebec
have had to eat their words.

The inspirational qualities that he has displayed in the last
two weeks make them sound like Jeremiahs—indeed, all of Mr.
Trudeau's critics have been floundering, including his opponents in the Conservative and New Democratic parties, who
appear as pygmies beside him.

He is a new kind of hero. Not only in Canada, but in the
global context as well. Out of the continuing tragedy being
enacted in Ottawa and Quebec, there is emerging a spectacle
of leadership in action, and a new image of Mr. Trudeau, who
already had attracted more world attention than any previous
Canadian leader.

Until We See More Clearly

LA PRESSE, *Montréal*
October 21, 1970
EDITORIAL BY CLAUDE GRAVEL

The FLQ thought it would liberate Québec. Because of the
FLQ Quebeckers are a little less free. The army is within the
walls of our principal cities. The War Measures Act has been
imposed upon Québec. Over 300 Québécois are held incom-
municado. The government of Québec has lost, in the last two
weeks, powers and an authority which it will take a long time
to regain. Liberties which until now were fundamental have
been suspended. The population is worried and its opinion is
difficult to measure.

No matter what our political options even the most methodi-
cal analysis leads to the conclusion that if this adventure is
prolonged the people of Québec risk losing their future in the
process. Even the members of the FLQ should be able to see
today the crisis they have led us into.

As these lines are written we assume that Mr. Cross is alive.

The government of Québec has told the kidnappers they will be allowed to go to Cuba; Mr. Trudeau's government has worked out an agreement with that of Mr. Castro. The terrorists must, for the good of Québec, accept the government's offer even if they find it clearly insufficient. We all want Mr. Cross to live; for humanitarian reasons and so the troubles now afflicting Québec will not get worse. There is still hope. Since last October 5 the kidnappers of Mr. Cross have, in their negotiations, been much more flexible than those who had kidnapped Mr. Laporte.

Let us hope they will understand that under the circumstances the freeing of the British diplomat is the best way to help the people of Québec. It is still impossible to foresee how this will end. It is too early to measure the consequences. Public opinion changes with each new event. We must slowly, once spirits have been calmed and when we can see clearly again, identify and correct the real causes of this despair and hatred.

Meanwhile, two facts must be emphasized before someone commits other irreparable abuses.

1) The population and particularly its leaders, must distinguish very clearly between ideas spread by legal political groups and the acts of secret terrorist movements. In periods of darkness people tend to look for scapegoats. It is a human reaction, sometimes understandable, but not at all reasonable. It must be avoided. Nothing would be gained. Such a reaction, by dangerously mixing the cards, would only create further problems.

2) At this moment 343 people are held by the police, who refuse to release their names for reasons that are perhaps well-founded but which begin to look questionable. Their families and all citizens have a right to know what is happening to them. At the suggestion of the Canadian Council of Churches, hardly an extremist group, independent observers are to have access to the prisons in order to visit the prisoners. It is the least we can demand in a society which claims to be democratic and humane.

Order is not a synonym for silence.

Youth's Other Voice

THE CHRONICLE-HERALD, *Halifax*
October 22, 1970
EDITORIAL

Imposition of the War Measures Act, predictably, has brought
out the placard-waving, professional protesters in some Canadian cities, at the University of Paris among some Quebec
students, and outside the Canadian embassy in Washington.

As usual, the protesters are firmly on the side of "Freedom".
The Canadian government's action in restricting the ability of
such revolutionaries as the FLQ (who evidently believe that
murder is a legitimate political weapon) to spread their ugly
creed and incite rebellion and the violent overthrow of legal
government, is offensive to these single-minded people. There
must be freedom for dissidents to speak and act against democratically elected authority, they insist. Yet when authority acts,
with the overwhelming support of the population, to protect
the fundamental freedoms on which democracy and good government are based, this is tyranny!

We have it from the Communist party of Canada, that the
War Measures Act (which even the federal government does
not claim is perfect and which it plans to revoke in favor of
some substitute legislation in the near future) " . . . is a declaration of war by the Trudeau government, acting on behalf of
monopoly, against the national social and economic aspirations
of the French Canadian nation."

What tired old cliches! What nonsense!

There is one highly encouraging aspect, however, of the
general reaction among Canadians to the emergency measures.
Not only have the "silent majority" found voice to express
their solidarity with the government in its defence of the nation
from enemies within. The great mass of the student population,
whose image for far too long has been tainted by the extremism, blind fanaticism, profanity, and violence of a minority
of anarchists and activists among their number, are speaking
out against revolution, against political murder, against violent
insurrection, against mindless politically-oriented vandalism.

More than this, they are speaking up for Canada and Canadian unity.

Both they and the great mass of their elders (including those in governments) must now be realizing that all of us have contributed, unwittingly, to the present crisis. Through apathy, laziness, indifference; complacency, a tendency to downgrade democracy and ridicule politicians, in speech and writing, and an excessive tolerance of destructive and violent dissent, we have put democratic government and the freedoms it embodies in peril. Already we have paid a high personal price to learn this lesson. But Canada's ordeal, and her reaction to it, may also have put other nations which practice and value western-style democracy, on their guard.

A United Front

THE LEADER-POST, *Regina*
October 22, 1970
EDITORIAL

There have been calls by many politicians, including Prime Minister Trudeau, for calmness on the part of all Canadians during these troubled times in the province of Quebec after the kidnappings, murder, and ransom demands by the Front de Liberation du Quebec.

What they feared in particular was what could be called an English-Canada backlash. Fortunately, there has been very little evidence of this.

Roger Lalonde of St. Victor, president of the French-Canadian Cultural Association of Saskatchewan and the Western French-Canadian Federation, alluded to it this week when he said he is concerned because some Canadians might equate the FLQ with all of the French-speaking people in the country.

Reasonable Canadians realize that the FLQ's actions are as regrettable to Quebec as to any other part of Canada. These crimes have united people of all ethnic origins in the country in their determination to support the government in its actions to eliminate a cancer in our society.

There should be no backlash to the legitimate programs to make Canada a nation in which both English and French—and all others—can live side by side in harmony.

As Mr. Lalonde said about the FLQ actions, "This may bring about the beginning of an era in which Canadians will strive to correct any intolerances that exist and to strengthen all parts of our society where we find a weakness."

Justice

LE DEVOIR, *Montréal*
October 26, 1970
EDITORIAL BY CLAUDE LEMELIN

How many times in the past have we heard Pierre Elliott Trudeau and the other doves of the federal covey speak out against abuses of power and arbitrary police action.

They have even at times understood that the outrages of a Duplessis can push unions and unionists to illegal action (scandal!), and even to violence (double scandal!).

This was in the past, remember. For here we have these men, having suspended the fundamental liberties of Canadians, revealing a total lack of concern for the use that the police forces of Québec are making of their terrible power of discretion, and having dissected, for our greater edification, the embryo of Québec democracy, they indifferently submit it to the risk of suffocation.

The instruments of repression with which Ottawa armed Québec's justice minister and police forces by invoking the War Measures Act would make a Duplessis jealous.

"In the same way that democracy is an aim in itself which must not be sacrificed to opportunistic consideration, it is true that in certain countries at certain times, federalism appears to have a fundamental value," wrote Pierre Elliott Trudeau ten years ago. It would seem that when two basic values are in opposition, opportunism can be overlooked.

This is perhaps why, among the thousands of congratulatory

telegrams Prime Minister Trudeau has boasted of having received, there was one that had come from the Colonels of Greece.

Keeping Our Heads

THE DAILY GLEANER, *Fredericton*
October 27, 1970
EDITORIAL

The London Sunday Times makes a reasoned assessment to the abduction and murder of Pierre Laporte and the unsolved kidnapping of James Cross. "The terrorists of Quebec have performed one service to the Western World. As their murderous adventure moves into its fourth week, the romance of the urban guerrilla should finally be seen for what it is. It is a story both morally sordid and intellectually infantile. This movement is not the ally of democracy. No one can doubt that democracy and the common good are safer in the hands of Prime Minister Trudeau than in those of the FLQ."

Most Canadians agree. The country is passing through a grievous period in its history, one bitter to endure and one which will be sad to remember. Yet the majority of Canadians have held their sense of proportion, keeping these things, terrible as they are, in balance with the general trend of events in the life of the nation.

We have just seen New Brunswick choose its government and legislative assembly by the orderly process of democratic balloting after a high-level election campaign. A few days ago Nova Scotia did the same. Montreal, scene of the most tragic events of the Quebec crisis, has also, by means of the ballot box, just given an overwhelming vote of approval to a mayor whose tremendous achievements are a matter of public record.

The proclamation of the War Measures Act, with its implications of insurrection and emergency, in no way curbs the liberty of thought, speech and action of the great body of Canadians. It bears down only upon one criminally subversive minority.

The world is taking the measure of Canadians in time of crisis and is finding that they are bold, resolute and cool when under fire.

Since I Was Three Years Old

THE SUN, *Vancouver*
October 29, 1970
EDITORIAL

Prime Minister Pierre Trudeau was being clever when he told the Commons yesterday that he acted in the current Quebec crisis on information already disclosed "and on information I have been accumulating since I was three years old."

He seemed to mean that he had used his best adult judgment. Those who recalled his life-long involvement in Quebec's intellectual, economic and political affairs were invited by implication to concede his unique competence to judge the temperament of the people and the timing of events.

But his answer will be regarded, at least outside Quebec, as more of a gallicism than an earnest effort to persuade. A claim to superior insight is less convincing to the plodding Anglo-Saxon mentality than the prosaic reasoning from cause to effect.

Is Mr. Trudeau now saying that it takes a French-Canadian to understand one? Does he now take the position that Quebec, indeed, is not "une province comme les autres"? And that the difference is inexplicable west of the Ottawa River?

If so, the prime minister need do little more than point to apparently authentic reports that a group of influential Quebecers had been preparing, before the armed forces came in and the War Measures Act was invoked, to set up a sort of provisional government with a softer response to the Front de Liberation du Quebec. It is impossible at this distance to visualize how this might have been done. What would be the mechanics of the takeover? How could a government fresh from the polls be pushed aside by the appeasers? Was this move envisioned as a sort of coup-by-consent?

The whole intrigue seems to make more sense east of the Ottawa than elsewhere. Mayor Jean Drapeau of Montreal admits its existence and Premier Robert Bourassa of Quebec says he heard about it but denies that it influenced a joint crackdown by the federal and provincial governments.

This affair may be given undue weight in the rest of the country by Mr. Trudeau's record of reticence in the Commons. Day after day, the prime minister has been fending off a barrage of questions about his administration's actions. His laconic responses, amounting to taciturnity, have left an impression of deliberate concealment. This has served only to egg on his questioners without adding much to the public's knowledge.

Once again it becomes necessary to ask the prime minister whether the time has not come, if it has not passed, to take the public into his full confidence, perhaps with a major speech on television if he prefers not to appear to be rising to the bait of political opponents.

It should not be beyond his talent to convey to Canadians at large some of the information that he has been accumulating for the past 48 years.

The Dangerous Simplifications of a Prime Minister

LE DEVOIR, *Montréal*
November 5, 1970
EDITORIAL BY CLAUDE RYAN

Mr. Pierre Elliott Trudeau was the guest Tuesday night of Louis Martin on the program Format 60. In the course of this discussion the Prime Minister of Canada summarized certain important chapters of the history of the past few weeks.

Mr. Trudeau's summary contained succinct judgments on the positions adopted by a number of persons (the publisher of Le Devoir among them) during the Cross-Laporte drama. We will try to correct certain facts, if only to ensure that history

will not have to be contented with this dangerously abbrevi-
ated official version of events.

The more we learn of these events the clearer it becomes
that at no moment since the kidnapping of Mr. Cross did Mr.
Trudeau feel seriously disposed toward achieving a negotiated
solution.

There was, at the very beginning, an appearance of hesitation, such as certain statements by Mr. Sharp and the broad-
casting of the FLQ manifesto on Radio-Canada. This hesitation was quickly overcome. The government's approach was
fixed as of the weekend that followed the kidnapping of Mr.
Cross. It would never change afterwards.

By refusing to negotiate Mr. Trudeau was following a familiar logic. He sees the FLQ members as criminals, mere bandits,
assassins. He believes that negotiating with them for the release
of Mr. Cross and Mr. Laporte would have undermined the
very foundations of society. "From the moment that governments give in to people like that on fundamental issues, governments cease to exist. It would have marked the end of the
State's authority." These words are Mr. Trudeau's. He states
his position. Whatever else we may think, we respect that
position. We respect it even more because we have followed
closely each step of the tragic dilemma that political authorities
had to resolve. And we agree, without reservation, that it was
up to them, and not up to citizens or private groups to take the
final decisions.

This said, it was nonetheless permitted to think differently
from the government. It is a basic right of those who did not
follow the government's line to refuse to allow their ideas to be
abused or laughed at by the leader of the government. That is
what Mr. Trudeau tried to do Thursday night. According to
Mr. Trudeau those who argued for a negotiated solution not
only betrayed their weakness but "they publicly supported the
aims of the FLQ" or at least "the intention of the FLQ that the
government give in to the demand for the liberation of prisoners." One might believe, reading these words, that Mr. Trudeau
willingly alters facts. The problem lies elsewhere: he cannot
understand. This chronic inability to see someone else's point
of view leads the Prime Minister to commit serious offences.

Some believed that the first concern of government at that time should have been the lives of Mr. Cross and Mr. Laporte. Without at all subscribing to the aims of the FLQ these people maintained that, given the terrible power the FLQ exercised temporarily over the lives of these two individuals, an attempt be made to save their lives by a negotiated compromise.

It has been written that these people pressured the government to surrender absolutely to the demands of the kidnappers. This is not what they thought. It is not what they said. They asked that the possibility of a negotiated settlement be explored to its limits: that is all. Since when has the idea of negotiations been synonymous with surrender.

Mr. Trudeau maintains that to foresee a negotiated settlement was a sign of weakness. He betrays a poor knowledge of the political and social evolution of the past half-century and a dangerous lack of understanding of certain realities of his milieu.

Because they did not understand the social and political dynamics hidden behind aggressive acts the leaders of many countries have unhesitatingly adopted a hard line against opponents who attacked them with violent methods. Mr. Trudeau and Mr. Bourassa state one day that the FLQ is composed of a handful of closely knit members. The next day one of their ministers says that the FLQ had infiltrated everywhere. What is certain is that behind the FLQ there exists a movement that runs much deeper than Mr. Trudeau is willing to admit: how else explain a recent survey that showed that 80 percent of the students in a major faculty of the University of Montréal support the aims of the FLQ.

The wish for a negotiated settlement took into account this difficult-to-measure reality. Though it was mostly intended to save the lives of Mr. Laporte and Mr. Cross this approach also foresaw, in the long term, the positive integration into the normal democratic process of elements which at this moment are tempted by violence.

Was this weakness? The very mention of nationalism or of separatism causes Mr. Trudeau to harden to the point where he cannot face facts. Prisoner of his own logic he cannot make room in his intellectual categorizations for facts that contradict his vision of things. This explains why, when confronted by an attitude opposite to his own, he reacts with inaccurate summaries and condemnation.

So long as the right to hold one's own views and to express them exists it will be necessary to tell Mr. Trudeau that we are not fooled by his casual simplifications. History will eventually tell us who in this affair were the most helpful allies of violence.

After the Fall

THE CANADIAN FORUM
November/December, 1970
EDITORIAL

A few poignant details seep through the language of autopsies and broadcasts. Pierre Laporte was apparently strangled with the chain of his scapular medal, and Rene Levesque wondered sadly and humanely how his murderers could kill a man they had lived with and talked to for several days. Rare moments in the days of gandiose hysteria and alarming repression we are now passing through.

Two men have been kidnapped, one atrociously murdered. Such things have happened before; they will happen again. Nothing we know so far (and so far those who supposedly know have told us almost nothing) justifies the suspension of law and civil liberties in the War Measures Act. The FLQ the cause of it all, shrinks at one moment to a handful of sadists, grows at another to include any and all of one's enemies, especially if one is a politician in power, and has at all times miraculous subversive powers. "These people", says Jean Marchand, the Titus Oates of the Cabinet, "have infiltrated every strategic position...every place where important decisions are taken..." (*Hansard* for 16 October, p. 224). Language such as this, and it has been echoed from coast to coast, repeated by a self-censored CBC, shouted in the House of Commons against the NDP members who alone opposed the War Measures Act, twists obscure causes and shaky evidence into vengeful arrests and wholesale attacks on any individuals or groups who can be made to seem children of darkness. The government's words and actions have evoked a frighteningly demonic response from a loud majority who are relieved to get away from the frustrations of rational argument and legal constraint. Now they can get down to the real business of casting out devils. Now they can trust utterly a government that clearly does not trust them enough to explain its actions. Now they can revert to their bigoted dislike of French-Canadians, hippies, radicals, of all those who threatened their sleepwalking lives. Now they can celebrate a new sense of national unity that typically and perhaps in the end tragically excludes almost half the population.

Let us make no mistake: *they* are the majority of our English-speaking fellow-citizens. No dominating foreigners sent in the troops, no order from Washington suspended our civil liberties, no outside agitators stirred up the witch-hunt that now seeks to discredit all forms of separatist activity in Quebec and radical activity in the rest of Canada. If we are to survive this plunge into righteous repression we must recognize how popular and how powerful it is. We must recognize that once we weaken our native defence to laws and traditions, Canadians will make repression rather than liberation their common cause. We have met the enemy, and they are us.

The advent of 1971 saw the early return of a problem inherited by the Trudeau Government: unemployment. A further issue the press began to develop in this year was foreign ownership of the Canadian economy. Their attention to this subject marked a welcome shift away from a preoccupation with the Prime Minister's personality to an increased emphasis on broader national issues.

Lumping It

THE EDMONTON JOURNAL
January 15, 1971
EDITORIAL

Last winter, as the number of Canadians out of work increased to the half-million mark, Prime Minister Trudeau refused to consider a change in his economic policy.

"Even if people think we are going to lose our nerve, we are not," he asserted.

When May unemployment figures showed 513,000 people still without jobs, Mr. Trudeau was even more emphatic about the policy which was fighting inflation at the expense of jobs and growth.

"If the Canadian people don't like it, you know they can lump it," he said on television.

By September, he was blaming unemployment on labor and business: "If there is high unemployment, it is because labor and business haven't co-operated voluntarily."

But in October, when Opposition Leader Robert Stanfield asked in the House of Commons whether the government was considering any new measures to fight unemployment, the prime minister replied: "The answer is no."

In November, the prime minister blandly conceded that further measures would be taken to relieve unemployment "if they are needed and if we have the money to implement them."

When he said that, the number of Canadians out of work was 476,000 and rising.

And In December, at the end of a year in which unemployment had averaged six per cent over the entire 12 months, the worst showing in nine years, Mr. Trudeau proclaimed that "inflation no longer exists in Canada" and that the government's "many, many" measures to combat unemployment were then taking effect.

It is hard to recall the "many, many" measures the federal government took last year against unemployment. And it is just as hard to find the effect claimed by the prime minister in the unemployment figures released this week.

At the time Mr. Trudeau claimed his measures were taking effect, 62,000 more Canadians were out of work than in the previous month. Compared with the same month in the previous year, 155,000 more Canadians were out of work.

The effect of Mr. Trudeau's economic policies is that 538,000 people were out of work in December.

This represented 6.5 per cent of the nation's working force, compared with 5.7 per cent in November, and 4.7 per cent a year ago. On a seasonally-adjusted basis, which economists believe to be a better indicator, December unemployment climbed to 6.6 per cent of the work force, compared with 6.5 the previous month.

The hardest-hit areas are the regions least able to stand the blow of mass unemployment. The highest rate of unemployment is in Quebec where nearly 200,000 workers are without a job, 8.4 per cent of the work force.

The time to have done something about this winter's unemployment was last summer, when Mr. Trudeau was telling Canadians that he wouldn't change his policies and they could like it or lump it.

We're lumping it now. And the worst thing about it is not the misery, heartbreak and human tragedy of this winter's unemployment. It is the fact that the government shows no awareness that there has been anything wrong with its economic record or that better, more effective, and less brutal policies are needed in the future.

Foreign Investment

THE FREE PRESS, *Winnipeg*
March 11, 1971
EDITORIAL

According to the Financial Post, the federal government will not be ready until summer at the earliest to announce its policy on foreign investment or until next year to enforce it. Meanwhile, the Post says, this long delay and uncertainty promote the sale of Canadian business concerns to United States buyers as the vendors move quickly to avoid possible restrictions later on. The additional uncertainty surrounding the government's taxation policy further encourages Canadian owners to dispose of their assets before new burdens are imposed on them.

Doubtless the government has pondered all these problems, but its inability, so far, to agree on foreign investment policy is not in the least surprising. For here it must deal not with some routine, day-to-day details of administration but with the entire future of Canada. And no one understands that fact better than Prime Minister Trudeau.

Herb Gray, minister of national revenue, who heads the cabinet study of investment, presumably is reading many reports and figures from his experts. But if he is seeking permanent principles rather than temporary, ad hoc remedies, he will find them close at hand in the considered, written thoughts of the prime minister (so different from his casual remarks in Parliament and press conferences). The cabinet may not yet have reached basic conclusions. Its leader certainly has.

His book and personal credo, Federalism and the French Canadians, goes far beyond constitutional arguments to survey the modern world economy and Canada's place in it. As he says, the capital of a rich country like the United States will tend to go wherever it can obtain the highest return and thus is attracted to countries like Canada. "The result is a sort of economic dependence which is sometimes described in such emotional terms as 'colonialism' and 'colonization.' This may give rise to simplified solutions: As Cuba has demonstrated, it is easy enough to get rid of American capital. But one must be prepared to accept the consequences. And there is no indication that a friendly country would be ready to supply Quebec with $300 million a year as Russia did for Cuba."

The prime minister's reference is to Quebec but it applies with equal force to the whole Canadian economy. The consequences of excluding capital would be nationwide. "The answer here," Mr. Trudeau goes on, "is not to chase away foreign capital, since the standard of living must then be lowered so that foreign capital can be replaced by indigenous capital. The answer, in the first place, is to use foreign capital within the framework of rational economic development; and, secondly, to create indigenous capital and direct it toward the key sectors of the future: computers, services and industry in the age of nuclear energy." Yet the Benson white paper, as it stands, would have precisely the opposite effects on foreign and indigenous capital formation alike.

Mr. Trudeau did not foresee the white paper when he wrote his book in 1965, but he clearly foresaw the growing interdependence of the world economy. Thus he quotes with approval this striking statement by Louis Armand, one of the greatest experts on technology in France: "To meet the needs of a new economy based on science it is no longer enough merely to be wealthy; you must be colossally rich. Actual needs destroy the idea of nations; they imply—and impose—great industrial complexes, and a sharing of manpower, markets and capital.... There are no longer any solutions on a national scale."

Yet it is precisely such solutions that some of Mr. Trudeau's colleagues, as well as the socialist Waffle group and other extreme nationalists, are demanding now. The prime minister thinks, on the contrary, that "if laws and constitutions create a situation that is not favorable to the entry and development of technology and technicians the country will be hopelessly outclassed economically and its industries soon outdated and inefficient. On the other hand, if technology is free to enter, the country must irrevocably step into the era of great communities, of continental economies. It will have to pay the price in terms of its national sovereignty."

These are deep waters and grave decisions, not of black and white but of rational compromises between unlimited, xenophobic sovereignty and unnecessarily slow economic growth— choices that no nation, not even the rich and powerful United States, can avoid. The nationalists, protectionists and isolationists pretend that we can have it both ways, without any cost, but Mr. Trudeau is not deceived.

Of Quebec he says that its economy "must not be isolated but open to the whole world, for then it will find new markets as well as the competition it has to expect." That doctrine is equally true of the whole nation, and especially of the West. Will the government's actual policy on foreign investment support Mr. Trudeau's principles, as expressed when he was a carefree private citizen, or deny them when he is a worried prime minister and necessarily a practical politician in a divided nation?

Foreign Capital Is Good for You-All, Says Trudeau

MACLEAN'S
June, 1971
STEVEN LANGDON

"My God, Langdon," I keep waiting for someone to say, "you're not still writing about foreign ownership? That's out-of-date, last year's issue." What he'll be trying to tell me, I'm afraid, is that the campaign against foreign control of our economy has become a cliché. And he'll be right: many Canadians are bored with the subject, some because the rhetoric is getting too shrill to follow, some because they think Ottawa's already doing something about it, some because they're doing very well, thank you, the way things stand.

That boredom, however, is a little unfortunate—and more than a little dangerous—because foreign ownership is growing faster than ever these days (the latest statistics showed a one-year increase of 13.3% in the assets of foreign-owned corporations) and, even more, because there are unhappy signs that the Trudeau government has abandoned any intentions it might have had of Canadianizing the economy. Perhaps the most indicative of these signs is that the Prime Minister has taken to using an impressive new argument against the movement for economic self-determination.

The new Trudeau position fastens onto one of his administration's more admirable priorities, the reduction of regional economic disparities. And it suggests, in effect, that we Canadians will have to choose which we want: economic independence or equitable regional development. Canadians, Trudeau told a Saskatchewan audience in February, "can't have their cake and eat it, too." If they oppose foreign capital, they prevent the new investment in poorer regions from which a fairer economy will grow. That, in the PM's view, explains why nationalism seems stronger in central Canada, "particularly Ontario...where you find the Mel Watkins and the Walter Gordons who think that enough is enough and they don't want any more foreign capital to develop their province; but they don't always realize that other parts of Canada ... wouldn't mind a little bit of foreign capital ... "

In political terms, it's a powerful argument. On the one hand, it plays on all the anti-Ontario feeling in the Maritimes and the West; on the other, it tries to convince people in Ontario that economic nationalism will hurt their fellow Canadians—and, since Quebec is one of those less developed regions, perhaps provoke the breakup of Confederation.

But, political advantage aside, how much validity has the Trudeau argument? Not much. There is no evidence that foreign investment is suddenly surging into the poorer parts of Canada. As a senior official I talked with in the Department of Regional Economic Expansion (DREE) concedes, most outside investment goes where it has always gone, to the richer regions, especially Ontario. In the face of that fact, it's difficult to see how foreign-capital inflows reduce regional disparities; if anything, they exaggerate the inequalities already existent in the country. Of course, the government is trying, through DREE subsidies, to influence the destination of new investment. But so far there is no proof that the approach has had much effect. DREE officials admit as much, and academic experts on regional development are even more scathing in their assessments (one told me the program was next to irrelevant).

So there is no way an effective policy of economic nationalism could make things worse. But—and this is the point—there are ways in which such a policy could make things better. Ironically, we have the U.S. Department of Commerce to thank for pointing out why this is so. The department published a detailed study this past winter that showed how little U.S. subsidiaries here depend on their parent companies for investment capital; less than 4% of the funds they invest in Canada come from head office. To a much greater extent than U.S. branch plants anywhere else in the world, U.S. firms in Canada finance their expansion out of their earnings in this country. Because so much of our economy is U.S.-owned, the patterns of that branch-plant investment determine the shape of our economy; and that means control (partial or complete) of that investment is the key to directing new expansions into the slow-growth regions. It is not foreign inflows of capital, but control of foreign firms already here, that will determine whether or not economically retarded areas of the country can catch up.

Economic independence, then, doesn't run counter to creating regional equality; on the contrary, it's a first step toward fostering that equality. And this is true whether we're talking about some kind of investment review board (as proposed by some spokesmen for the Committee for an Independent Canada) or about the more fundamental socialization program proposed by the Waffle group within the NDP.

The tragedy, of course, is that while DREE hasn't done much about regional inequality, it has done a lot to encourage foreign ownership—more than 66% of its grants ($46 million by the end of 1969) have gone to non-Canadian firms. Similarly, the lack of a strong regional development effort from Ottawa, including some measure of control of branch-plant investment patterns, has forced provincial premiers to go begging for capital wherever they could get it.

Canadians, it seems don't have their cake and don't get to eat it either, to go back to a favorite prime-ministerial cliché.

There is an alternative: a serious policy of nationalism. Its elements? First, an activist Canada Development Corporation, in which large foreign-owned firms would be required to invest some of their Canadian earnings. Second, a Canadian ownership and control bureau that would compel outsider corporations to meet our social priorities. (An all-party Commons committee suggested such an instrument last summer.) And third, some selective nationalization in critical parts of the economy, especially in the resource sector, where there seems no other way to ensure Canadians maximum benefits from the underground assets the U.S. so badly needs.

It could be done—but it won't be done unless Canadians keep raising hell about independence. That's why that boredom I mentioned at the beginning is so dangerous; it might weaken such public pressure. And at a time when Ottawa is not about to move unless it is pushed very, very hard.

A Pressing National Problem

PRAVDA, *Moscow*
May 18, 1972
K. GEIVANDOV

Ottawa—The statement of the Canadian Government on the question of foreign capital investment in the country and the tabling in Parliament of the bill providing for certain measures to limit the takeover of Canadian private companies by foreign firms, has again drawn the attention of Canadian public opinion to one of the most difficult problems facing the country.

The Government statement and the bill were accompanied by a voluminous—523 pages—report: *Direct Foreign Capital Investment in Canada*. This is the result of a protracted effort by a group of Government-appointed experts, who, after examining an enormous quantity of factual material, have come to, quite frankly, some rather disturbing conclusions for Canadians. "The level of foreign control over economic activity in Canada is already significantly higher than in any other industrialized country, and this level continues to rise," stated the authors of the report.

Confirmation of this conclusion was shown in the report by the fact that approximately 60 percent of all their manufacturing industry is under foreign control, and that in several branches of the manufacturing industry, such as oil and rubber, foreign control exceeds 90 percent. The authors of the report directly name those concealed by such a seemingly abstract expression as "foreign control." "Approximately 80 percent of all foreign control over the manufacturing and mining industries of Canada," they point out, "is in American hands."

American domination of the Canadian economy is not news to Canadians. On this score warnings have sounded for a long time. The publication of the following report, undertaken on the initiative of the Canadian Government, is noteworthy because its authors insist on the adoption of urgent measures to slow or limit further expansion of this genuine cancerous tumour in the Canadian economy. Otherwise, they say, it could happen that one fine day Canada would cease to exist as an independent country. The report indicates three basic ways foreign capital, particularly American, continues to penetrate the Canadian economy. These are the creation of Canadian subsidiaries by foreign monopolies, the expansion of already existing companies, and finally the acquisition of Canadian firms which the owners have decided to sell for one reason or another. This last way is the least used for the penetration of foreign capital into Canada, accounting for less than 10 percent of all direct foreign investment.

However the provisions of the bill tabled in the Canadian Parliament are aimed specifically at this last way. Why? This question is being asked at the present time by the bill's many critics and they are not getting a satisfactory answer....

Economic Policy and the Evasions of Mr. Trudeau

LE DEVOIR, *Montréal*
November 15, 1971
EDITORIAL BY CLAUDE LEMELIN

If the Trudeau government were to retain as a general statement of policy on foreign investment a version of the preliminary and abridged Gray Report published in Canadian Forum last Friday it would be offering to the Canadian people one of the most remarkable and most exciting documents it has given birth to since assuming power. Whereas the list of white papers published by Ottawa since 1968 have disappointed by their superficiality, the "Memorandum on regaining Canadian control of the national economy" would, if adopted and implemented by the government, produce a fundamental transformation in the economic structure of the Canadian economy. In other areas, notably constitutional reform, the social security review, employment policies, regional development policy... the reformist promises put forth by the Trudeau government before 1968 have resulted in bitter disappointment; one can even say there has been a definite regression with respect to the directions undertaken under the Pearson regime. Will the same be true in areas of economic control? The comments so far on this by ministers, the divergent views within the cabinet revealed by the Gray report and the possibility therefore that it will be shelved or retained in a version so adulterated as to be insignificant all lead us to fear that we are about to lose the last of our illusions.

By the spring of 1971 most Canadians preferred to forget the trauma of October 1970. But at least one voice was eloquently raised to re-examine Trudeau's handling of the whole affair and his behavior during his first three years in office.

Dilettante in Power: The First Three Years of P. E. Trudeau

SATURDAY NIGHT
April, 1971
JAMES EAYRS

There are times when telling the truth becomes too painful to be borne. Since their crisis of last October, Canadians have been living through such times. As a result our recent past is in danger of becoming irremediably distorted.

People protect themselves against the recollection of excruciating experience by developing what W. M. Medlicott, reflecting on the problems of writing recent history, describes as "a system of unacknowledged reticences amounting almost to taboos on some matters of great importance." They furnish their minds with "a body of folk-history with its own standards of appraisal and condemnation, and even its own rules of evidence: a simplified version of past events which politicians need and must accept because it provides the working assumptions on which they base their programmes."

Already in these last few months our protective layer of folk-history has become a thick veneer. What really happened gets harder to make out. Two examples:

It lay within the power of the government of Canada to save the life of Pierre Laporte. It chose instead to gamble with his life. Pierre Laporte was murdered. The government of Canada bears inescapably a measure of responsibility for his death. No naming of bridges, no scholarship fund, no widow's pension, alters that reality. Yet it is a reality too painful for most Canadians to bear. They distort their past accordingly.

A second example. The government of Canada is now making a determined effort—though not determined enough—to reduce unemployment and social unrest in Quebec. Without the revolutionary challenge of the FLQ and its supporters, its efforts would not be anything like so determined. There are times when terrorism pays off, and we are witnessing such a time. Here again is a reality too painful for us to bear. We hide from it, or run away.

All this makes especially difficult an assessment of the leadership of Pierre Trudeau, who came to power three years ago in April, 1968. . . .

We must now go back three years to the spring of 1968—Centennial Year plus 1. Statesmen everywhere are wilting, ailing from tired blood. L.B.J.'s just about to call it quits. Kosygin looks even more haggard than usual. Mao overcompensates by skinny-dipping in the Yangtze. In Ottawa the odd couple of Confederation glower across the aisle of the House—a pair of fighting cocks frazzled by a decade's scratching.

But see who's returned from Tahiti, fresh as his pink carnation, looking good like a prime minister should. Canadians, surfeited during the Diefenbaker years with a style of politics that was all passion and no reason, buffeted during the Pearson years by a style devoid of passion and reason both, respond to the promise of "*le raison avant la passion*," the heady mixture of Cartesian logic and Gallic verve. "What shall we do, Sir," asks the executive assistant to the Minister of Justice, "about the Abortion Bill?" "Pay it!" snaps Pierre Trudeau.

Trudeau's credentials for his high office included at least one certificate of guarantee—that of Marshall McLuhan. "He is as tribal as the Beatles," gushed that guru. "With the unconcern of the enormously erudite and the socially assured man of wealth, Trudeau... correctly assumes that all top level experts in any field of endeavour are hopelessly copeless."

Correctly? Marshall McLuhan, what are you doin'? Sure, you look for confidence in your leader. But in a leader of such brief apprenticeship you look for diffidence, too.

Diffident Trudeau is not. He even tried to make his brief apprenticeship a virtue. "Perhaps I am partially a Mc-Luhanite," he mused to an interviewer after six months' taste of power. "One of the arguments I used in the leadership campaign, when they said 'You don't have experience, how can you aspire to be a prime minister?', was, well, in the rapidly changing world, the experience isn't always very useful ...What you learned in a previous context can hamstring you." The priceless extra of inexperience. Walk right in, sit right down...

Now it's true that treatises on statecraft don't dwell upon experience. That's because they all take it for granted. Plato's philosopher-kings are trained in governance for half a lifetime before they give an order. For the same reason that a St. John's ambulance first-aid course (admirable for cuts and sprains) doesn't qualify for neurosurgery, or a few hours logged in a Piper Cub won't get you into the cockpit of a 747. Trudeau was no philosopher-king when he took over. He was more like Walter Mitty in the Cabinet Room—a dilettante in power.

A dilettante is "one who interests himself in an art or science merely as a pastime and without serious study." It is an appellation Trudeau detests. "It became a cliché to call me a dilet-tante, just because I didn't live on the same rhythm as other people." The interviewer from the *New Yorker* records that when the Prime Minister told her this, "he was clearly an-noyed; his eyes were icy blue." But if the cap fits, wear it.

What does experience do for a statesman? It gives him the confidence to change his mind. It gives him the wisdom to admit mistakes. It gives him the courage to override his pre-cedents. It gives him the fortitude not to run on his record.

A dilettante in power, when rudely surprised, reverts at once to principle—it's all he has around. But it may be the wrong principle. He is hamstrung, to be sure—not by what he learned, but by what he never learned.

There are such things as the lessons of history, and they are all the more serviceable when taught by experience. The lesson of how to retreat from an untenable position. The lesson of how not to over-react in crisis. The lesson of how to be generous in triumph. "Appeasement from strength is magnanimous and noble." So wrote a prime minister who waited thirty-four years in parliament, in and out of office, before being called upon to lead his countrymen in their finest hour. Trudeau waited three. Then came not our finest hour but our meanest. Or so it seems to me.

"In spite of long periods spent wandering about the world," writes Leonard Beaton of Trudeau, "he understands very little and does not know it." Agreed that travel, especially on foot, only narrows the mind. But our leader's inexperience has mattered least in the international affairs. It may even have done us some good. It has helped us climb down from that lofty plateau of preoccupation with foreign policy to which we'd been led by L. B. Pearson—the pied piper of infantile internationalism—and where we had little business being.

There are two achievements of Trudeau's foreign policy worth talking about. I don't count what he did at Singapore as an achievement worth talking about. "Saving the Commonwealth" is all very well, but saving it for what? Besides, it remains to be seen that it was saved. The kind of salvage operation that's done by tinkering with the communiqué is the cheapest thrill of personal diplomacy. It's an exercise for bureaucrats, who don't need to follow through. You win the battle of the communiqué, but you haven't won the war.

What is worth talking about is Trudeau's China policy. Here I have to concede that travel did broaden his mind. The Prime Minister is an old China hand on a modest scale. In 1960, he and some companions roamed the mainland for a month. You don't learn mandarin in a month, but you learn that China is a reality as well as an image—be it an image of the red menace or the image of the yellow peril. Trudeau may be unique among the leaders of the West in having shaken the hand of Mao Tse-tung.

Recognition was not only an idea whose time had come, it was an idea long overdue. It would have been possible merely to go through the motions. Recognition could have been proffered on terms the Canadian Government knew Peking could not accept—some version of a "Two China" policy that did not involve breaking with Taiwan. Such a strategy, known to insiders as "negotiating to failure," seems to have been considered at first. But the government made up its mind to negotiate to success. The chargés are now in place, the ambassadors will follow. Whether they will merely cower in their compounds remains to be seen. But at least a route of communication has been channeled between China and the West.

Next, Trudeau's NATO policy. The new China policy required the agreement of the new China. But the new NATO policy—whatever it might be—could be carried out despite the hostility of all concerned.

"Hostile" may be exaggerating the response of NATO governments to the news that Trudeau was reconsidering Canada's twenty-year-old commitment to the defense of Western Europe. "Worried" is no exaggeration. There was the worry of bureaucracies everywhere faced by uncertainty and the prospect of change. Western Europe was worried lest a Canadian withdrawal stimulate the Soviet appetite for adventure, or, like the first in a row of falling dominoes, touch off retreat all down the line. The United States was worried lest Canada catalyze a mood of isolationism and encourage the demand that U.S. troups be recalled from overseas. Some Americans were shocked as well as worried.

To the extent that this apprehension was genuine—rather than feigned on behalf of the *status quo*—it arose through unfamiliarity with Trudeau's style of policy formation. The Prime Minister can be cautious to a fault, but that does not prevent him keeping dire options open until he wants them closed, nor does it inhibit his asking questions of the kind that, in a politician, seem provocative to the point of perversity. Just as he could ask a mining community looking to him for better housing if it had thought of the day when the ore body runs out, so he could ask his chiefs of staff if they had thought that

NATO might be no longer necessary. It was unnerving while it lasted, but it was not to be taken seriously, just another aspect of the Trudeau manner.

A number of proposals were considered. Canada should get out of NATO, Canada should get out of NORAD, Canada should get out of defence and into foreign aid. By April, 1969, the debate had gone on a year, the debaters were repeating themselves, the Prime Minister looked bored. No consensus had emerged. The country was still confused—though perhaps at a higher level of confusion than before the debate began. A NATO deadline—the twentieth anniversary fell due in a few days—brought a mousey decision from this mountainous labour. Canada would remain a member of the alliance. But we would begin pulling back from Europe.

It was not a bug-out, elegant or otherwise, just a scaling down. A land force of 2,800 men and an air element of 2,200 men would be combined in a single unit for an interim period of three years. By January, 1972, it is planned that no Canadian forces in Europe will have access to nuclear weapons—a reminder that in 1963 Trudeau had called Pearson "a defrocked priest" for accepting access to such weapons.

Throughout the foreign policy review, Trudeau maintained a pose of impartiality—"letting a hundred flowers blossom and a hundred schools of thought contend." But if this was the correct way of handling contradictions among his advisers, it did not mean he had no thoughts of his own. Once or twice he allowed these to be glimpsed. "We are not threatened by communism or fascism or even by atomic bombs," the Prime Minister remarked at Queen's University in November, 1968, "as much as we are by the fact that very large sections of the world go to bed hungry every night and large sections of our society do not find fulfillment in our society. I am less worried about what is over the Berlin Wall than about Chicago and what might happen in our great cities in Canada."

It is the hallmark of the dilettante that he does not follow up his insights. Trudeau stated our great strategic problem three years ago: how to keep our society together, peaceful, prosperous and free. Beside this central challenge, all issues called "defence" fade into inconsequence. Or else acquire from it whatever consequence they have.

He stated the problem without solving it. The defence budget is what it was and is going to go higher. But we can't afford to keep on diverting our limited resources from the central front of Euro-British North America to the periphery of Western Europe. With the St. Lawrence as turbid as it is today, it is blind to keep watch on the Rhine. What does it matter whether Canada remains in NATO, remains in NORAD, remains in the Commonwealth? What matters is that Canada remains. . . .

The Prime Minister is not to be blamed for all of last winter's discontents. But he is to be blamed for much of them. For the high rate of unemployment. For too much law and too much order. For the intensity of separatism which threatens the unity of Canada.

Nothing identifies a Canadian more quickly than the saying "I'm not an economist, but . . . " I'm not an economist, but you don't have to be an economist to know that Trudeau's a lousy mechanic in the garage of capitalism. His defence of his economic policy at Regina in February recited every error, every half-truth in the book.

He said a little bit of inflation leads to runaway inflation with the same inexorability that a little bit of pregnancy leads to a full-term baby. It isn't true. He said a "strong" dollar—one close to par with the American—means a strong economy. For Canada the opposite is true.

He said a severe winter causes our high unemployment. But that isn't true either. Other countries have severe winters and low unemployment—Norway, Sweden, the Soviet Union, for starters. Winter ought logically to increase demand for labour— the people who shovel us out. What we have here is the latest variation on a very old refrain—that geography and history have made us hard to govern. It seems to me I've heard that song before. It has an old familiar score. "It became fashionable," writes Professor Nicholas Mansergh of the statecraft of Mackenzie King during the 1930s, "to emphasize the precariousness of Canada's export markets but not the value of her exports; to speak of regional and cultural tensions within but not of the growing sense of unity; of the conflicting pulls of geography and history to which indeed every 'settled' country is subject, but not of the immense strength of Canada's position in the heart of the English-speaking world."

But in our era of post-Keynesian economics and high technology, to put the blame for unemployment on old man Winter is surely the ultimate in fuddle-duddle determinism—what medical people call an insult to the brain. Only Trudeau could get away with it. Only a dilettante would try.

Is it simple parsimony? Or is Trudeau's reforming zeal more Savonarolan than humanitarian, seeking to cure society's ills by scourging it? As between money losing value and people losing jobs, Trudeau opts unhesitatingly for people losing jobs. Asked last year whether he was fully aware of the suffering imposed by an unemployment rate of five per cent, he replied: "Yes, and it can go to six." Since then it's gone to eight. The end is not in sight.

Hardest of all for a dilettante in power is to do nothing in a crisis. Everything conspires to goad him into action, make him press the button. He fears that otherwise it will be said that inexperience betrayed him into inactivity. Yet all too often what is required in a crisis is precisely inactivity—masterly inactivity, controlled inactivity, but inactivity nonetheless.

Trudeau's response to his first crisis in office was the ultimate of escalation. Nothing is more damaging to democracy than to send troops into its streets—unless it is to suspend its civil liberty. Trudeau sent troops, suspended civil liberties—and called his critics bleeding hearts.

This bleeding heart does not suggest that the response of the Prime Minister of Canada, on receiving the unprecedented message from the Prime Minister of Quebec—"We are facing a concerted effort to intimidate and overthrow the government and democratic institutions of this Province through planned and systematic illegal action"—ought to have done nothing. What he ought to have done was to find out whether it was true.

People being terrorized have a right to be protected. But only two people—the kidnapped hostages of terrorists—were

being terrorized and both were beyond protection at that point.
Other people panicked.

For this condition there's a well-known remedy. It's called
the fireside chat. In times of crisis, when the nation is roused
from its accustomed private preoccupations to apprehensive
awareness of danger, it is the Prime Minister who through
press and radio and television must play the father figure,
providing reassurance and guidance and hope.

Well, where is our father figure as the kidnap crisis gathers
momentum? Hiding out at Harrington Lake, his profile low,
his dander high. Meanwhile his ministers rave as if FLQ terrorists have blown their minds:

"These people (Jean Marchand declared) have infiltrated
every strategic place in the province of Quebec, every place
where important decisions are taken ... There is an organization which has thousands of guns, rifles, machine guns, bombs
and ... more than enough [dynamite] to blow up the core of
downtown Montreal.

O still small voice of calm.

The troops go into action—peacekeepers in their own country. Almost all applaud their presence. But it is fraught with
peril for our future....

The danger in using troops as police is that it's habit-form-
ing. One becomes accustomed to their face. But it is not the
face of freedom, it's the face of friendly fascism. Machine guns
at the palace. The knock at the door at five a.m. Don't say
such things can't happen here. They've already happened here.
And each time it happens makes it easier the next—easier, and
more likely....

As in the Spring of 1968, so in the spring of 1971. The Prime
Minister remains uncompromisingly opposed to separatism and
special status. Here is his 1962 argument against them: "Every
national minority will find, at the very moment of liberation, a
new minority within its bosom which in turn must be allowed
the right to demand its freedom. And on and on would stretch
the train of revolutions, until the last-born of the nation-states
turned to violence to put an end the very principle that gave it
birth ... Now there is something for Quebec's Separatists to
sink their teeth into; if there is any validity to their principles

they should carry them to the point of claiming part of Ontario, New Brunswick, Labrador, and New England; on the other hand, though, they would have to relinquish certain border regions around Pontiac and Temiskaming and turn Westmount into the Danzig of the New World."

This is not reason before passion, it's chop-logic before passion—the pleading of a casuist. One hears across the years the voice of Père Bernier, Trudeau's childhood tutor: "*Bravo, bravo p'tit Pierre, comme tu es drôle!*" Except that it's the work not of a child prodigy but of a mind formed by then for forty years. It's not national self-determination that's absurd, it's Trudeau's argument against it—a model of *reductio ad absurdum*.

Even so, it makes a powerful case—especially when put (as Trudeau puts it) with utter sincerity and intellectual and emotional conviction. Yet it is not an overpowering case. His notion of nationalism as impoverishing is an hypothesis, not an axiom. Much of French Canada is unconvinced.

Just how much is hard to say. Separatism has yet to be put to a test of its strength. The closest it's come to such a test was the Quebec election last April. René Lévesque's Parti Québecois polled twenty-four per cent of the votes—even if a gerrymandered voting system awarded it only eight per cent of the seats.

What do these figures mean? Can they be read as a mandate for "independence now" by a quarter of the Quebec electorate, and well more than a quarter of the French-speaking electorate? Or was their vote just a protest against poverty and a response to the personality of the leader? It must be remembered that many of his supporters occupy key positions in the communications sector—the schools, the colleges, Radio-Canada—and that often it's not the size, it's the ferocity.

On the fringe is the Front. PQ and FLQ haven't much in common. The Parti Québecois is pledged to peaceful change. The Front is pledged to violent revolution. The Parti Québecois is reformist. The Front is terrorist. The Parti Québecois seeks an independent Quebec. The Front seeks world-wide liberation—an apocalyptic takeover by Third World freedom-fighters. The Parti Québecois is part of Canadian society. The Front is at war with Canadian society.

They have kidnapped and they have killed, but that does not make them ordinary criminals. What drives these young terrorists to such desperate extremes, to such a depth of alienation? Poverty is only part of it. The young terrorists of Quebec, unlike Weathermen in the United States, were mostly born and bred in poverty. But if their poverty were all that mattered it would be easy to buy them off. They are not to be bought off.

The basis of their power, the key to their commitment, is their sense of moral indignation, their sense of moral superiority to the corruptions of the society they will continue to harass if they cannot actually destroy. Men are moral beings, as I. F. Stone has noted; "and to take from the terrorists their moral justification is the only way to strike at the heart of the terror spreading round the globe."

I concede at once it is easier to recite this diagnosis than to recommend a regimen of cure. But the right diagnosis must precede a cure. I do not think Pierre Trudeau has the diagnosis right. He is philosophically an anti-nationalist. He believes French-Canadian nationalism, insofar as it seeks fulfillment outside the ambience of a federal state, to be a wayward and irrational force. Above all, he believes in his own ability to control that force—as if it were an aircraft lost in a storm, and he the voice of ground control. He is unimpressed by the lesson of history—that when a nationalist movement meets stubborn federal power, the result of their collision is partition or civil war. He does not think things will come to that in Canada. He believes history doesn't repeat itself, it's only historians who repeat one another. As a Canadian I hope he's right. As an historian, I fear he's wrong.

Canada's fifteenth Prime Minister will not go down in history as a reticent man. The subject of greatest press comment in February of 1971 was the Prime Minister's foul language. Taunted by 400 strikers on Parliament Hill, Mr. Trudeau invited them to "mangez de la merde." Not one to forget members of Parliament, Mr. Trudeau dismissed an astonished opposition M.P. with a brief phrase seldom heard in polite company. The Prime Minister later insisted it had been "fuddle duddle," and one newspaper, looking on the bright side, congratulated the nation for having elected a leader able to swear well in both official languages.

Of course Pierre Trudeau is not one to stand still for long, and soon after he had ceased exchanging oaths, he was exchanging vows. A brief truce with the press resulted as all wished the P.M. and his young bride well.

Look Who's Married

THE OTTAWA JOURNAL
March 5, 1971
EDITORIAL

"Society cannot become mature without the full participation of women."

The speaker was Pierre Trudeau, bachelor, Wednesday evening in Toronto. Thursday evening he became a husband.

It is good news on every count. First, for their happiness. Second, because two halves are better than one. Third, because the Prime Minister will learn something of the art of compromise which is not his strong suit in politics. Fourth, because the general well-being of a man with a wife and home is likely to make more bearable the crushing responsibilities of being Prime Minister. Fifth, because there is a great deal to be said for having a chatelaine in 24 Sussex and adding grace and gaiety to the affairs and ceremonies of state.

That speech to a Liberal banquet Wednesday evening about the quality, ability and charm of women and how the Royal Commission report should be implemented must have been the longest and most public proposal of marriage on record. Did Margaret Sinclair make him thus pledge his government's policy on women as a condition of acceptance? If so, that man has met his match.

Matrimony of State

THE CHRONICLE-HERALD, *Halifax*
March 6, 1971
EDITORIAL

Record national unemployment, paralyzing blizzards in Quebec and the Maritimes, the opening of the Conservative leadership contest in Nova Scotia, sky-rocketing residential tax assessments in Halifax, high prices and high taxes all round— all these pressing matters faded, temporarily, into insignificance when the nation was told that Prime Minister Trudeau, claimed to be Canada's most eligible bachelor, had been married at a secret Vancouver ceremony to Miss Margaret Sinclair.

We wish the prime minister and his bride great happiness.

Mr. Trudeau has always insisted on his right to enjoy a private life. Yet, because he is prime minister and, because he was until Thursday evening, a confirmed bachelor who enjoyed visiting theatres, restaurants and similar establishments often in the company of beautiful, and sometimes famous, women, he was forced to spend many hours of his "private" life in the glare of publicity.

Now that Pierre Elliot Trudeau is no longer a bachelor, will his appeal, particularly to Canadian women, diminish? Will marriage, which at one time was being urged upon him, as though it was not a strictly private matter for him to decide, make the Trudeau image less, or more, agreeable to the romantically inclined floating voter, taking into account that his bride is an attractive young woman of 22?

After an initial shock, and a realization that the old Trudeau image (which not every Canadian appreciated), has gone forever, Canadians and Canadian politicians will undoubtedly get used to the idea of a charming and permanent hostess at the prime minister's residence whose atmosphere, like that of any other home, will be enhanced by the presence of a gracious chatelaine.

To The Bride's Health

LE DEVOIR, *Montréal*
March 8, 1971
CLAUDE LEMELIN

From the moment of his entry into the federal arena, the possibility of a state wedding aroused murmurs of anticipation. A Wedding March, it was said, will ensure his election; but he managed to get elected without it.

The cynics, the unhappily married, the vicious tongues were jubilant: without doubt Pierre Trudeau was an inveterate bachelor. As with Mackenzie King the new Prime Minister would renounce the support of a wife, some were already wondering what sort of crystal ball would come to illuminate his moments of solitude.

But the promoters of matrimony quickly overcame this disappointment. Twenty-four Sussex simply could not be deprived of a chatelaine. From East to West the provincial chancelleries put forth their most nubile offerings, for the honor was great and who could say what might be the effect of a wife's whispered word at a federal-provincial conference. Québec had an embarassment of choices and opted finally for the loveliest of actresses. Ontario counter-attacked with its blondest of daughters. From Regina Ross Thatcher sent out the country beauties that grew wild in the province. From Newfoundland Joey Smallwood boasted of the salty freshness of the sirens of the Atlantic. Even America, to seal the continental alliance, tendered the charm of a Brooklyn star. Only Wacky Bennet retained his reserve.

"There are many lovely things in my British Columbia," whispered the fox of the Pacific. He had taken the measure of his man. Pierre Trudeau went to see for himself: Vancouver, Mount Garibaldi, the Okanagan Valley, the sumptuous slopes of the Queen Charlotte basin. He returned often. Everyone dismissed it as a habit. It seemed the Prime Minister was invincible and that he would continue to change with the seasons, now a brunette, now a blonde upon his arm. The jealous began to whisper: will nothing convince this man that it is not by spending oneself that one accumulates riches? The perfidious chimed in: such frivolity in affairs of the heart is the precursor of instability in public affairs.

A strategist chuckled: this seeming capriciousness is calculated, said he. A bachelorhood that has been preserved for so long is too precious to be lightly abandoned. Why give it up when the polls are at their peak?

So much calculation should have been suspect. The brunette and the blonde were for the parades. In the secret recess of his heart Pierre Trudeau had installed a fine flower of the Rockies. Having sunk her roots there Margaret will bloom. Some will say the wife is very young but what better to bridge the generation gap.

Blanc de Blanc, Bordeaux, champagne, take your pick: we must drink the health of the bride.

May They Have All the Best!

THE SUN, *Vancouver*
March 5, 1971
EDITORIAL

Their fellow Canadians wish all the best to the happy couple. To Pierre Elliott Trudeau may we add, "Lucky fellow!" to have won such a lovely young lady.

The prime minister can be counted on to do the unexpected and this is what he has done in quietly appearing out on the Pacific Coast for a date so few people in his own inner circle seem to have been aware of. He has acted in his own way and, whether unexpected or not, it is a matter of delight to millions in this country who appreciate his lack of stuffiness.

Mr. Trudeau is young in spirit and has now proved that he is not, after all, the unapproachable bachelor. It remains to be seen if having a family responsibility will change his pace and outlook.

British Columbians are doubly pleased that he has chosen a British Columbia girl. Once again, may they have the best of everything.

Mr. Trudeau After Four Years in Power

LE DEVOIR, *Montréal*
July 20, 1972
EDITORIAL BY CLAUDE RYAN

Other than the Prime Minister's personality, two main factors contributed to his success in 1968: the insurance policy he offered English Canada about Québec and the promise of a renewal in the country's political life. On each of these points the charisma of 1968 seems to have faded. On Québec Mr. Trudeau remains true to himself. He declared in 1968 that a vigorous policy of linguistic equality would cure Québec's malaise. He has not only put that policy into place, in the face of mounting criticism from English Canada, but does not hesitate to say that it is not advancing quickly enough.

The facts show that this policy has not forced the retreat of nationalism in Québec but has aroused widespread resentment in English Canada. One would have thought that Mr. Trudeau would have readjusted his sights and enlarged his view of the problem, taking into account the realities he had ignored in 1968 and which now stand in his way. Far from having evolved, Mr. Trudeau seems to be frozen once and for all in his conception.

This rigidity has hardly helped him in Québec where the proponents of sovereignty have continued to gain ground and where the views of someone like Claude Castonguay seem in the eyes of many to be a more accurate reflection of public opinion than Mr. Trudeau's.

We begin to doubt that these views can succeed a second time in English Canada. English Canadians are realistic. They seek above all peace with Québec. How can we reproach them their conclusion that that peace is no more assured now than it was four years ago. The English-language press was greatly impressed in 1968 by the very modern philosophical and technical abilities on which Mr. Trudeau's leadership seemed to rest. They spoke with admiration of the clear leap into the future that Canada would be forced to make under the leadership of the program and computer specialists that surrounded Mr. Trudeau.

Four years later the country is becoming aware that it has given itself as a leader a man who is a cautious and conscientious manager but who is not the prophet that had been expected.

CHAPTER 4

THE TRUDEAU MINORITY 1972-74

"Here, David — just cut on the dotted line."

The Pierre Elliott Trudeau who went forth to face the Canadian electorate in his first attempt at re-election as Prime Minister was not the same politician they had enthusiastically embraced four years earlier. The boyish charm and highly personalized campaign style evident in 1968 had given way to a low-key almost complacent approach to the voters. The Prime Minister who had personally won the day for the Liberal party now remained in Ottawa for the first several weeks of the campaign, leaving the travelling and hard work to his more pedestrian cabinet colleagues. And what of the idealistic rhetoric of '68—the calls to vote for a "participatory democracy" and work together to build a "just society"? Four years later they had become musty and slightly embarassing relics from another era, pushed into obscurity by the bland smugness of the new party motto, "The Land Is Strong."

Few policy differences separated the major parties, with the exception of NDP leader David Lewis's fiery attacks on the "corporate welfare bums." Conservative leader Robert Stanfield, switching roles and playing hare to Trudeau's tortoise, crossed the country repeatedly with earnest denunciations of the government's mishandling of the economy, but offered few substantial policy alternatives apart from tax incentives for business. The Prime Minister finally emerged from Ottawa in early October to begin a curious sort of non-campaign that took the form of a donnish series of low-key "dialogues" with the Canadian people, in which he tried to portray a country bathed in the glow of quiet optimism, marching forward together in steady Liberal progress. It didn't work.

Press reaction was highly variable. Traditional Liberal papers like The Montreal Star, The Ottawa Citizen, Winnipeg Free Press, and Vancouver Sun supported the government's bid for re-election but with little enthusiasm. The Globe and Mail and Montreal Gazette backed the government with certain reservations, but The Winnipeg Tribune withdrew the support it had enthusiastically given Mr. Trudeau in 1968. The widely-read Toronto Star endorsed the Conservative Party for the first time in fifty years, citing the government's poor performance on the unemployment issue and its unwillingness to control foreign ownership as reasons for their dramatic change of political heart.

Perhaps because of the low-key, often dull nature of the cam-

paign, the on-the-spot reporter who had been the centre of media election coverage in 1968 was now being pre-empted by the editorialists and feature writers. Canada's press was now turning its reflective powers to the task of evaluating four years of Trudeau government.

Wake Us Up Next Week

THE PROVINCE, *Vancouver*
September 2, 1972
EDITORIAL

We'll wait—yawn—while you get over the thundering excitement that hit you with the news of yet another—yawn—general election. After months of punditry setting the national election for October, Prime Minister Trudeau has pulled a surprising switch for him, and done what everybody said he would do.

There's no doubt it will be a bigger election than the one British Columbians have just gone through, but there is no sign that it will produce a comparable upheaval, although the view from here may be a little distorted.

Surveys of various kinds suggest that British Columbians, who tend to leap more quickly on and off bandwagons than most other Canadians, may be ready to skip away from Mr. Trudeau in bigger numbers than people in the rest of the country.

But the timing of this election call may mitigate some of that feeling. A major survey this newspaper did in May showed that unemployment and labor problems topped the list of voters' worries. Mr. Trudeau calls his election right after assembling Parliament to end the dock strike here, and making sure that another potential strike, by the grain-handlers, doesn't shut the port either.

That can't fail to help him. He will be hurt, however, by an unfortunate anti-Quebec feeling, fostered to a great degree by Premier Bennett's actions and comments. This is an issue Mr. Trudeau will have to deal with squarely when he campaigns here if he hopes to save a few seats.

It will be an interesting campaign for several reasons, despite the initial yawns. Mr. Trudeau has taken a moderate line on U.S. investment when there are more strident nationalist voices being heard than there have been for years.

And he has been under savage attack on his employment record, although by world standards it's not a bad record at all.

Will it be a rational campaign? Will emotionalism, especially out here, cause much heat and little light? Should be interesting.

Four Fuzzy Years

MACLEAN'S
October, 1972
JOHN GRAY

Looking back now on the past four and a half years of Canada's political life, it is a shock to realize how little has changed. After the frantic Diefenbaker-Pearson decade, in the wake of Centennial year and Expo 67, the election of 1968 seemed destined to be a turning point. Many people felt Canadian politics would never be the same.

The essence of that expectation was one man—and that, undoubtedly, was the flaw. Pierre Trudeau, it is true, was a new kind of party leader. He seemed so rigidly intellectual, determined, courageous, unassuming, frank, even antipolitical. His image was so different from those who preceded him that he was virtually an assault upon the system.

That Trudeau campaign of 1968 made him, calculatedly, many things to many people. But there was one overriding impression: that he was sanely progressive. Remember the intellectual community? They had flounced uncertainly for years between liberalism in the Liberals, nationalism in the Conservatives, socialism in the NDP; suddenly they were all Trudeauites. "The Man For Tomorrow," one Toronto magazine called him....

It is doubtful that any Canadian prime minister came to office with quite the same fascination with the sheer mechanics of power as Pierre Trudeau. He was, and is, absorbed by the technique of government, and even before he entered politics he was sure that the tools for the job would be superior to those of any of his predecessors: "Such tools will be made up of advanced technology and scientific investigation, as applied to the fields of law, economics, social psychology, international affairs, and other areas of human relations; in short, if not a pure product of reason, the political tools of the future will be designed by more rational standards than anything we are currently using in Canada today." ...

For all the innovation and imagination of the *mechanics* of policy, the actual policies of the Trudeau government have been notably unimaginative. It has been suggested that Trudeau and his staff have been effectively hypnotized by the process.

The exceptions always cited, such as the Arctic Pollution Bill and Opportunities For Youth, were conceived and approved apart from the normal policy process. The first came from Trudeau's special assistant, Ivan Head, with little help from External Affairs as a sophisticated method of establishing Canadian sovereignty over the waters of the Arctic. Opportunities For Youth, like the more recent Local Initiatives Program, was put together in a blind panic to take some of the sting out of unemployment.

A more significant measure of the Trudeau government is apparent in those policies that evolved after a long, careful and elaborate period of gestation. These were the "priority problems" so carefully defined in the early months of the Trudeau administration: Tax reform, native peoples, status of women, urban affairs, housing, election expenses, business competition, social policy, drugs (particularly marijuana), and foreign ownership of the Canadian economy.

Each of these reviews resulted in recommendations for sweeping and sometimes radical changes in public policy. On each of these issues, the Trudeau cabinet retreated in confusion and embarrassment. Either cabinet ministers rejected the recommendations handed to them, or they hastily watered down their own initial policy at the first sign of criticism. Each retreat was inevitably camouflaged with a flourish of rhetoric about bold progress. A Liberal cabinet minister (and not a crackpot outsider) recently complained to a friend that "this government has run away from more pressure groups than any government I've ever seen. It wants to be everybody's darling." ...

The government has been notably influenced by the strength of conservative voices in the cabinet, led by Mitchell Sharp and Jean-Luc Pépin, who have campaigned for the interests of the business community. Although this faction failed to dilute Bryce Mackasey's labor legislation, they were triumphant on other crucial issues such as tax reform, election expenses, business competition and foreign ownership. The foreign ownership policy eventually produced by the government remains one of the least explicable of the past four and a half years. Before the issue became any kind of public cause, Trudeau had written about it very knowledgeably in his days as a gadfly academic. Indeed, he went so far as to suggest that governments had taken no action to restrict foreign ownership because their hands were tied by election contributions—"the fund providers must always preserve their rights."

In this one essay, Trudeau managed to tie into a neat bundle two of the problems that would confront his government 15 years later. Foreign ownership has been the subject of two task force reviews and long study by a parliamentary committee. Election expenses were studied by a prestigious committee of inquiry and a parliamentary committee. On both issues, the studies were excellent: in both cases, the resultant legislation was a farce.

Still, 15 years is a long time and Trudeau has shown no recent inclination to wave the banners of nationalism. He prefers to talk vaguely of the splendid variety of ways in which his government has reinforced "the Canadian identity." Nationalism seems doomed as an election issue. Stanfield worries whether restrictions on foreign ownership might not be regarded in other parts of the country as "southern Ontario imperialism," but even he scorned the government's legislation. David Lewis, who would like to debate the issue, will probably end up talking to himself.

The Prime Minister started with apparent conviction in the field of Canada-U.S. relations. After President Nixon's emergency economic measures last year caused renewed doubts about the viability of old-style dealings, Trudeau began making comments about the need for greater independence and new friends, like the Soviet Union. That trial balloon lasted just a couple of months before Trudeau abruptly cut the string and began talking earnestly with old Dick Nixon about fantastic breakthroughs.

The government's reluctance to legalize the simple possession of marijuana and hashish, as recommended by the Le-Dain commission, is more understandable. It is doubtful that the general public, which still equates marijuana with heroin and cocaine, is ready for such a change. It is equally doubtful whether the government would have been prepared to make any substantive changes on such a touchy issue, no matter what their high-powered commission recommended. But why did they set it up in the first place?

In fact, the Prime Minister has been feeling pangs of unrequited love from those he has sought to serve. On an open-line radio show during the summer he expressed delight that the callers were not "people bitching about their own private problems."

Yet, in spite of changes in the man, the Trudeau government cannot be identified as merely conservative. Nothing is quite that simple. The two major defectors from the cabinet have split in quite opposite directions. Eric Kierans began preaching policies much closer to those of the NDP; but when Paul Hellyer left the seats of the mighty, he began to mutter darkly about Communists being in control in Ottawa.

Looking back on Trudeau's term of office, the outstanding impression is that, with few notable exceptions, Trudeau has remarkably few political goals. The most obvious exception has been his view of the constitution and Quebec's role in Confederation—Quebec would be helped economically and French would be equal as a language to English in the federal government, but there would be no jurisdictional privileges for Quebec and no romantic sympathy for French-Canadian nationalism. From the Official Languages Act to the War Measures Act, he has been true to those goals.

In general, however, the Prime Minister is not readily identified with goals or purposes. His own definition of the role of government is to anticipate problems and to avoid crises. That is like saying that the ship of state must stay off the rocks: it says nothing about a destination.

We Will Have Some Goodies

LE DEVOIR, *Montréal*
October 10, 1972
CARL DUBUC

"Watch out," Mr. Trudeau blares in Shawinigan. "We'll soon be announcing some goodies in the area of recreation." There have been a number of salty comments in this election but this is the first time we get a sweet one.

In any case let's not wait for the goodies. And as a Lapalme worker told me, licking his chops, "It's better to get promises of candy than to be told to eat shit."

Trudeau and the Two Cultures

LE SOLEIL, *Québec*
October 11, 1972
EDITORIAL BY GILLES BOYER

The direct tone which the Prime Minister has always used as much in the Commons as with ordinary citizens is still evident in the current election campaign. Depending on one's view his manner is labelled "arrogant" or "courageous honesty." One thing is certain, Mr. Trudeau's style is the same with his French-language compatriots as with those of the English language. It is applied equally in his native province, Québec as in Ontario or the West, whether it concerns separatism or special status, the need for French in the civil service and in the national capital or the place of wheat policy within the national economy. In this regard, Mr. Trudeau is different from our traditional politicians. Instead of appealing to the chauvinism of each province, which would be the easy route, he attempts to place the problems within a national dimension.

If this frankness is arrogant then the Prime Minister was being arrogant recently at a meeting in Ontario. In a Liberal riding (Grenville-Carleton) in an Ottawa suburb, where there are many anglophone civil servants, Mr. Trudeau did not hesitate to deal with a subject that is traumatizing anglophone civil servants in the federal capital: bilingualism in the federal civil service. Because French is occupying an increasingly important role, English civil servants are feeling insecure. Before his own Liberal partisans from the Ottawa area, a certain number of whom fear and misunderstand the application of the Official Languages Act, the Prime Minister stated clearly that French Canadians will not wait another hundred years to be able to communicate with their government in Ottawa. He added that he had little sympathy for those who say they favor the Official Languages Act but cannot accept its implementation.

The affirmation of cultural differences raises problems. It is difficult to accommodate, since differences cause national tensions. These cultural differences tend to transform themselves into political differences that risk fragmenting the country: separatism, special status for one or many provinces, etc. If the Trudeau government insists on cultural and linguistic differences it is very cautious of the latter which strains national unity or the efficient functioning of a central government, which is the same thing. But that is precisely what lends credibility to his actions in regard to Canadians of both languages, in that it assures that differences will exist within the framework of Canadian unity. In this regard Prime Minister Trudeau remains true to the logic of his political philosophy. He seeks to establish the two cultures while refusing appeals to the nationalism of one linguistic community. He has proved this once again before the voters of Grenville-Carleton.

The Liberal Record: Good in Spots

THE OTTAWA CITIZEN
October 19, 1972
EDITORIAL

It has been a strange election campaign. Compared with 1968, the voters have seemed restrained, detached, perhaps a little cynical. Compared with all four elections in the 1960s, the mood of Canada has been hard to read.

The canonization of Pierre Trudeau that took place between April and June in 1968 was unreal, if not blasphemous. He warned that he could not fulfill the extravagant hopes that were placed in him, and he was right.

Let us now then, in the relatively unheated atmosphere of the 1972 campaign, look at the government's record and try to assess whether it deserves another term. The Citizen does not intend to be dogmatic about this election. It is a matter of human judgment, and our judgment is as capable of error as yours. We are simply going to set out some of the considerations that seem to us important, and draw conclusions from them.

Mr. Trudeau and his Liberals were elected in 1968 primarily on the national unity issue. The leader's charisma, his political sex appeal, was important; it certainly added to the Liberal vote. But the voters decided primarily, we believe, because they thought he and his party were better fitted than any alternative to hold Canada together against the threats of political separatism and economic disparity.

On the test, the government has justified our confidence. Canada has not split up. Separatism is on retreat. Long-range efforts to strengthen those regions of the country where poverty is most severe have been pursued with vigor.

In the crisis of 1970 the government courageously refused to treat with terrorism. Despite the tragic fate of Pierre Laporte, that decision was right—as shown by many incidents of terrorist blackmail in other parts of the world since then. Terror grows by what it feeds on; there can be no compromise with evil on that scale.

On the other hand, the proclamation of the War Measures Act and the results that flowed from it were unnecessary and excessive. There was no insurrection, not any real threat of it. There was criminal activity, for which the normal weapons of the law sufficed.

The Trudeau government, as it promised, pursued consistently the goals of a formally bilingual nation and a bilingual public service. Unpopular as that may be in some sections of

Ottawa, we believe it to be necessary and just if we are serious about sustaining Canada. Important objectives are not achieved without some sacrifice.

Mr. Trudeau's greatest failure has been in economic policy, specifically in unemployment. This stubborn problem is more serious today than when the government took office, despite the relative affluence of the employed. The obtuse economic policies pursued by the government during the first half of its term must be judged largely responsible for that sorry situation.

More briefly, we give the government high marks on what it has done for the physical environment—in the Arctic, at Stockholm, and, to the degree that constitutional barriers allow, across the land.

We give it good marks on foreign affairs. It took important initiatives with China and the Soviet Union. It made a sensible retrenchment in NATO. It stood up well to President Nixon's tough economic challenge. Its policy on foreign ownership was feeble and half-baked—but better than a strident nationalism that could damage Canada far more.

On one issue we give the prime minister zero marks: the financing of elections. In the spring of 1968 he said that this matter had top priority. Indeed it should have, for it bears upon the fundamental question of how truly our democratic machinery reflects the people's will. Four and a half years later nothing effective has been done.

It was a spotty record—very good in some areas, poor in others.

Smartest Mouth in Town

SOUTHAM NEWS SERVICES
October 26, 1972
CHARLES LYNCH

With Trudeau, Heading East—The Trudeau campaign has as much snap, crackle and pop as a bowl of porridge but the people seem to be eating it up.

The prime minister ladles the stuff out in carefully measured amounts, as though recognizing the public's limited ability to absorb such wisdom.

The land is strong, say the Grit slickers, meaning you've never had it so good. Trudeau's speeches are a mixture of that and his belief that his opponents have never been so stupid.

In giving his glowing account of the first four Trudeau years and expressing the certitude that four even better ones are in prospect, he permits himself several exaggerations, perhaps to show that in addition to having the smartest mouth in town he knows something about gut politics.

One of those exaggerations is his description of the state the country was in when he came to power in 1968. After hearing him describe it in his Victoria speech, one correspondent who wasn't in the country at that time said: "God, it must have been awful."

Trudeau spoke of scandals and assorted uncertainties, violence in Quebec, regional disparities of the most awful kind, wheat surpluses unsold, the dollar going to pot.

Lester Pearson would be interested to hear he had left Trudeau and the country such a dismal inheritance; the implication is that if Trudeau hadn't descended into our midst at that critical moment, we would have been doomed.

The odd thing is that I remember 1968 as a very good year and I suspect it was that way for most Canadians. The only spooky thing that happened was Trudeaumania, an unexplained phenomenon believed to be related to the virus that causes lemmings to rush into the sea. . . .

He still has the power to compel, inspire or provoke a crowd into irrational behavior, as he did in 1968 and as John Diefenbaker did in 1958. It is a power that Stanfield lacks and that Lewis, lacking the aura of vested authority, can only dream about.

Trudeau denies his audiences a chance to explode while he is speaking; he turns his sentences down at the end, rather than up. He doesn't drone them as he used to and doesn't sound bored as he always does in the House of Commons or at new conferences. What he seeks to convey is controlled excitement and unabashed pride in his accomplishments. The message is that no one could have done better.

He is introduced as a man of greatness, strength, vitality,

warmth and compassion, although we never have had a politician with less of those last two qualities.

He has come to proclaim that Canada no longer has an identity crisis and is no longer an unknown country, to her own people or to foreigners. In his four years as prime minister, Canadians had pulled it all together.

I suspect that what that reflects, as much as anything, is how little Trudeau knew of Canada before he became prime minister. What has happened isn't so much that we have discovered ourselves—Trudeau has discovered Canada and like some early explorer, he's taking the credit.

Picking holes in the Trudeau approach is as easy as it is fruitless; his audiences eat the stuff up, relishing the lack of humor, sharing flights of fancy that would bring snickers if delivered by any other. There is something of the Adlai Stevenson approach in all that, except that Stevenson had warmth and humility, which may explain why Stevenson was a loser, while Trudeau is a winner.

By his own admission he has reached into almost every facet of our national life and everything he has touched, he has improved. No other prime minister in our history has ever dared to make that claim.

The Trudeau File

LA PRESSE, *Montréal*
October 27, 1972
EDITORIAL BY VINCENT PRINCE

Prime Minister Trudeau was elected in 1968 by making the people of Canada believe in the creation of a just society.

A just society has many elements. It involves a program which comprises every aspect of the country's internal politics and its foreign relations. The aim of justice is to fill individual needs, those of the different classes of society, those of the different regions of Canada and those of the nations with which we deal.

It is understood that such an objective cannot be fully realized. But how close have we come? That is the question we wish to answer in this brief evaluation of the pros and cons of the last four years of the Trudeau administration.

On the positive side we can point to the following accomplishments.

1. The review of our foreign policy: The Trudeau government has reduced Canadian military participation in NATO. It has established diplomatic relations with Communist China and the Vatican and it has improved the links with Russia. The last two efforts have increased our wheat sales.

2. A greater affirmation of Canada's sovereignty: Here we can point to the efforts to retain control of the Arctic, legislation to extend our fishing zones and the timid effort to reduce American control of our economy. Some of Mr. Trudeau's trips abroad have also emphasized the unique Canadian personality.

3. Policies which, on the whole, have contributed to the maintenance of a healthy economy: The rate of new job creation has been higher than that in most other industrialized nations. Our trade level has been maintained despite American import restrictions. Wages have increased by 55 percent since 1968. New initiatives such as Opportunities for Youth, Local Initiatives Programs and subsidies for regional development have surely had an effect in this regard.

4. Improvements for the poor: Tax revision has allowed a more equitable apportionment of the tax burden in favour of low-income earners. Old age pensions were indexed to the cost of living. Unemployment Insurance was made more generous for the unemployed. Efforts were also made to make our environment more "liveable," through measures against pollution, the creation of national parks etc. The Labour Code was brought up to date.

5. A greater respect for human rights: The Trudeau government introduced three modifications to the penal code and began a certain reform of our penitentiary system.

6. Extension of the bilingualism policy begun under the Pearson government: The Official Languages Act was the principle element of measures taken by Mr. Trudeau. The progress to date within the public service is not very convincing but the francophone minority outside Québec places much hope in this new attitude of the federal government.

On the negative side there are the following items.

1. The continuing constitutional impasse between Ottawa and Québec: If Mr. Trudeau has been sensitive to the recommendations of the Laurendeau-Dunton Commission on bilingualism he has not shown the same concern in regards to the status of Québec within Confederation. His rigid attitude is largely responsible for the failure of constitutional revision and the increased separatist activity in Québec.

2. The increase in unemployment: The number of unemployed reached 4.7% of the work force in 1969, 5.9% in 1970, 6.4% in 1971 and 7.1% in September of this year. This level causes concern even if we consider that the unemployed are not all heads of families and that this is, in part, the price we have had to pay to fight inflation more effectively than other countries.

3. The repression during the October Crisis in Québec: Many people in Québec remain convinced that it was not necessary to resort to the War Measures Act and that in any case the law was in many instances applied without discretion.

4. The lack of progress in eliminating tensions within the country: Regional development policy has not greatly reduced the economic disparities between the different regions. The Eastern farmers have not received as much attention as those of the Prairies. Ottawa intervened quickly to end a legal strike in Pacific ports but allowed an illegal strike in the St. Lawrence to fester.

5. The continued foreign strangle-hold on our economy: Despite the timid efforts mentioned above, the Americans, for example, still control nearly 60 percent of our manufacturing sector. Our trade is not sufficiently diversified.

The Decision

THE CALGARY HERALD
October 27, 1972
EDITORIAL

During the past four days all four serious parties in this election have been examined in these columns. They've all been found wanting.

It would be a temptation next Monday to pull the covers up and stay in bed. But people can't preserve freedom by doing that. And maybe it is when the decisions are the most difficult that it is most important to vote.

All parties have contributed to the emptiness of the campaign now winding down. Social Crediters, New Democrats, Conservatives and Liberals alike have proceeded with one cautious eye on their own internal problems—and the other fixed firmly on the past.

The things Canadians are really worried about—the declining value of their money, whether there will be jobs a year or so from now, what it will be like when they retire, what to tell their children about drugs and crime, what life is coming to in the cities, what morals are coming to, whether it's good to work or better to loaf—haven't been faced by any of the so-called party platforms or by the leaders.

Voters feel all the values that underpin their lives slipping away or changing beyond recognition, and all they're getting from the democratic process is a bunch of politicians playing that increasingly private game of holding or seeking office.

The Liberals and Conservatives have to bear most of the blame because they are the major parties, the ones that are supposed to have the resources and the brainpower to come up with some ideas. There is a temptation to cast a plague on both their houses and vote for one of the little parties. But that's no way to run a democracy, either, out of spite. And the little parties have been even less coherent than the big ones, anyway.

So what to do? It is a decision preceded by a lot of mental anguish. But Canadians have endured from their government too much arrogance, too many contradictions, too many failures and too much confusion in the conduct of their business during the past four years.

In 1968, the majority of Canadians gambled on the charismatic but unknown man named Pierre Trudeau, and it hasn't paid off.

Now, we should seriously consider gambling on a known,

honest, sincere and non-charismatic man named Robert Stanfield.

It could pay off.

The Choice

THE FREE PRESS, *Winnipeg*
October 28, 1972
EDITORIAL

The quiet election campaign of 1972 has drawn to a close,
leaving the experts wondering what the quiet means. Is a majority of voters happy with things as they are? Are voters
quietly contemplating a change? Or are they merely apathetic
to the urgent issues the country faces?

If it is the latter—and there appears to be a consensus that it
is—the voters are doing no more than reflecting the attitude of
all the parties toward the major issues. Of these by far and
away the most important is the state of the economy—spirall-
ing inflation and rising prices coupled with high unemployment. No party has had the courage to grasp the nettle and say
that if elected it would halt or slow inflation by controls on
prices and incomes. The Liberals have argued that Canada's
rate of inflation (over five per cent annually at last reckoning)
is not so bad—not as bad as that of some other countries; and
that the number of people out of work must be measured
against the number with jobs. The Conservatives would tackle
the problem with another commission. The NDP has said that
it is "not ill disposed" toward controls, but David Lewis doubts
if Canadians would accept them—an easy out.

Of the various parties' credibility in other areas, there is little
more to be said now than there was when Prime Minister
Trudeau first announced the election. The government remains
open to criticism in many areas—the unemployment insurance
mess, a non-existent labor and strikes policy, increasing spending and higher taxes, confusion in defence and foreign affairs
leading to a deterioration of Canada's prestige abroad. But the
Liberals can also point to some accomplishments. The separa-

tism issue is not the painful problem today that it was some months ago. There has been substantial revision of the Criminal Code. Tough legislation has been introduced to protect Canada's environment including the Arctic. There has been a spate of laws to protect the consumer. With an assist from nature around the world, the government through its wheat policies has markedly improved the lot of the Prairie farmer.

The credits must be balanced against the debits; and then the whole must be set against what the other parties are offering. Again the answer is, as it was two months ago, not much. The Conservatives seem to have no clear-cut policies whatsoever. Mr. Stanfield claims that a vote for the Liberals is a vote for taxes. But his proposals, it has been estimated, would cost taxpayers another $2 billion a year. The NDP's main plank has been Mr. Lewis' simplistic attack on corporations. All his proposals, if implemented, would put the nation's bill up by another $4 billion a year. And, as was pointed out on this page on Thursday, the best that Mr. Stanfield can hope for is a caretaker Conservative government, with another election in the near future. Mr. Lewis is honest about NDP hopes. The most they hope for is to form the opposition or, at least to elect enough members to hold the balance of power in a divided house.

All of which leads one, however reluctantly, to the conclusion that there is really no choice but the Liberals. It is a reluctant choice that many voters are not going to make happily or with much enthusiasm. Their hope must be that, if a Liberal government is re-elected, it will waste no time getting down to work to put its house—and the nation's—in order. There is no guarantee that it will. But there is more chance of a Liberal government being able to do so than a government of any other party.

Early on the night of October 30 television screens began to bring the bad news home to Liberal Party organizers and candidates. Soon after the polls closed a Liberal debacle in Ontario began to unfold; within several hours the Trudeau government would see 23 of their sitting members from that province defeated by Conservative candidates. The government was virtually wiped out in the West, but managed to retain 56 seats in Québec. When the recounts had been completed several days later they showed the slimmest of minority governments: Liberals 109, Conservatives 107, NDP 31, Social Credit 15, Other 2.

The political hangover suffered by the Liberal Party the morning after their surprising near-defeat would not be eased by the post-election press reaction.

A Liberal Defeat

LA PRESSE, *Montréal*
October 31, 1972
EDITORIAL BY VINCENT PRINCE

As this is being written the results of yesterday's election are still unclear. The gap between Liberals and Conservatives is so small that we cannot know who, Mr. Trudeau or Mr. Stanfield, has succeeded in electing the most candidates, although it is certain that we will have a minority government.

Whatever happens, there's no doubt that the Liberals were the big losers in this confrontation and that the country can expect another election soon, an election which should this time clearly favor the Conservatives.

A solid Conservative wave made itself felt yesterday west of Québec. If Mr. Trudeau hangs on to power the Conservatives will surely hasten to overturn him in the House before the electorate changes its mind. They might well be able to count on support from the NDP which also made important gains yesterday and now holds the balance of power. If, on the other hand, Mr. Stanfield is called upon to form a government he will no doubt be tempted to repeat what Mr. Diefenbaker did in 1957. Mr. Diefenbaker called a session during which he had passed highly popular laws and immediately after called an election which resulted in an unprecedented victory. The only thing that prevents the first hypothesis is that the NDP may realize that a hurried call for an election might be as bad for it as for the Liberals. A stronger showing by the Conservatives in a new election might submerge the third parties. This occurred in 1958. Whatever happens the country seems more divided now than ever. French Canada voted Liberal while the English provinces leaned the other way. The two solitudes have confirmed their continued existence. . . .

Send for Mr. Stanfield

THE OTTAWA CITIZEN
October 31, 1972
EDITORIAL

The Citizen has not supported the Conservative program or the Stanfield team. But orderly change is one of democracy's chief benefits, and it is vitally important that our leaders and our institutions should respond when the people speak.

A fundamental weakness of the Trudeau government has been an insensitivity to the needs of the people. Now it is up to the prime minister to respond, and his graceful words late last night suggested that he will do so. We hope he will advise the Governor-General to send for Mr. Stanfield.

Mr. Trudeau need not draw the conclusion that the election result requires his retirement from political life. He has made a tremendous contribution to Canada, particularly in his work on our most serious problem—the tensions between French and English-speaking Canada. At his age, he can expect to make many important contributions in the future. We urge him to stay on as a vigorous and lively leader of the opposition.

To Mr. Stanfield we offer congratulations on a great political achievement. Should the burden of office fall upon him, we wish him well in bearing it.

The Conservative party has won the victory.

The standing in the House of Commons is virtually a tie. The constitutional position is open to a variety of possible responses. The political prospect is unstable, to put it mildly. But the message is clear.

When an entrenched government such as Prime Minister Trudeau led in the last Parliament is cut down to equality with the official opposition, and with two other opposition parties holding substantial blocks of seats, it ought to resign.

Although it would be constitutional for Mr. Trudeau to hang on and wait for the verdict of Parliament, we believe it would be politically unwise. It would appear to ignore a thumping vote of non-confidence from the people.

Six out of 10 Canadian voters have expressed dissatisfaction with the Liberal government's performance. Even if Robert Stanfield's Conservatives have been able to convince slightly fewer than four out of 10, they offer the only viable alternative.

A Precarious Minority

THE CHRONICLE-HERALD, *Halifax*

October 31, 1972

EDITORIAL

Whatever else may be said about yesterday's federal general election, the cliffhanger results could hardly be considered anything else but a victory for Robert L. Stanfield and his Progressive Conservative party and a rejection of Prime Minister Pierre Trudeau and his administration's program in a number of major areas....

For his part, Mr. Trudeau will have no choice but to realize that his rapid, almost startling descent from majority government resulted from widespread unhappiness over many of his major policies, not the least of which was his administration's methods of implementing its plans in the area of bilingualism.

Just as surely, it resulted from general disillusionment with the government's job program, as well as its economic and taxation policies, and it indicated a continued lack of enthusiasm for his administration's efforts to tackle the serious problem of regional disparity.

The election results will provide considerable food for thought, as well, to political pundits quick to notice that with the cooling off of Ontario's love affair with the federal Liberal party, Quebec rejected Conservative overtures and solidified its position as the only real and major power base of the Liberal party.

For Mr. Stanfield, the election results enhanced his prospects immeasurably, solidifying his position at the helm of the PC party and placing him in the enviable position of a man on the way up....

As for the many, many polls forecasting wide margins between old-line party standings after Monday's vote, the pollsters gave proof to a theory attributed to former prime minister John Diefenbaker: polls are for dogs.

Like a worried, almost rejected suitor, the Prime Minister reacted to his electoral rebuff by offering Parliament and the Canadian people an ambitious list of proposed legislation in the January Throne Speech. The inertia of the past eighteen months was thrown out and replaced with the promise of action. "The Land Is Strong" was forgotten and the press responded more positively.

Burnishing the Image

THE GLOBE AND MAIL, *Toronto*
January 5, 1973
GEORGE BAIN

IT NEVER RAINS BUT IT POURS
or
THIS PROGRAM TAKES IN EVERYTHING BUT
LAUNDRY

*We've worked out a program we're sure will do
To burnish the image as good as new;
There's social security, jobs for all,
We're taking on housing and urban sprawl,
Amendments are coming on Income Tax,
And measures for moving old railroad tracks;*

We'll deal with inflation, we'll make you fit,
We'll sweeten the lot of the aged a bit,
And wouldn't old Bennett have been impressed?
— We've even discovered the Golden West.

Western Liberal: Do you know how the West was lost?
Pierre E. Himself: No, but if you hum a couple of bars, I can fake it.
We continue:

We've bills relating to field and stream,
Another allowance-for-families scheme,
For corporate immigrants: yet-new terms
(We're putting more natives on boards of firms).
We've plans for improving the IDB
And tightening the rules of the UIP
And still to make sure that we're back in grace
Oh, see how we've wrapped in a fond embrace,
A threesome which simply ensures our health
— The Mounties, the Queen and the Commonwealth.

Trudeau Learned Election Lessons

THE TORONTO STAR
January 5, 1973
EDITORIAL

It was a hard lesson that Canadian voters had for Prime Minister Pierre Trudeau but he has proved a willing learner.

Stripped of his majority and humbled by the Progressive Conservatives, Trudeau and his cabinet have rallied to produce a program for this session of Parliament—however brief—that promises the kind of legislation that almost certainly would have won him a decisive victory a few months ago.

He now deserves a chance—as the New Democrats have promised him—to translate this statement of good intentions into solid legislation. There should be no more talk of the government's downfall in a few days or weeks. The Liberals have earned the time to prove they mean what they say—even though it is so different from what they were saying in 1972.

The reshuffled cabinet obviously took to heart the lesson from concerned Canadians that the tide of foreign investment has to be diverted into channels that offer this country a maximum of benefits and a minimum of difficulties.

In a broad extension of the Liberals' previous position, the Speech from the Throne recommends that Parliament pass measures dealing with direct foreign investment, ownership and control of resources, sale of land to foreigners and easier access to foreign technology.

The government proposes to re-introduce its bill to set up a review board to screen foreign take-overs, a measure too weak and narrow to have much significance. But the speech indicates the government is prepared to extend the screening to cover all new direct investment from abroad. This would allow the cabinet to influence not only the kind of foreign investment that was entering Canada but where it might locate. This is a significant step forward in a continuing battle to be masters of our own economy. It has been recommended by various government task forces—most recently in the Gray report—and deserves support from all parties in the House of Commons.

In addition to a re-appraisal of its foreign-investment policy, the government has laid a new and necessary emphasis on a co-operative approach with provinces and regions on economic matters. The Throne Speech comes close to proposing regional economic policies, an issue of vital importance to the have-not areas of Canada that bear the brunt of unemployment.

Economic policies to reduce unemployment are promised the highest priority in the legislative agenda and properly so. Details are scarce but if the government proposes to produce more jobs by reviving the economy—at the risk of more inflation—it has made a mistake in failing to propose wage and price controls. The opposition parties will have to take a close look at these economic manoeuvres. Without controls, the pledges to fight both unemployment and inflation appear contradictory.

Another top priority went to social policy and here the government promises two significant moves. It will take further steps towards a guaranteed annual income by extending guar-

anteed benefits to the blind and disabled. It also offers a more
co-operative hand to Quebec. Provincial policy, apparently,
will play a much larger role in social security. This is an
essential recognition of differing priorities in different parts of
the country.

While applauding the intent of the Trudeau government in
its new reincarnation, it's too soon for rafter-ringing cheers.
Proposals to deal with disclosure of election expenses appeared
in other Throne Speeches, we remember, without anything
significant happening. And the cabinet may yet use its promise
to consult with the provinces as an excuse for inaction on the
foreign investment measures.

But the agenda for action in vital legislative areas is clear in
the Speech from the Throne. They are the kind of policies
Canadians have told the Liberal government they want, and
the cabinet has responded. Parliament should give the government a chance to translate its good intentions into legislation.

Generalities

THE FREE PRESS, *Winnipeg*
January 5, 1973
EDITORIAL

If promises and proposals were the criteria of a speech from
the throne, the speech delivered at the opening of Parliament
on Thursday would be a winner. The speech, outlining the
minority Liberal government's plans for the coming session,
contains something for just about everyone—from higher pensions and a guaranteed income for some Canadians, to more
housing, incentives to business and industry, and what appears
to be a new and more prominent place for the West within
Confederation. Above all it is a speech primarily constructed to
enlist the support of Mr. Lewis to maintain the government.

Throne speeches are expected to contain only a general outline of the government's program. More was expected of this
one, however, if only because of Prime Minister Trudeau's
statement a few days ago that this speech would be concerned
with specifics rather than generalities. Perhaps Mr. Trudeau's

definition of specific is not that which is generally recognized; for while the speech covers a multitude of subjects, it does so only in the most general way. . . .

Most striking, and most disappointing, in its absence, is any indication that the government intends really to come to grips with the two major problems facing the Canadian economy—unemployment and inflation. It assigns the highest priority to these issues; it hopes to expand job opportunities, promote stable economic growth and attain "reasonable price stability." But it hopes to do so by the same methods that have proved abject failures in the past—more money for local initiative programs and job training; a large capital works program; changes to the Income Tax Act and to tariffs; more assistance to business; an extension of the work of the Industrial Development Bank, and so on. These, and other proposed measures, may all be of some help. But they are like giving a man a sticking plaster when he is bleeding to death from his jugular vein. All that the speech specifically states about fighting inflation is that a joint Senate-Commons inquiry will be made into food prices. If this is all that the government has in mind to fight unemployment and inflation, the country can prepare itself for another year of high unemployment and mounting inflation. The latter problem will be solved only when the government has the political courage to impose controls on prices and wages—as Britain and the United States have done. If it fails to do so, it will forfeit what public support it has, and will not deserve to remain in office.

The decimation of the Liberal Party in the West could hardly be blamed entirely on the actions of the first Trudeau government or its lacklustre 1972 re-election campaign. Anti-Liberal, anti-central Canada alienation can be traced to numerous economic factors including Western anger at a national tariff policy that protected central Canadian manufacturing indistries without offering similar benefits to Western agriculture.

July of 1973 saw the first major attempt by the Trudeau government to deal with Western disaffection: the convening of the West-

ern Economic Opportunities Conference in Edmonton. The now-conventional Canadian wisdom that minority governments are more responsive governments appeared to be borne out.

New Forum

THE EDMONTON JOURNAL
July 27, 1973
EDITORIAL

This week's conference between Prime Minister Trudeau and the four Western premiers was held in a Mount Royal College conference room called "the forum." And now that we know what limited headway was made during the three days of talks we wonder whether this wasn't really the wrong forum in which to deal with the West's problems and its feeling of alienation.

The Western Economic Opportunities Conference wasn't a failure, despite the somewhat gloomy assessments of certain premiers. On at least two major points the West scored significant gains, and the meeting was worthwhile for them alone.

In the key area of transportation the premiers wrung from Ottawa the right to full disclosure of transportation costs, which will provide them with badly-needed ammunition in their battles against discriminatory freight rates. They also obtained permission for provincial government participation—albeit on a limited scale—in the establishment of new banks, which would be located in the West and more responsive than existing institutions to Western financial requirements.

In addition, there were all kinds of "goodies" doled out by Mr. Trudeau's cabinet colleagues, and nobody is going to turn them down.

However, in larger terms, the conference fell far short of expectations—or at least hopes.

Try as he may, Mr. Trudeau can't convince us that the two major federal concessions and all those gifts amount to a "new national policy," the goal he himself set at the start of the conference. "Policy" implies a well thought out course of action towards achieving a definite objective. A series of press releases and ministerial announcements aren't the same thing at all.

In fact it is kind of insulting to the West that Ottawa should try to placate us this way, especially after the prime minister declared to the recent Liberal get-together in Vancouver that he had new insight into our problems and realized there was a lot more involved than just freight rates.

If Mr. Trudeau and his government really had a new national policy for the West, then it should have been spelled out in a comprehensive program covering agriculture, industrial development, transportation, minerals, and so on....

Calgary: No Touchdown But a Few Yards Scored

THE LEADER-POST, *Regina*
July 28, 1973
EDITORIAL

... The four Western premiers were there, alert, explanatory, persuasive and insistent, essentially asking for the makings of a national development policy that would best serve Canada and the West in the 1970s and beyond. They had done their homework.

The well-mounted attempt to put across the oft-repeated Western message once more was clear enough. But the communication of ideas requires both a transmitter and a receiver, and there is no clear indication on the part of Prime Minister Trudeau and the cabinet ministers who accompanied him to Calgary that the receiver was tuned into the message. They were unmoved....

There was no disclosure at Calgary, after three days of discussion, of the emergence of a new comprehensive national development policy to replace the Sir John A. Macdonald policy of 100 years ago.

Premier Blakeney perhaps summed it up succinctly enough.

"I regret to say," he said, "that after three days I do not see the progress toward that national policy which I might have liked to have seen." . . .

There were few signs that the Trudeau government intends to change the National Transportation Act in any major way that would reform a freight rate structure that discriminates against meaningful economic development in the Prairies, and that, after all, was the biggest and most fundamental Western beef.

But was it [the conference] an utter failure? Here the answer is clearly no, and here's why.

● By all the laws of communications that play such a major role in Canada's national life, there simply must now be a greater understanding of the West among Ottawa civil servants, and a greater commitment by the Trudeau government to make sure that myopia never again sets in.

● The excellent way the four Western premiers presented their case augurs well for a renewed sense of regional common purpose that transcends political differences. Messrs. Schreyer, Blakeney, Lougheed and Barrett gained stature as statesmen through their participation and there was no sign of ideological thrust in the positions put forward by any of them. They and Mr. Trudeau came through as Canadians first, advocates of special attitudes molded by the inevitable geographic and psychological exigencies of a sprawling federation like ours second.

● And at least some progress was made toward the drafting of a new national development policy. Surely that's far better than no progress at all.

The initiative is now in the hands of Western MPs of all parties. It is up to them to keep the flame of legitimate Western aspirations burning bright in Ottawa's corridors of elective and bureaucratic power, hopefully without the ideological coloring that so often blunts the thrust.

Meanwhile, it would be well for Mr. Trudeau and his cohorts to remember one transcendental fact about "Western alienation."

We aren't trying to get out of Confederation and the mainstream of Canadian life. We're trying to get in.

From West to East

THE TELEGRAPH-JOURNAL, *Saint John*

July 28, 1973

EDITORIAL

Considering that the prime minister and the four western premiers got together in Calgary to discuss western economic opportunities, a surprising amount of what surfaced bears directly on the Atlantic region and, indeed, this region was often mentioned in the discussions.

Many topics were broached, but transportation clearly dominated the talks. The western concern with that, and the determination that a national policy that for a century has been designed to build and maintain Ontario and Quebec as the manufacturing centre of Canada must be changed, were such familiar themes for Maritimers that the conference might well have been in Fredericton or Charlottetown.

The West didn't get all it wanted. Observers on the scene concluded that if things don't begin to improve visibly, the western premiers will be on the warpath again in six months or a year.

Maritimers, promised in 1967 that regional policies for them would be developed and included in the National Transportation Act, which never was done, may be somewhat wryly amused at the West's chagrin over Ottawa's refusal to promise to embed new policies in the act for the West.

In all, though, the West lustily challenged the idea that the western (and eastern) hinterland of this nation must exist merely to supply raw materials and agricultural products to the prosperous plants and factories of the "golden triangle of the St. Lawrence Valley," as one westerner put it. The prime minister agreed and said a new "national policy" was needed with the aim of providing a balanced and diversified economy in each region.

Sounds like a recipe for a lovely pudding. Suppose we'll ever get to taste it?

The Economy of the West

LE SOLEIL, *Québec*
July 31, 1973
EDITORIAL BY GILLES BOYER

The Calgary Conference on Western Economic Opportunities could not hope to solve the particular economic problems of that region nor the feeling of political "alienation" the West says it feels in regard to the central government and the rest of the country. The Western premiers, presenting a solid front to the federal cabinet, nevertheless expressed views that showed their own individual interests. In so doing they have increased their participation in the shaping of national policy. This can be seen as compensating for the West's poor representation in the federal government. The Premiers put before the central government the economic interests the West believes it has a right to demand within a national policy.

Because of their agriculturally-based economies the Prairie provinces could demand a "special status" within Canada. In the far west British Columbia, cut off by the Rockies, could do the same. But then so could the Maritimes on the basis of their particular history and so could Québec because of its particular culture. Ontario, in the middle, would then be the only province willing to integrate with the rest of the country. One can only conclude that granting special status to one province or region would risk setting off a chain reaction across the country that might shatter a structure already straining under the burden of centrifugal forces. The differences that arise from the agricultural economy of the Prairies or the isolation of British Columbia in relation to the industrialized and urbanized economies of the two central provinces must be resolved without recourse to a solution that would grant these regions sole control over their economic or political particularities. It is only at the national level that different, but not necessarily divergent, interests can be reconciled. This excludes a formula that would isolate provinces or regions. Attention to regional differences must not lead to regional compartmentalization. This would be fatal to a country such as ours, which already finds it difficult to resist the strong attraction of its neighbor to the south.

The goodwill generated by the Western Economic Opportunities Conference was short-lived, particularly in Alberta. Six weeks after that meeting, the Prime Minister announced the creation of a two-price system for domestic and exported Canadian oil, with Ottawa pocketing a good portion of the export revenues. Apart from ensuring that the Americans would no longer get Canadian oil at the bargain basement prices they took for granted, the government was trying to ensure that the entire country and particularly energy-deficient Atlantic Canada shared some of the oil wealth. The Alberta government, riding high on its growing mountain of oil money, was not amused.

Bad Policy

THE CALGARY HERALD
September 15, 1973
EDITORIAL

The federal government has finally come to the logical conclusion of its recent behavior. It has told the oil industry and the province of Alberta to go to hell. The interests of the hinterland are to serve the interests of the Ontario-Quebec consumers.

The forty-cent-a-barrel export tax will create a two-price system. Canadians will receive the existing price. Americans will pay extra. Ottawa pockets the difference.

Thus the two-price system, which is worth considering on its logical merits in national terms just as the Lougheed plan for two-price gas is worth discussing in provincial terms, combines the worst of both worlds.

No extra revenue flows to the producers of crude oil. Where do they get the millions of dollars—the hundreds of millions of dollars—necessary to explore for and find the new oil reserves the country so desperately needs in the long term?

All Energy Minister Donald Macdonald can say is that the $15 million a month the tax produces might be spent to assist the industry. If past experience is any guide, that motive bespeaks a maximum of federal government interference and an absolute minimum of genuine assistance as the actual result.

Even while the deficiencies of the plan are catalogued, it must be admitted that there appears to have been a vacuum available for Ottawa to move into. There are real indications that Canadian crude was under-priced in terms of the realities of the bellwether Chicago market.

The Canadian oil industry seems to have been slow to adjust its price to the level the traffic would, in fact, bear. The Alberta government has so far contented itself with intervention in the price of natural gas and has left crude oil to find its own market level.

It is not entirely surprising that the National Energy Board, according to one attempt to divine federal motives, felt that it was not honoring those provisions in its governing legislation which call upon it to ensure not only adequate reserves in Canada, but a fair market price for exports.

But the resolution of this problem could have been a heaven-sent opportunity for Ottawa to at last demonstrate some knowledge of the oil industry and some appreciation of Western sensibilities.

The problem could have been a splendid catalyst for genuine federal-provincial-industry contact and discussion to evolve not merely an answer to a short-term market anomaly, but the beginnings of a genuine energy policy for Canada. The ground work could have been laid for a detailed presentation to the full-scale federal-provincial meeting on energy that Premier Lougheed has called for and the federal government has not rejected.

Instead, Ottawa chose to act unilaterally. Its methods are crude and rude. Its policy is bad. It is bad because it frustrates development of the industry. It is bad because it denies the true owners of the asset—Albertans—potential revenue opportunities. It is bad because it will lead to a new and meddlesome federal presence in the industry. It is bad because it repre- sented an opportunity for genuine consultation and that oppor- tunity is now lost.

Finally, the policy is bad because it seeks to insulate the central regions of Canada from the realities of the market, without properly understanding the equally powerful realities of the producing region.

Tax Return

THE EDMONTON JOURNAL
September 21, 1973
EDITORIAL

Energy Minister Donald Macdonald has certainly been vocal enough of late, whether announcing some new oil policy or reversing his field on what should be done about a pipeline to Montreal. So we can't understand why he has been so uncom- municative on another topic, one of pressing interest to this province, its people and its government.

The subject in question is the newly imposed oil export tax and what portion of it Ottawa intends to turn over to the producing provinces, the owners of the resource. All we have heard thus far from Mr. Macdonald are hints, suggestions and vague statements.

What, for instance, does the minister have to say about Conservative Leader Robert Stanfield's flat statement that the full amount of the tax—estimated at $15 million per months— should be returned to the provinces from which the oil is produced?

If Mr. Macdonald's two-price oil policy protects Canadians from paying more for petroleum products by eliminating exter- nal market pressures, fine. Any move that combats inflation is welcome, even though we question why this particular industry was singled out.

But what about the revenue Alberta loses under the 40-cent- per-barrel export levy? Premier Peter Lougheed claims the tax will cost the Alberta economy $300 million. Now this may not

amount to much in the Ottawa Big League, where Mr. Macdonald and his cabinet colleagues throw around millions of
dollars with abandon (remember Bonaventure?), but for Alberta the figure represents one-fifth of the provincial budget.

Even in its wilder moments the federal government can't
expect Alberta to suffer this kind of loss, especially when tax
revenue from a provincially-owned resource is pouring into
Ottawa's coffers.

Lougheed Is Not Kadhafi

LA PRESSE, *Montréal*
September 20, 1973
EDITORIAL

If the premier of Alberta, Peter Lougheed, were Colonel Kadhafi he would announce that his province will cease deliveries
of oil to Canada so long as there exists a federal tax of 40 cents
on each barrel of oil exported to the U.S.

But Alberta is not Libya and Lougheed bears little resem-
blence to Kadhafi. He resembles more the Québec Deputy Minister for Intergovernmental Affairs, Arthur Tremblay, who admitted he has no global strategy *vis-a-vis* Ottawa, than an oil
king holding the upper hand on President Nixon.

There will therefore not be an Alberta oil war. Alberta will
not separate from Canada. At least that is the indication given
in Mr. Lougheed's televised address Tuesday night.

Federal circles have always feared, since the birth of the
separatist movement in Québec, that it would have a "contagious" effect on other provinces. "You will export your poison"
predicted one of the Federal government's closest advisors. At
Québec, within the offices of the Bourassa government, the
"separatist poison" is neutralized by carefully nurtured counterweights. As for Alberta, it would be presumptuous to assume that the anger of its premier is anything more than
another episode in the history of bad relations between the
West and the Eastern provinces.

Some advice about chopsticks from Premier Chou En-Lai during visit to Peking in October 1973.

Winding up the 1974 election campaign with Energy Minister Donald Macdonald at a Toronto Island picnic. *(CP Photo)*

Above: Presentation of *Between Friends/Entre Amis* to President Ford in Washington, June 16, 1976. *(CP Photo)*

Right: In Cuba with Castro during late January 1976. *(Public Archives Canada— PA110807)*

Left: With President Carter at the White House, February 21, 1977. *(Wide World Photos)*

Below: A pirouette for the press at Buckingham Palace, May 7, 1977. *(CP Photo)*

On the reviewing stand for St. Jean Baptiste parade with Sacha *(left)* and Justin in Vankleek, Ontario, June 25, 1978. *(CP Photo)*

The Trudeau shrug at a news conference following the three-day conference on the economy in Ottawa, November 29, 1978. *(CP Photo)*

A thorough survey of Pierre Trudeau's press coverage will reveal that his most consistently favorable copy comes from two sources: foreign press coverage in general, and Canadian coverage of his foreign travels and international policy initiatives. This pattern can be clearly seen at work in October of 1973, as the Prime Minister made his first official visit to China since the establishment of Sino-Canadian diplomatic relations in October 1970.

Warmly Welcome the Distinguished Canadian Guest

THE PEOPLE'S DAILY, *Peking*
October 9, 1973
EDITORIAL

Pierre Elliot Trudeau, the Prime Minister of Canada, arrives in Peking today for an official visit to our country at the invitation of the government of the People's Republic of China. The distinguished Canadian guest comes to China from far away, bringing with him friendship of the people of Canada. The people of China wish to extend a warm welcome to the distinguished guest.

There has been profound traditional friendship between China and Canada. During the second World War, the people of our two countries sympathized and supported each other, in our struggle against the Fascist agression. We will never forget that Dr. Bethune sacrificed his own precious life for the cause of liberation of the Chinese people. His noble spirit of internationalism has always been a learning example for the Chinese people....

China and Canada have different social systems, but we all stand for the development of our friendly relations on the basis of the five principles of mutual respect for sovereignty and territorial integrity, mutual non-aggression, non-interference in each other's internal affairs, equality and mutual benefit, and peaceful co-existence. In October, 1970, China and Canada established diplomatic relations. It was a great event in the history of Sino-Canadian relations, and has opened up broad prospects for the development of friendly relations between the people of our two countries. . . .

Prime Minister Trudeau has always actively promoted the development of Sino-Canadian relations. In 1960, he came to visit China. During this visit, he will discuss and exchange views with our country's leaders on bilateral relations and various international issues of common interest. We are confident that this visit will further deepen our understanding and enhance our friendship. We sincerely wish him success on his visit. We also wish that the friendship between the people of China and Canada will continue to flourish.

Realistic Canada-China Relations

THE FREE PRESS, *London*
October 18, 1973
EDITORIAL

The series of agreements reached between Prime Minister Trudeau and Premier Chou En-lai during talks in Peking are not momentous enough in themselves to warrant more than passing notice on the world stage. They serve as a formal base for Mr. Trudeau's symbolic visit to China, but little more.

Yet the fact that Canada and China have been able to make the headway they have toward practical and timely relationships is one of the world's diplomatic bright spots of recent years.

China is moving into a new era of international contact—not only as a Pacific power of vast potential but as one of the pivotal nations of the world. It is of increasing importance that Canadian relationships with China continue to be well-founded and realistic.

The significance of the altered Chinese stance has been illustrated in the parade of Western leaders to the Chinese capital. Last year it was President Nixon. French President Georges Pompidou preceded Mr. Trudeau by a few weeks. Britain's

Prime Minister Heath is planning a visit for early in the new year.

An examination of the range and scope of Canadian contacts with China will show that they compare well with those of any Western nation. Indeed, Canadian agreements with China have been instrumental in extending Chinese relationships elsewhere.

China's relations with other Western powers are likely to grow rapidly. It is an advantage therefore that with Canada they have already grown considerably. There is substance in the fact that Canada and China are marking the third anniversary of full diplomatic relations, while taking significant steps in the areas of trade, immigration, consular services, and medical, scientific and cultural exchanges. Some Western powers are still only making preliminary overtures in these areas.

Journey to Peking

THE EVENING TELEGRAM, *St. John's*
October 18, 1973
EDITORIAL

The Chinese people are noted for being polite and hospitable to strangers. It seems they are also a grateful people if we can judge from the kind of reception that has been given Prime Minister Trudeau, his expectant wife and the members of the Canadian party who have just completed a week-long visit to China.

It is universally recognized by now that it was Canada's action, initiated by Prime Minister Trudeau several years ago, in recognizing the Communist government of China that opened the way for membership in the United Nations and acceptance by the United States. It is also a matter of record that, despite the controversy which still surrounds the career of the Canadian doctor, Norman Bethune, (who became a hero of the Chinese revolution) his memory still evokes a favorable response in Peking and elsewhere in the People's Republic of China.

The result has been that the journey to Peking has been a notable success. It may not have received the extraordinary coverage of President Nixon's visit to Peking nearly two years ago; but it has been noted that Mr. Trudeau spent an hour and a half with Chairman Mao Tse-Tung, half an hour longer than the U.S. president!

The Long March Toward the Third Option

LE DEVOIR, *Montréal*
October 29, 1973
EDITORIAL

The visit to the People's Republic of China by the leader of the Canadian government from October 10 to 18 is undeniably the most successful foreign relations maneuver undertaken by Mr. Trudeau since his accession to power. Announced with an equal degree of modesty and meticulous preparation, Mr. Trudeau's visit to Peking, though briefer and less spectacular than his tour of Asia in 1970 and his Russian sojourn in 1971, has nonetheless produced impressive and concrete results in the areas of trade exchange of delegations, and a program of cultural, medical and technological exchanges.

More important in the long term, Mr. Trudeau has been able to present with greater force and precision than ever before, during his long meeting with Chou En lai, the new view of the world that has recently enlightened our foreign policy. Though the execution of that policy is not always convincing, Mr. Trudeau was able to define more clearly for his Chinese hosts the place that Canada intends to occupy in the universe. It is no small matter judging from the conclusion Mr. Trudeau has drawn from these meetings, that the leaders found a "surprising compatability," according to one diplomat, between the new Canadian vision and that which serves as the backdrop for Chinese diplomacy since the cultural revolution;

and this despite the profound differences of opinion that exist on many specific problems.

The Canadian Prime Minister has solidly planted in Asia the Chinese segment of the long march begun by Ottawa to achieve the "third option" of its foreign policy. This "third option" was described by External Affairs Minister Mitchell Sharp in a remarkable essay published in October 1972, but which was unfortunately lost in the noise of the election campaign. The effect of the minister's statement greatly exceeds the theme that brought it about: Canadian-American relations. Its aim is in fact, to reshape all of Canada's International relationships on a more multilateral basis.

The Ottawa-Alberta oil dispute flared up constantly during and after the period of minority government. The issue was often seen in the wider context of conflicting federal-provincial jurisdictions, and here Alberta received a very articulate ally in the form of Montréal's leading intellectual daily paper, Le Devoir.

What Does Alberta Want?

LE DEVOIR, *Montréal*
November 7, 1973
EDITORIAL BY CLAUDE LEMELIN

Is it merely a question of money that opposes Ottawa and Alberta on the question of Mr. Macdonald's tax on oil exports? One would tend to believe so judging from the fact that Premier Lougheed and his colleagues have concentrated their attacks on this element—certainly the most spectacular but not necessarily the most important—of Ottawa's new oil policy. The tax increase announced last Friday from 40 cents to $1.90 a barrel seems to support this conclusion since the financial stake in this federal-provincial conflict is large—some $600 million per year if the new rate is maintained. No provincial treasury can ignore such revenues, especially if it believes it has a right to it.

There are however other motives behind Alberta's anger which are linked to the positions defended these last few years by Québec in other sectors, such as cultural and social affairs.

The Lougheed government has seen in the recent decisions of the Trudeau government an intrusion into the legislative sphere of the provinces and the start of a frontal assault on autonomy—some would say sovereignty—of the provinces. Alberta believes it is justly defending against Ottawa provincial rights to the ownership and management of the natural resources within its territory.

Unfortunately for Edmonton, the federal powers in the area of international and interprovincial trade are much more firmly founded within the constitution and are much harder to oppose than the "spending powers" and other constitutional inroads used by Ottawa in areas that concern Québec. This means that the Edmonton-Ottawa conflict will have to result in political compromise. The two governments each have exclusive powers which however overlap on the question of international or interprovincial movement of Alberta's oil. It will be in the interest of all to find a solution which will contain an agreement on the application of these powers.

The interest of the other provinces and the sympathy that Québécois should be feeling for Albertans in this negotiation is obvious if we imagine the reaction of Québec if Ottawa ever decides to impose a tax on the exportation of iron, asbestos or copper.

Plan Together

THE CALGARY HERALD
November 14, 1973
EDITORIAL

With a certain amount of hedging, the federal government has denied any intention of using relevant sections of the BNA Act to extend its jursidiction to Alberta's tar sands (although the story that said: "active consideration" was being given to the idea was not denied.)

In any case, Albertans are just a bit more nervous today than they were yesterday. And that is quite nervous indeed.

The state of relations between the national government and this energy-rich province was already at a low enough ebb, without reminders of the fact that Ottawa just might have the power to take from the provincial government its great ace in the petroleum hole.

But speculation about future intentions is a luxury that no one in Canada can really afford any more. An energy crisis is gripping the entire world. This country is vastly more fortunate than most, as the only nation in the Western Hemisphere that produces more crude oil than it uses as a matter of course.

But instead of rejoicing, the nation is tearing madly at its own throat. The problem stems from the unusual distribution of Canadian oil. Past transportation logic, and government policy, has resulted in a situation where half our production, at least, goes to the United States, while an approximately equal amount is imported to serve the needs of Eastern Canada.

Thus we are thrust into a fog of export taxes, import cutbacks, unfulfilled promises, accusations of bad faith, to the extent where everyone in the country is unsettled.

Ordinary Westerners and Easterners are slandering one another in the cruellest possible terms. There is widespread talk of a national election, and perhaps a provincial one, too, being called on the energy issue. Alberta has said it won't talk further to federal Energy Minister Donald Macdonald, until an atmosphere of trust and co-operation has been restored. For their part, people in the East are reading into an Alberta statement, that mentioned the "economic waste" of selling oil cheaply, overt threats of cutting off oil to customers in Ontario.

It has gone too far already. Now with the big guns of the constitution under discussion there are ominous signs that matters may go disastrously farther in the near future. As passions grow there may not be much time left to cool things down before the row gets out of hand altogether.

It is absolutely essential that the people involved, regardless of personal and policy provocations of the past, sit down once more and try to establish intelligent policy planning—not for

Alberta or Ottawa or the East or the West, but for *Canada*—
before we collectively do irreparable damage to ourselves. . . .

*Before the 1972 election the Trudeau government had played
down the importance of the monarchy in Canadian public life.
But this attitude changed noticeably in the aftermath of the
Liberals' near defeat at the polls. By 1974 writers in both French
and English Canada were remarking upon the Prime Minister's
newly awakened sensitivity to the virtues of the royal connection.*

Why Trudeau, in 1973, Became a Monarchist

SATURDAY NIGHT
January, 1974
JOHN MUGGERIDGE

One of the most remarkable events in Canadian politics during
1973 was Pierre Trudeau's sudden appearance in the ranks of
the royalists. Trudeau, after all, was the man whose cabinet
was so often accused of creeping republicanism. He was the
destroyer of royal emblems, the by-passer of Her Majesty's
loyal Commons, the TV democrat, the man who would be (so
they said just a couple of years ago) president. But then 1973
brought us the courtly Trudeau, the effusive welcomer of royalty. Could this be the same man who, according to John
Diefenbaker, once rated skiing and even snowshoeing above
the Monarchy?

A conversion of some sort had clearly taken place. Whether,
to quote Dief again, it was of the Damascus Road variety was
doubtful. Vision is not the specialty of our prime minister. He
is a thinker of dreams rather than a dreamer of them. One can
imagine him arguing that Ottawa is worth a royal visit to the
West. Less acceptable is the theory that a sudden access of
filial affection prompted him to get in touch with the Palace.

Pierre Elliott Trudeau, it may safely be assumed, is not about to join the Canadian Monarchist Association.

To do him justice, his attitude towards monarchy has always been strictly pragmatic. While it works, keep it. If royal visits raise national morale, let there be royal visits. If platitudes about the Crown being a symbol of national sovereignty heighten our sense of unity, let Her Majesty speak platitudes. And if the sort of breast-beating which Indians have learned to expect from white men sounds better coming from royalty, let there be royal breast-beating. The Prime Minister publicly endorsed such a functional approach when he told Canadians that the Monarchy had served them well in the past and that "they should realize when they are well off, and not try to change a thing that is working reasonably well."

Hardly the sort of appeal to set the Ottawa River on fire, but forceful enough in its way. The argument that British institutions should be retained on the grounds that under them Canadians have been reasonably well off is as old as our history. The heart has its reasons which reason knows nothing of. So, according to a long and honourable Canadian tradition, has the pocket-book.

Write "and the Liberal Party" after "Monarchy" in the Prime Minister's speech quoted above, and another dimension to his new-found royalism becomes apparent. The Queen, one must remember, is symbolic head not only of the Canadian people, but also of the Canadian government. "By Appointment to Her Majesty" is as valuable a trademark in politics as it is in marmalade manufacturing. The fact that a particular confection is spread on Buckingham Palace toast raises it above the common herd of breakfast foods. The Queen, who can afford the best, likes it. It must be good.

The same dignity by association attaches to the party which happens to strike it lucky in a general election. Overnight its leaders become Ministers of the Crown. The list of clever compromises and vague promises once known as a party platform is elevated to the status of Speech from the Throne. No wonder, then, that the federal Liberals, having taken a royalist tack, should stress their own special constitutional relationship with the Queen.

Proudly they admitted that what she said as Queen of Canada reflected government policy; gladly they confessed last summer that her speeches were the work of government speech-writers. The divinity which does hedge the king could be made to go round them, too. And because pragmatism is so firmly entrenched as a Canadian virtue, even Robert Stanfield, having said that Trudeau was trying to derive as much political advantage as he could from his association with the Queen, added: "I don't suppose one can blame him for that." ...

The problem facing Liberal ideologues today is not that of demonstrating their party's unique capacity for achieving progress without tears, but rather that of quieting anxiety about changes which it has already helped to instigate. The so-called conservative reaction of the 1970s takes the form of a long, hard look at the Just Society. It is not Trudeau's personal charisma which has deserted him so much as his reputation as a wise and all-seeing technocrat. Hence the debacle of October, 1972. Nowadays people want anchors rather than rudders. The answer to electoral gains by the Progressive Conservatives is conservative Liberalism.

This is where the new loyalism comes in. Monarchy fills the need for an anchor. It is something intangible but permanent. It cannot be bought out by foreigners or polluted with oil spills or corrupted by media or blown up by terrorists or slaughtered on the highway. It won't go on strike. It doesn't lend itself to being taxed. ...

Plus c'est la même chose; plus ça change. So you can sum up the myth and reality of Canadian development. Beneath what looks like a calm and unbroken surface we have gone through all the pains and vicissitudes of post-industrial society. In these times of dissolving social relationships and loss of moral direction, it is in the interests of our official myth-makers to stress the outward calm of our history. When the bombs are falling there is nothing like a rousing sing-song; I remember during the Blitz in a school cellar belting out "We're here because we're here because..." and deriving comfort from it. Whistling in the Canadian dark takes the form of talk about the Peaceable Kingdom, and appealing to the Monarchy as our very own Canadian Rock of Ages. The Queen, according to the Montreal *Gazette*, brings to all occasions the reality of history and "a sense of the permanence of the values that make life worth living." "In a world losing its sense of history," says the *Globe and Mail*, "she is history." . . .

The fact that our federal government wants the Queen to be thought of as Queen of all Canadians, not just of one or two ancestral strains, does not necessarily bring about a meeting of minds among us. Trudeau's invocation of the monarchy in 1973 may be compared to a conjuring trick which aims not at pretending to saw a woman in half, but at creating the illusion that her two already severed halves are united. His new slogan was: "Queen or Chaos." It may bring in English-Canadian votes, but it won't prevent the chaos.

The uneasy but legislatively productive alliance between the Liberals and New Democrats came to an end eighteen months after it began. In the debate that followed the presentation of John Turner's second budget, the government was defeated by the combined Conservative-NDP opposition by a vote of 137 to 123.

Fly in the Ointment

THE DAILY GLEANER, *Fredericton*
May 9, 1974
EDITORIAL

The effete government of the day has fallen, toppled from its lethargic legs by a unanimous combined vote of Conservatives and New Democrats.

The nation heads toward a July election with mixed emotions. Prime Minister Trudeau says Canadians do not want an election. But this can hardly be the case when more than half of their elected representatives thought otherwise. And Mr. Trudeau himself could have avoided one by having the Governor-General ask Robert Stanfield to form a new government.

That would have saved the country a lot of money—perhaps $30 million—for election expenses are skyrocketing too, giving new thrusts to the inflation on which the coming campaign is expected to centre.

But Mr. Trudeau could not take that course and retain his political integrity. He is going to fight it out on the hustings. He is going to stand on his record. And if the battleground is to be the high cost of everything, that record is not a good one.

For inflation took off on him and he could never get it in hand with the phlegmatic measures he adopted. He would not cut government spending; he would not get away from deficit financing; he would not control wages and prices; he would not contain strikes in the public service—and that is a particularly dark mark on his books for every wage increase wrenched from the pocketbooks of the taxpayers was inflationary: he would not abandon the welfare state philosophy that those who work owe those who do not work a living: he would not give the business sector a chance to make the free enterprise system function.

It is remarkable that, even with NDP support, he lasted as long as he did.

The fly in the ointment is that he may secure a minority government position again for his party, in which case it will be the mixture as before, with David Lewis doing handsprings for him over a short period, then becoming disillusioned with the partnership which he knew from the start could never be an enduring one. And no one wants another situation like that.

Perhaps the best hope is that Robert Stanfield can dig up enough votes from Ontario and—though unlikely—Quebec to be able to form a coalition with Real Couette and his Creditistes. There is an alliance which would make sense and, in all probability, good legislation. Give the Social Crediters a couple of cabinet posts and get them thinking about dollars instead of funny money and Mr. Stanfield would have something. Wishful thinking, perhaps but a whole lot better than the Trudeau-Lewis axis around which the political life of Canada has lurched for a year and a half.

Election 74

THE EVENING TELEGRAM, *St. John's*
May 10, 1974
EDITORIAL

It had to come. The Liberal minority government had run out of ideas; the NDP had run out of time; the Creditistes were totally ineffective; the PCs were frustrated and hungry for power which they felt had been snatched from their grasp barely eighteen months ago.

Mr. Trudeau, sanctimonious again, immediately began cozening the electorate. The country doesn't want an election, quoth he. When does the country ever really "want" an election? However, when it comes, they accept the fact and take their place in the battle lines. The unfortunate feature, however, about federal elections, as previously pointed out, is the dreadful length—two months, eight weeks—it's much too long!

Because the campaign is so long, and because the election will cost a great many millions of dollars, the people may decide to do a real job this time one way or another, and put in a majority government that will be able to stay there and govern effectively for its full term.

Mr. Stanfield and Mr. Lewis say the main issues will be the cost of living and inflation. They'd better be able and ready to offer some really convincing proposals or programs showing how they would keep both from rising. But, it's likely to be many smaller, closer-to-home issues that will decide the final result.

What we could see emerge from the confusion and general disenchantment in the country is a return to a strict two-party system again, with the splinter parties drastically reduced in size, even eliminated. The NDP, under David Lewis, has lost a lot of its credibility and he will have a big job to restore faith.

The campaign will be the key and the personalities of the leaders vital. But the Liberals can't depend on Trudeaumania any more and the PCs will have to brighten up the Stanfield image. It's true that the tortoise did finally beat the hare in the race ... but don't forget that's a fable and this election is a real life affair.

CHAPTER 5

MAJORITY REGAINED 1974-76

The National Sport

*I*n *preparation for the July 8 election, the Prime Minister quickly set out on a fast-paced campaign that included a four-day swing by train from Sydney, Nova Scotia, to Montreal. Accompanied by Margaret and Sacha, he made stops in 20 separate constituencies and delivered three major speeches. Unlike the 1972 campaign, this time the Liberals were offering a list of specific legislative programs, including new housing, transportation, agricultural and consumer policies. The importance of strong leadership was also stressed.*

Robert Stanfield's main target once again was the Liberals' unimpressive economic record. As an alternative he offered the familiar incentives to business and a new idea: a 90-day wage and price freeze followed by a period of selective controls. This proposal—derided by the Liberals, given half-hearted support by his own party, and hedged and over-qualified by Stanfield himself —would become the Conservatives' undoing. Meanwhile, the NDP under David Lewis continued to denounce the now-familiar "corporate welfare bums" and call for a redistributive tax system and a massive new housing program.

By 1974 many leading newspapers, including the influential Globe and Mail, *had concluded that six years of Trudeau government was enough. But whatever the final judgment of the press, editorialists and reporters alike seemed impressed by the rejuvenated Trudeau and his energetic campaign.*

Mr. Trudeau's New Incarnation

LE DEVOIR, *Montréal*
June 4, 1974
EDITORIAL BY CLAUDE LEMELIN

The journey of the "Trudeau Express" through Eastern Canada has confirmed that the Liberal leader has turned in the crown of abstraction and the sceptre of reason of the Philosopher-King for the simplistic, rousing, and frankly partisan harangue of the "traditional" politician. Some observers, dazzled by the intellectual qualities and mannerisms of Mr. Trudeau thought him incapable of such a reincarnation. Others, so often bored by his monotonous reading of speeches written for him by others thought him devoid of natural eloquence.

They were forgetting that Pierre Elliott Trudeau spent the bright electoral days of his youth following from husting to husting the great orators of Québec politics. From the time of Taschereau to the end of the Duplessis era he railed against dishonestly simplistic rhetoric, the defense of what seemed to him indefensible, the appeal to public passion that only hid from the populace its true interests.

From that has come the enduring disdain of the present Prime Minister for "traditional" politics and politicians which led him to impose upon himself, when he entered the parliamentary arena, a style which depended exclusively on reason, which rested its arguments on logic, which sought to hide none of the complexity inherent to the governing of men.

That this "new" political style was based upon tenacious and sometimes perverse illusions is attested to by the numerous flights of demagogy that have occurred, more or less consciously, from 1962 to 1972. It was necessary that events prove the ineffectiveness of his reasoned approach for these illusions to evaporate and for Mr. Trudeau to find himself on the barnyard floor, where the past masters of Canadian and Québec politics had so often and with such success put the bridle on the electoral beast.

But as soon as he found himself there, as soon as he admitted being there, the Liberal leader found himself quite comfortable at that level, for one does not fight a whole generation of politicians as ferociously as he did without the risk of contamination.

Absorbed almost by osmosis during an unusually long political youth, the tricks of "traditional" politics were waiting for Mr. Trudeau to exploit them; and he has been doing so with great ability since the start of this election campaign. The more things change the more they are the same? Not quite. Let us concede that Mr. Trudeau's new political incarnation is not the reincarnation of Casgrain and Rinfret, Talbot and Duplessis. The ideologue of Cité Libre knows enough to retain his moral elegance. If his reasoning is now simple and sometimes simplistic it is never deliberately dishonest or malicious. If his attacks on political opponents are stunning they are never cheap and are aimed at ideas rather than men.

If the defence of Liberal policies has become vigorous it does not present these as panaceas or models of perfection.

On top of everything, this man who was once so jealous of his private life that he berated the press for pursuing his girl friends does not hesitate today to place himself, his wife and his family in the forefront of his political action.

"In 1972, my campaign never really got off the ground; but this year I've found the secret: I have a train and I have Margaret," he shouted in Truro. Mrs. Trudeau has been at his side since the dissolution of Parliament, smiling gently, accepting bouquet after inevitable bouquet of red roses, allowing herself occasionally an unforeseen gesture which charms the crowd. This omnipresence of Margaret Trudeau in the Liberal campaign—strategists are not shy about saying that they fully intend to exploit any Margomania—does not seem to embarrass Mr. Trudeau.

Mrs. Trudeau is not only a presence on stage but also has a place in her husband's speeches. The Liberal leader no longer hesitates to talk about himself, about his marriage, about what Margaret has added to his life. "She has certainly made me happier; but has she made me richer? No it would be too much to say she has made me richer," Mr. Trudeau replied to someone from the crowd.

In Rogersville he spoke of having been charmed on his last visit by the local monastery and of having entertained the thought of retiring there at the end of his political career.

"But I've changed my mind, you see, first of all because I got married and I don't think the monastery would want me with my wife and children and secondly because I've decided to stay in politics." This new political language of his is always more flavorful in French than in English, the grandson of the peasant from Napierville reaching back to the sources of Québec's heritage. It was only necessary for this man, so often ranked in the "English" camp, to begin to speak more in order for us to discover his true origins.

Let us say finally that Trudeau the politician seems more comfortable in his skin than was the Philosopher King he has just discarded. He says he is enjoying himself more this year than during his three previous election campaigns. He is perhaps happier with himself on the hustings this time. This is perhaps because this time he believes more in what he's saying.

The National Dilemma

THE GLOBE AND MAIL, *Toronto*
July 1, 1974
EDITORIAL

Canadian voters are faced with an unhappy dilemma. The country is in the grip of two-figure inflation, which most of the economic facts indicate will accelerate. Probably the only hope we have of containing that part of inflation which is domestic in origin is a strong majority government with the will to take the unpopular measures necessary to live within its means and to require Canadians to live within their means.

The prospects—barring a hidden surge not visible or some dramatic development before next Monday—are that Canadians will not elect such a government. They exhibit no great faith in either of the two major parties or their leaders. They are afraid of a future full of rising prices, greater labor unrest and the possibility of a recession; but nobody has advanced any clear program for dealing with these difficulties. What are the chances that either Liberals or Conservatives will bring them a measure of safety?

The Liberals have had since 1968 to show what they could do. They started with a large majority, a strong mandate. Before the end of their first Parliament, Prime Minister Pierre Trudeau announced that with tough measures which had greatly increased unemployment, inflation had been beaten.

Inflation had not been beaten. Unemployment persisted. Generous amendments to the unemployment insurance plan made unemployment attractive to many who had not before been in the work force, but condescended to join it for a few weeks to gain benefits. The benefits were so costly that they laid a heavy burden on the genuine workers. The civil service, first frozen, grew enormously. Public services, notably those

supposed to be offered by the postal department, were frequently unavailable.

In 1972 the electorate told Mr. Trudeau what it thought of
his policies by giving him the slimmest minority government
possible. He promised to mend his Government's ways. The
mending has been so ineffective that inflation is higher than
ever, interest rates are appalling, too much money is being
printed, the civil service continues to grow and the Government budgets for deficits when it should be budgeting for
surpluses and cutting back its spending.

The Prime Minister has gone about the country, moreover,
promising to spend hundreds of millions more—an inevitable
source of further inflation. The Government's only real stab at
fighting inflation has been to cut taxes on manufacturing and
processing in an effort to increase supply to meet demand.

To stay with the Liberals would seem to make certain that
we live with mounting inflation, until the recession—or even a
bust—arrives.

Conservative Leader Robert Stanfield has done a somewhat
better job of looking inflation—the country's root problem—in
the eye. He proposes a temporary income and price freeze,
followed by perhaps as much as two years of price and wage
controls, the controls to be negotiated with the provinces, labor
and business. Such controls have seldom worked very well,
even in wartime when they were powered by patriotism. Mr.
Stanfield has not been able to give a satisfactory explanation of
how he would persuade the people—and the people would
have to be persuaded—to make them work now.

But Mr. Stanfield has also promised a balanced budget. That
—or better, a surplus budget—is essential if inflation is to be
tempered. The government must set an example of living
within its means if it hopes to persuade Canadians to do the
same. It must flatten the belief that one should buy now, on
credit preferably in order that the paying may be done before
prices rise and in less valuable dollars.

Mr. Stanfield has also promised to shake up, perhaps remove, some of the top civil servants who have been considerably responsible for the economic policies which produced the
crisis in which Canada finds itself. That could be good. They

may have been valuable civil servants in the circumstances of early times; but times have changed, new outlooks are needed.

Mr. Stanfield's political team, such as is visible, does not overwhelm one with confidence. He has a few good men; there may be some dark horses in the bush. But the team now in office, though better known, has not been very effective.

It is a sad choice Canada faces; the Liberals who have promised much and delivered little; the Conservatives whose proclaimed intentions give hope, but whose strength is unknown.

In The Globe and Mail's view the Liberals have had their chance and flunked it. It is time to send in a new team, the Conservatives, and develop as much faith as possible that change will be for the better. Canada can no longer afford the inflation patterns of the Liberal years.

The Election and the West

THE CALGARY HERALD
July 4, 1974
WILLIAM GOLD

On balance, the rigors and rhetoric of this election campaign don't seem to have been as damaging to Confederation as earlier seemed both possible and probable.

This time the spectre of damage involved mainly the West. This made it the first election of the last several not to be dominated either openly or indirectly by the real or imagined threat of Quebec seccession.

During those years there was no time for the West or the Maritimes to assert their grievances, which in the case of both regions are of real importance and of historic origin. So perhaps it is a measure of the basic health of the country that it was tacitly assumed this time that one of the nether extremities, the West, could be permitted to play a role of sorts.

At issue in Alberta are two sets of conflicts relating to oil and gas alone. One is the rights of Albertans as producers and owners of the products, versus the rights of the people of

Central and Eastern Canada as consumers either direct or
potential. The second dichotomy revolves around the right of
the Alberta government to collect money from Crown-owned
resources on behalf of the people of this province, versus the
right of the federal government to do the same on behalf of all
Canadians. . . .

The second of the two confrontations is what has lingered on
into the campaign. Neither the government of Alberta nor the
oil industry has ever fully accepted the principle of the export
tax on oil exported to the United States, nor the manner of its
imposition without consultation or advance notice last September.

And certainly there has been very little acceptance at all
around here of the provisions in Finance Minister John Turner's budget of May 6, which would have the practical effect of
tripling the federal income tax payable by many oil companies.
This he achieved largely through the unusual device of rendering money paid to the provincial government in royalties cal-
culable as income.

There is no question this will hurt the oil industry. There is
equally no question that Ottawa feels it has a duty to assert its
presence. Because it chooses not to confront the provinces
directly—all of them being politically stronger these days than
Ottawa—the squeeze was put on the industry.

This is an unfair, dangerous, and stupid tactic. It is a serious
misuse of the power of office. No government has an auto-
matic right to penalize A because it seeks to change the policies of B. It is the epitome of arrogance to assert anything of
the sort. Yet the Liberals unblushingly advance that policy and
such bullet-headedness ought properly to contribute to their
defeat Monday just as surely as it did in 1957. . . .

Red in Québec, Red in Ottawa

LE JOUR, *Montréal*
July 6, 1974
EDITORIAL BY YVES MICHAUD

Red in Québec, red in Ottawa. In a column by its editor the Liberal daily Le Devoir has openly declared its unconditional support for the Liberal Party of Canada and its leader Pierre Elliott Trudeau. "When he believed himself to be a Prince," writes the editor of Le Devoir, "Mr. Trudeau was often agreeable and arrogant. But the experience of the last two years have made him more flexible and humbler."

Read this and die laughing. The Trudeau of 1970, his eyes filled with hate at the time of the Laporte affair, has become the peaceful lamb of federal politics, an advocate of compromise, a smooth negotiator, a velvet Prime Minister. He has been touched by grace and repentance. Amen!

But no matter what the Liberal daily Le Devoir says, a vote for the Liberal Party of Canada is a vote against Québec, and particularly against attempts to increase and consolidate the power of Québec. It's obvious that the federal Liberals have as a first objective—and they are not far from achieving it—to demolish, to the benefit of a centralizing power, what an entire generation of Québécois have tried to build: a government which belongs to us and which is faithful to our best interests.

I refuse, for my part, to believe that this is only a dream. And I will continue, supported by a million others, despite Trudeau his works and his new humility, to fight for my idea of Québec till the day when the centralizers and the sappers of Québec's dynamism will have laid down their arms. No matter how long it takes.

The Prime Minister's hard work and combative campaign style produced results on election night, as the Liberals held their own or gained seats in every province. The heavy losses suffered in the 1972 election in southern Ontario and British Columbia were recouped and when the final results were in, Canada had a majority government: Liberals 141, Conservatives 95, NDP 31, Social Credit 11, Other 1.

A Personal Victory

THE GLOBE AND MAIL, *Toronto*
July 9, 1974
EDITORIAL

In spite of the pundits, in spite of the polls, in spite of the most vigorous campaign ever staged by a Conservative Leader, the Liberal Party has won a most decisive victory. It is a personal victory for Prime Minister Pierre Trudeau. Not for Trudeau-mania, this time, but for the work, effort and energy that he put into his campaign. He went to the country this time and did not, as he did in 1972, wait for the country to come to him.

Mr. Trudeau has been returned to office with a majority, with most of his senior lieutenants still beside him, and with a number of new members of high promise. Even more important, he heads a Government that is far more representative of the country.

The parties that brought him down have been chastened, the principal architect of the May defeat in the House has lost his seat.

The opportunities that lie ahead of Mr. Trudeau are immense. So are the temptations. Obviously Canadians are convinced that their Prime Minister will avoid the greatest of these, which is to return to the arrogance of the early years, the arrogance that brought the rebuke of 1972.

Mr. Trudeau faces not only opportunities but problems, problems of grave dimensions. The gravest of them all is the one that Conservative Leader Robert Stanfield emphasized so eloquently—perhaps too eloquently—the problem of halting runaway inflation....

There are other worries aplenty for the Government. In too many parts of the country too many people are still out of work. Our transportation system, in the word of the responsible minister, is a mess. Premier Peter Lougheed of Alberta is waiting to do battle on energy and anything else he can think of. Decisions on pipelines wait while the tankers are being built that will threaten our West Coast with the worst kind of pollution. But all of these pale beside the agony of the economy itself.

Even on the morning of victory, the thoughts are sobering.

A Useful Election

LE SOLEIL, *Québec*
July 9, 1974
EDITORIAL BY RAYMOND DUBE

Canada will enjoy political stability during the next four years thanks to yesterday's election which returned the Liberals to power with just enough seats to form a majority government. It was a narrow victory, since it wasn't until the British Columbia vote had come in that the Liberals were certain of a majority in the House.

A decisive victory at least over the Conservatives and the New Democrats, the two big losers of the day, while the Social Crediters, to everyone's surprise, lost only three of their 15 seats. A decisive victory as well if we consider that all ministers, except Jack Davis, were re-elected without much trouble.

Yesterday's vote confirmed the view of those who foresaw that the election would be won or lost in Ontario. And the Liberals made a bigger comeback there than expected. They made a few gains in Québec, but less than they expected, the Social Credit putting on a better show than anticipated. A few gains in Manitoba were enough to guarantee the parliamentary majority. As for the West—it voted almost exactly as in 1972, particularly Alberta; this was foreseeable in view of the Trudeau government's position during the oil crisis. Once again Canadians have demonstrated their strong regional differences and most of all the split that exists between East and West.

The Lesson of Yesterday's Election

LE JOUR, *Montréal*
July 9, 1974
EDITORIAL BY YVES MICHAUD

Canada renewed its pledge of loyalty yesterday to the same masters who have governed it since 1968. This time Mr. Trudeau has been returned to power unequivocally, with the support of the two key provinces, Québec and Ontario. For we in Québec, yesterday's election had little meaning beyond the confirmation that power continues to slide towards a state which is increasingly centralizing, uniform, assimilationist and disrespectful of the so-called federal nature of Canada.

During the campaign Mr. Trudeau and his Québec shadows carefully guarded themselves from dealing with the fundamental problems that arise from our participation in Canada. In accordance with the Liberal's idea of how the country is organized the election was run as if the provinces did not exist. Mr. Trudeau announced policies dealing with housing, urban transportation, consumer protection, and other areas without consulting the provinces. As in the past these will be implemented where and when he chooses and the premiers of the provinces, somewhat like regional administrators, will have no choice but to accept the decision.

Mr. Bourassa has already acquired this habit. The personal defeat suffered by Bill Davis in Ontario yesterday will likely lead him to practice his genuflections. For if there is one lesson that emerges from last night's results it is the growing tendency of the Canadian electorate and, unfortunately, of a part of the Québec electorate, to favor a central government which is increasingly powerful, omnipresent, final arbiter of all decisions, able at whatever price to impose its will on the governments within the federation. That is one conception of how a country should be organized. Most nations have developed within a centralizing model, entrusting to a single level of government the most important decisions of their collective life. It is precisely because we are a nation that many of us reject the Canadian model. Another lesson of yesterday's election is that we are right to raise a solid opposition to the government of Mr. Trudeau and to his provincial followers. If the country were headed by Mr. Stanfield, who realizes better than Mr. Trudeau the present extent of federalism, progress toward political sovereignty for Québec might have been slower and more painful.

Pierre Elliott Trudeau on the other hand, solidly installed at the head of the country, makes things easier. He represents both our domination by outside forces and our dependence: domination by interests, a majority and a government which are foreign to us, a growing dependence on a central power which intrudes increasingly into our affairs, leaving the government of Québec a little less than the powers of a large school board. There are nearly a million of us who reject that kind of Canada. With or without Trudeau. It is here in Québec that we build our future. Not in Ottawa.

The Road Ahead

THE CALGARY HERALD
July 10, 1974
EDITORIAL

Having won the election, Prime Minister Trudeau ordinarily would be expected to go ahead and implement his campaign promises. For the good of the country, however, many of these promises would best be forgotten until Mr. Trudeau deals with more urgent issues that he mostly ignored during the campaign.

Inflation is still the most urgent priority. Most of the country evidently rejected Robert Stanfield's proposals for dealing with it. But the problem remains. To say it is an international problem, and shrug it off, is no policy at all. If controls aren't the solution, the government must seek other solutions. Something more substantial than the impotent Food Prices Review Board is needed.

Mr. Trudeau's performance prior to the election was less than encouraging. It has been estimated that he pledged new government spending in excess of $2.5 billion. To capitalize a proposed national petroleum company would cost $500 million. The real value of this and other, similar projects remains highly debatable.

More government intervention is inherent in almost all of Mr. Trudeau's promises. Some of his ideas for untangling the transportation snarl—freight rates based on real costs, more efficient ways of getting grain to the markets—sound useful and even overdue, but he also would have the government buy freight cars, operate passenger trains, and even try to run a bus service. All of this costs money. The whole package, from transportation to housing, would cost a lot of money. Even proposals aimed at more Canadian ownership of the economy represents a rechannelling of scarce resources.

It adds up to too great a strain on the economic resources available at this time, and it is inevitably inflationary. In many areas it probably isn't even efficient. There is still no reason to believe a federal bureaucracy can run a railway better than a railway company regulated by government controls.

There is so much Socialism involved in so many of the promised programs that they appear to represent a low bow in the direction of the NDP. One of the positive results of the election was that it eliminated the need for any more genuflecting of this sort.

Leadership was the issue, Mr. Trudeau said. Ignoring the hard fact of inflation while redeeming campaign pledges with spending in the billions isn't the kind of leadership that's needed now. Mr. Trudeau has his mandate—and with it the requirement that he exercise it responsibly.

An "Eastern" Majority

THE PROVINCE, *Vancouver*
July 10, 1974
EDITORIAL

As the Liberals bask in the glory of majority victory, Prime Minister Trudeau at least has shown himself keenly aware of a potential weakness in the government he'll lead for the next four years. He has his majority but it's not the "national" majority he really would have preferred to handle the very serious problems Canada now faces.

Any majority, of course, is better than the situation he found himself in after the 1972 election. That election reduced his base essentially to Quebec, from which he governed with the help of a New Democratic Party that made demands far beyond the "mandate" given it by the voters.

Alone among Western leaders harassed by the problems of inflation he has emerged stronger and presumably less inhibited in his search for solutions. That's a credit more to the style of forceful leadership he developed during the campaign than to his actual performance over the last two years.

Yet his majority is still based essentially on Eastern Canada or, more particularly, on Ontario and Quebec. The Liberals made some marginal gains in the Atlantic provinces and they made a remarkable comeback in British Columbia. But even in those areas the Conservatives remained strong and on the Prairies they remained virtually impregnable.

So the Liberal majority actually represents a badly divided Canada, one that may be no easier to govern than it has been over the last two years.

Mr. Trudeau's mandate comes from the industrial heartland of Canada, from a highly sophisticated and diversified economy that, despite all its problems, has been riding the crest of an inflationary boom. It was obvious that the people of Ontario, industrialist and wage earner alike, were scared away from the belt-tightening policies Tory Leader Stanfield had proposed to deal with inflation.

With such a relatively narrow power base Mr. Trudeau's problem will be to try to reconcile the interests of that diversified economy in the East with those of the emerging resource economy of the West.

In developing resource policies for the West, particularly in energy, Mr. Trudeau will be dealing from weakness. The East wants cheap or at least relatively cheap energy. The West, particularly Alberta where he didn't win a single seat, wants to encourage a petroleum industry based on the highest prices available on the world markets.

In his victory speech, the prime minister regretted his party hadn't done well in the West but renewed a pledge he made at the Western economic opportunities conferences a year ago to apply federal policies fairly. The question is: will the Quebec-Ontario axis let him?

There's the rub in the majority given him by Monday's general election. Parliament may work better now, but Mr. Trudeau has his work cut out to make the majority work well for Canada as a whole.

The Spring of 1975 marked a significant anniversary in Canadian politics: it was now ten years since Trudeau, Marchand, and Pelletier had decided to enter federal politics.

The Three Doves Ten Years Later

LE DEVOIR, *Montréal*
June 10, 1975
EDITORIAL BY CLAUDE RYAN

In this era when images crumble so easily and where unexpected accidents are so frequent in politics it is no mean accomplishment that the three doves who first made their appearance on the Federal scene in 1965 should be able to celebrate the tenth anniversary of that event with each of them still at his post.

Approached first by Maurice Lamontagne and Lester Pearson, Jean Marchand was the initiator and backer of the experiment. It was normal that the celebration of this decision that could not have been taken without him should have been held at his home. But the wager that was made in 1965 by Jean Marchand, Gérard Pelletier and Pierre Elliott Trudeau extended far beyond their own persons. The fate that has befallen each man is not as important as what happened to that wager.

In 1965 Mr. Marchand, Mr. Pelletier and Mr. Trudeau prepared themselves to inherit a power that was open to whomever could sieze it. Ottawa's power had been weakened under two minority governments. Pushed from all sides the central government was blamed by some for making too many concessions to the provinces, notably Québec, and by others for not going far enough in trying to understand. While Québec did not question its very membership in the federation it demanded an increasingly higher price for its participation. The orthodoxy of the Quiet Revolution required that we busy ourselves with the creation of a strong government in Québec. Satisfied with a more or less increased measure of bilingualism at other levels there was no thought about the possibility that a minority group might influence the arena of federal affairs. The strength of Mr. Trudeau and his colleagues was their early understanding that such a course led straight to separatism. From the moment of their entry into politics, while proclaiming their preference for federalism, they stated their belief that the Canadian experience could not survive without a better representation from francophones in the running of the central government, the acceptance by all provinces of common rules of the game and of a central government wielding real power.

The wishes of the three doves have been realized beyond all expectations as far as participation in the exercise of power. The three doves had promised to acquire their equal share of power. They have been called upon to take a much fuller power than had been foreseen. Not content to merely accept the challenge of power, they have used it in these past years in a manner which, far from being harmful, has placed Canada among the best-governed, most open and most tolerant countries in the world. This is no small accomplishment for a trio of Québécois who committed themselves ten years ago to the conquest of a veritable political Himalaya.

The three doves formed an extraordinary team which has retained its solidarity even if the roles assigned have not followed the original model. No other team of French-Canadian politicians measures up to them in terms of complementary personalities, culture, competence, knowledge of their milieu and the best of modern methods. One inevitable question arises now that, for at least one of them, the experience seems to be drawing to an end: have the three doves created a new equilibrium that will finally rout separatism or have they merely held the fort with dignity and intelligence for ten years?

In terms of their generation Mr. Marchand, Mr. Pelletier and Mr. Trudeau have no doubt won their wager. But in terms of the generation following them they have on the contrary lost much of their plumage, having suffered a loss of influence in the circles which were once their sources of support (universities, intellectuals, artists, unions). The final answer will come from the next generation, which already promises to be very different. But much depends upon the succession which the three doves have prepared: on that front, the horizon is more obscure . . . and more troubling.

Future Canadians May Regard Trudeau as a Success

SATURDAY NIGHT
June, 1975
PETER DESBARATS

The longer Pierre Trudeau stays in office, the less people have to say about him, at least in print. This year is his tenth in Ottawa and the silence surrounding the anniversary so far speaks volumes, all of them cryptic. An outside observer, say from *Pravda*, might assume that some sort of conspiracy exists. Trudeau's photograph appears regularly in newspapers; his image is seen often enough on television screens to create the impression of close news coverage. But as far as studied comment and critical assessment goes, nyet. Our Russian would find the pattern misleadingly familiar if not particularly enlightening.

Anthony Westell of the Toronto *Star* wrote a book several years ago called *Paradox: Trudeau as Prime Minister*, and everyone since then seems to have accepted the idea that there's no explaining the man. Few people even try nowadays. In the Press Gallery in Ottawa, critical comment has faded away to a few isolated bleats from journalists who, on principle, don't like anyone left-of-centre or east of the French-English boundary along the Québec-Ontario border. Even the politicians seem to have given up. When was the last time you heard a Conservative or New Democrat say anything biting about the Prime Minister?

In the House of Commons, Tom Cossitt, the arch-Tory from Leeds, rides Trudeau about the size of his personal staff; the mysterious overseas missions of Trudeau's own Kissinger, Ivan Head; the Prime Minister's armoured limousines; and his new swimming pool. Once you've waded quickly through these shallows, you discover that there's no deep end.

Is the man too deep? That could only be established if a number of attempts to plumb the depths had failed; but the record simply shows a slow withering away of enterprise after a fairly normal beginning.

In the early 1960s, before he entered federal politics, Trudeau was often the subject of journalistic interest as a rather singular Québec intellectual with a taste for civil liberties and federalism. For a long time, people in English-speaking Canada couldn't get him quite straight: Was it Trudeau, or Elliott, or Elliott-Trudeau? It seemed impossible that someone so utterly English in ideas, political ethics, and social habits could really be French Canadian.

But at that time, if there was some confusion about Trudeau, there was no shortage of attempts to explain him. His ideas, of course, were there for everyone to read. The social habits of a wealthy but quiet bachelor, of impeccable political background but apparently without political ambition, might have seemed curious; there was no mystery about his views on democracy, justice, language, Québec nationalism, and many other subjects. By the time he decided to run for Parliament, the intellectual self-portrait was remarkably detailed by Ottawa standards.

Between 1965 and 1968, with a little encouragement from the Liberals and the collaboration of Trudeau himself, almost everyone made a terrible mistake. That was the playboy period. Millions of words were written about the hippie who came out of Québec, via Cuba, China, and the London School of Economics, to lead the beautiful Canadian people into the promised land. It was nonsensical, but at least it was a portrait that you could get your teeth into. Many did, and ripping it apart was an exercise that left more scars on the journalists than the Prime Minister. They came out as dupes; he emerged as a non-playboy but not much else, unless you went back to the portrait of the early years in Québec, rapidly fading and becoming less relevant.

The whole exercise made everyone so cautious about Trudeau that the discarded playboy image has never been replaced by anything of equal clarity. Instead, we have accepted the out-of-focus "paradox" as the best substitute.

Raw material isn't the problem. Atop his earlier writings there is now a heap of old campaign speeches, transcripts of interviews with journalists as well as off-the-cuff sessions with various audiences, and Hansard. Despite his prickly relations at times with journalists, Trudeau has always held the required number of press conferences. He still meets smaller groups of journalists from time to time for informal sessions. No one can accuse him of keeping the press at arm's length, except when he jabs at them, which used to happen more often in his early Ottawa days when a few journalists still dared to tangle with him.

The Prime Minister is neither inaccessible nor mysterious. He answers political questions in detail and recently even answered a few personal ones about his marriage to a much younger woman. In either language, he speaks precisely. It can't be said that the documentation is scanty or obscure.

If the conspiracy of silence isn't on Trudeau's part, presumably it originates among his observers. And I suspect that a good part of the explanation may be as simple as the old adage turned upside down—that good news is no news.

There's almost nothing that a political journalist hates more than praising a politician. His audience suspects him of credulity; at worst, of being in someone's pocket. Cynicism is a reliable coin for journalists; admiration is a devalued currency that runs the risk of being proved counterfeit at any moment.

This might seem to be an almost simple-minded explanation for the lack of comment about Trudeau. But the two facts are there, whether or not you link them together: little evaluation on the journalists' part, lots of success on the Prime Minister's.

Take his own objectives as a start. When he decided to enter federal politics in 1965, when he was forced on the Liberals as the price they would have to pay to acquire labour leader Jean Marchand and newspaper editor Gérard Pelletier, Québec was undergoing one of its periodic crises of nationalism in the superheated context of the 1960s. There was violence in Montréal and a widespread assumption, at the extreme ends of both sides, that Québec could easily become another Algeria.

Trudeau entered federal politics as an outspoken opponent of separatism and an advocate of establishing a meaningful French presence in federal politics and the federal bureaucracy. These objectives were unfashionable then in Québec and derided in many parts of English-speaking Canada, but Trudeau persevered.

A decade later, the terrorist FLQ seems as faded a political force as the French-Canadian patriots of 1837. Separatism is still a vital element in Québec, where many problems between French and English remain unsolved; but the stability that has prevailed for the past several years achieves one of Trudeau's main objectives. The amount of money being spent on bilingualism helps to fulfil another. The federal programme is so comprehensive, and such an established part of the Ottawa scene, that Conservatives now feel they can scrutinize it without opening themselves to charges of racism.

Future Canadians probably will be more aware of Trudeau's success in achieving his original political objectives. We're still too close to the transformation, and too uncertain about the outcome, to applaud with much confidence. But if there are Canadians in future, including those who live in Québec, the first Trudeau decade will be remembered as a critical time when one man's vision imprinted itself on the nation, and the man himself matched the challenge.

All this has been consistent with Trudeau's personal background and our own political history. More remarkable have been Trudeau's successes in areas where he predictably might have failed. As an electoral campaigner, for instance. His comeback between the elections of 1972 and 1974 contradicted one of the axioms of politics: that a majority Prime Minister who slides into a minority is on a fast trip to oblivion. But despite the virtuoso character of this unusual campaign, there have been relatively few attempts to analyze what happened.

In his own cabinet, to give another example, Trudeau has developed into an effective leader. Older ministers, despite fond personal recollections of Lester Pearson, don't hesitate to compare the two to Trudeau's advantage. Most often the comparison is between Trudeau's decisiveness and Pearson's inability to make up his mind and clearly communicate a decision to his colleagues. Trudeau's ministers expect him to have precise positions on issues; they've learned that his commitments to them are equally clear. The only two defections from his cabinet, involving Eric Kierans and Paul Hellyer, were both surgically clean processes that left the political integrity and special reputations of all parties intact.

The Trudeau administration, to date, has been remarkably

clean. It was a point of honour for Trudeau, as well as good
politics, to refuse Labour Minister John Munro's resignation
earlier this year in the early stages of the Hamilton harbour
scandal. Evidently no one was going to spoil the image of
Trudeau's administration unless he had a better reason than
the one Munro offered to the Prime Minister.

Trudeau is an ethical politician, not primarily a tactician.
The Richard Nixon mentality saw politics as an exercise in the
management and retention of power. A great deal of this has
slopped over into Canadian political life; in particular, I recall
the premier of one of the largest provinces discussing another
premier in private strictly in terms of his ability as a political
strategist, without any reference to his larger goals. Trudeau
understands politics in terms of social problems and aspirations, and this ethical sense was cited to me recently by one of
his Québec colleagues as the secret of his durability in politics:
"He always knows where he stands on an issue. If you don't
have that sense of certainty in politics, the pressures and compromises soon destroy you."

His metamorphosis in the House of Commons has been,
when you think about it, as surprising as the development of
an aloof academic into an effective team man within the cabinet. The freshman MP who lounged in ascot and sandals under
the horrified gaze of John Diefenbaker is now as commanding
a presence in the House as the old Chief ever was, although he
isn't as flamboyant. Trudeau's influence is noticeable when it
suddenly isn't there. During his absence in Europe this winter,
the government's initial response to the dredging scandal, as it
was being called, became progressively sloppier as House
Leader Mitchell Sharp prevaricated and Transport Minister
Jean Marchand played the clown. The government gave every
sign of being defensive and apprehensive. On the Prime Minister's first day back, the atmosphere in the House shifted completely, leaving the Press Gallery and the entire scandal suspended in mid-air for a time. Discipline returned to the government front benches; and on the other side of the House,
cautious respect again became the rule.

Parliament rarely sees flashes of the Trudeau temper nowadays, but the cutting edge is never far beneath the quiet answers. There's little mercy for the opposition backbencher who presses too hard. Even veteran MPs have been scolded into fuming silence by the Prime Minister for aiming too low during the excitement of Question Period. Younger members who try the Prime Minister's patience are sometimes told to stop being stupid, in almost so many words.

They used to call this arrogance but that label seems to have come unstuck. Trudeau now watches his manners in public; in Parliament, the opposition parties are cautious about treading on his toes.

Trudeau's success in retaining power has its own dangers. There are many signs that he's gradually losing the intellectual originality that distinguished him in Ottawa at the outset. When he used to speak, even about the most hackneyed political subjects, he always sounded as if he had worked things out afresh within his own mind. But you can only do this for a short time, particularly when repetitions of the same questions, over and over again, train you to deliver copies of familiar answers. After a decade in politics, his vocabulary remains remarkably free of the official clutter that overwhelms the thought processes of many politicians. Trudeau can still say what he thinks, but his thoughts have less inspiration from original experience now, and less time to mature.

Among his prospective perils, at the moment, is a resurgent separatism in Québec feeding on the mistakes of Premier Robert Bourassa's government. If the Parti Québecois ever takes power in Québec, Trudeau will lose his main political base and his credibility as a negotiator for federalism in one swoop.

But that may, or may not be, in the future. Up to this point, his achievement has been remarkable. Why doesn't anyone remark on it? If Canadians really are a nation of losers fretting about national survival, we should presumably be fascinated by a political leader who has survived far longer than most in the western world, and who wears his success with such aristocratic nonchalance. There must be some reflection of ourselves in this political success story that no one seems interested in telling.

*On September 24, 1975, Pierre Elliott Trudeau went on national
television to announce one of the great about-faces of his political life: the imposition of wage and price controls. The same
basic program advocated a year earlier by opposition leader Robert Stanfield and derided by the government was now official
policy. While generally welcoming the government's effort to
control inflation, the press was very conscious of this abrupt
change of economic direction.*

A Symbolic Act

THE CALGARY HERALD
September 25, 1975
EDITORIAL

It all depends on how much how many people are willing to
believe.

There are at least two ways to run a country. There are the
ways of the experts who know, quite correctly, that such economic simplicities as wage and price controls won't logically
work.

And there are the ways of the people; the people who know
instinctively, and also quite correctly, that times of trouble
require simple demonstrations of leadership onto which ordinary people may cling.

After a long and profitless flirtation with the experts, Prime
Minister Trudeau last night turned back to the people. He
offered Canadians leadership; and thereby risked our rejection.
Was it enough leadership, in time?

After lunch with all 10 provincial premiers, Mr. Trudeau as
of last midnight changed the nature of Canada. Today he asks
Parliament to appoint a super, extra-judicial administrator with
powers to roll back price increases and set aside wage raises in
large sections of the marketplace. And he said his own vast
federal bureaucracy would observe the 10 per cent guidelines.

Today in Canada millions of people are disturbed and
frightened. They have watched inflation eat away at their stan-

dard of living. They have watched powerful companies, unions, governments (and yes, politicans) use raw power to grab off a self-protecting and disproportionate share.

But has this sense of concern translated itself from a desire to see others restrained, into a willingness on the part of ordinary people to restrain themselves as individuals?

This isn't the first war on inflation declared by Pierre Trudeau.

Back in August, 1969, the man who gave Canada majority government for the first time in six long years went on national television.

He described inflation as the worst threat facing Canadians. He created the prices and incomes commission under Dr. John Young. But he said that mandatory wage and price controls simply would not work.

He said the same thing when President Nixon invoked limited controls a couple of years later—and when he allowed Canada's own toothless commission to die altogether.

When Conservative Leader Robert Stanfield urged controls at election time, Mr. Trudeau sneered. He went on to interpret his victory as the implied refusal of the Canadian voters to accept such controls.

During the months after that he and his finance minister, John Turner, argued endlessly that inflation was an international thing that could not be brought to heel by any one country alone.

Last night the prime minister didn't say a word about any of those things. He spoke as though the obvious recent desire of many Canadians to demand more of the country than its wealth can provide was the only cause of the problems now besetting us.

It is a tremendous reversal of policy and outlook. It is not Mr. Trudeau's first about-face, but it may be his biggest. He almost certainly did it in response to popular demand.

People were saying the experts could go hang. They wanted leadership. Now Mr. Trudeau has acted with force and decision. The next move is up to the people and their non-political leaders.

What Now, Mr. Trudeau?

THE SUN, *Vancouver*
December 29, 1975
BRUCE HUTCHISON

Translated from the sleek patois of politics into simple English, what is Prime Minister Trudeau really trying to tell us?

He is telling us, first that his government has been grotesquely wrong in its economic calculations for the last seven years, that its budgetary spree (with the full support of the opposition parties) has produced a shattering financial hangover, and that the government is now doing precisely the opposite of what it planned and promised in order to win the election of 1974.

Mr. Trudeau is telling us, secondly, that his anti-inflation program has got away to a chaotic start because it was thrown together in panic, at the eleventh hour, under the shock of John Turner's resignation. Consequently, this loose package stolen from the Conservative party, and botched in the theft, is bursting at the seams already and must be tightened up, drastically and soon, or will fall apart. So will the government and the national economy.

Mr. Trudeau is telling us, thirdly, that the cuts in his spending plan (a nice little raise for members of Parliament blandly ignored) are mere tokens, symbols and cosmetics, quite meaningless until we see how much will actually be spent next year.

Even when Donald Macdonald brings down his first budget we shall not know for sure how much expenditures, deficits and debts will increase because supplementary estimates, the old grab bag of every government, will be introduced later on.

Most ironical of all, Mr. Trudeau is telling us that "the federal government accepts its full share of the burden in this crucial national effort."

The burden! As if anyone but the ordinary citizen could bear it in statutory taxes and the extra unofficial tax of 10-percent inflation. As if the government could spend any money but that of the public. As if the government had not sought re-election but had been conscripted, against its will, for heroic sacrifice. Mr. Trudeau's irony is inflated like the currency.

Brilliant as a philosopher, unequalled as an actor but in economics a dismal flop, he is fighting for his survival, for his place in history, for a vindication of his life's work. If nothing more than his personal future were involved the fight would be interesting as a human drama but not very important otherwise. Unfortunately we are all involved—our money, our style of living, the future of our children and our country.

For that reason the prime minister's success is the most important business immediately before us. To confuse our opinion of him as a man with our own self-interest in him as head of the government would be a dangerous mistake.

Until we find a better one—a wistful thought when the Conservative party has become a shambles of competing leaders—Mr. Trudeau is the only prime minister we have. His government may also be a frightening spectacle but it is our only government. With it we must sink or swim for some time yet.

Anyhow, Mr. Trudeau is right in saying that the outcome of the inflation struggle will depend mainly on "you, the people," not on his government. It is hardly an exaggeration to say that the nation must save itself in spite of its 11 governments. But after the false public promises of all their politicians, and their own private failures, the Canadian people, even now, have not faced up to the burden that no government can carry.

That fact, indeed, presents the greatest obstacle to Mr. Trudeau's success. In a climate of prosperity, however uneven and fragile, it is difficult to persuade the people that they are living far beyond the nation's means, especially when the government and opposition parties have long encouraged unlimited demand on limited supply and paid the bill with IOU's now being called in by our creditors.

While all these things are implicit if not plainly stated in Mr. Trudeau's speeches, it is explicitly clear that he has only begun his retreat from unreality as he prepares, very late, for a new advance.

To this reporter his most significant and perhaps least noted statement is that he will soon tell us how our society must change its "values" and adjust itself to a new way of life. So, of course, it must because an impoverished world cannot always support the prodigal habits of North America. Assuredly there

will be changes, most of them unpleasant. But Mr. Trudeau
has yet to tell us what values and what kind of society he has
in mind.

Finally, he is telling us that, after all our mistakes, we are
now testing whether any free society can govern itself and long
endure in freedom. And if this is a faint contemporary echo of
a nobler speech at Gettysburg we might also remember Lin-
coln's other warning that "it is not best to swap horses while
crossing the river."

In a river running high these days we have a single horse for
the time being and a single anti-inflation policy. To destroy
that policy with pin pricks and debating points, to lose the
good in the pursuit of the perfect, would be the ultimate
lunacy. But we seem quite capable of committing it.

*Apart from the election of the Parti Québécois, the most emo-
tional and divisive political issue faced by the Trudeau government in the 1975-76 period concerned the language of aviation.
French-speaking pilots and air traffic controllers, who did not
have the right to use their own language at the major (non-visual
flight) airports in Canada, were insisting on a change in this
discriminatory system. The English-dominated Canadian Airline
Pilots Association and Canadian Air Traffic Controllers Association began a vigorous campaign against extending the use of
French, raising the spectre of potential death in the skies if
bilingualism were implemented and threatening strike action. The
government finally defused the problem temporarily by placing it
under study.*

*The Québec press and public were shocked and outraged at the
attempted supression of their language rights at federally administered airports, and it is fair to say that Mr. Lévesque profited
handsomely from the issue. Not a single newspaper in English
Canada gave its unqualified support to the French-speaking pilots and air traffic controllers. Analysis and explanations of the
issues at hand were vague and often confusing, and editorial
reaction ranged from support for those opposed to the extension
of French to a verbose sort of fence-sitting that did little credit to
anyone.*

Racism in the Air

LA PRESSE, *Montréal*
October 16, 1975
EDITORIAL BY JEAN-CLAUDE DUBUC

This is not the time to give in to verbal excess. But it is necessary to call things by their names. And at the moment, the word racist best describes the attitude of the airline pilots who have decided to go on strike next Saturday. Well-disguised racism. They speak of security, of francophones in Toronto who risked causing serious accidents by addressing the control tower in French; they speak of English as the International language of aviation; they accuse their opponents of narrowness of mind and similar failings. In other words everything is mixed in, more or less consciously confounded to protect ignoble interests.

Because if the pilots are not aware of confusing facts then they are not intelligent enough to transport us in safety; if they are aware of it then they are practicing a totally unacceptable racism. It is absolutely false to pretend that the use of French in Québec by francophone pilots in their communication with the control tower is dangerous. The pilots association declares "We consider that the utilization of two languages rather than one is certainly more dangerous. All aviation authorities recognize this fact." Which would mean that this danger exists everywhere in Europe, in the Orient and elsewhere. Because at Charles de Gaulle airport two languages are spoken, as at Orly and at Brussels and Frankfurt and Amsterdam, Peking, Tokyo, Madrid and Rome. In all these places English is spoken as a universal language along with the local language. The French pilot can land in his language, as can a Chinese pilot, or Japanese, Spanish or German. But the Québec pilot does not have the right to speak French over his own soil. Those who wish to prevent them are their anglophone compatriots.

We must face the facts with pain and disappointment. It is racism which has slated a strike for Saturday. Even the least fanatical of nationalists cannot tolerate this fact. The Bourassa government's silence on such a serious issue is pitiful. In other parts of the country some are ready to prosecute Prime Minis-

ter Trudeau who, last week, allowed the Concorde to land in
French at Mirabel. Racism knows no limit.

Those Are the Rules

LE DEVOIR, *Montréal*
December 12, 1975
EDITORIAL BY MICHEL ROY

Five years after the adoption of the federal Official Languages
Act two francophone air controllers are suspended for communicating to each other in French while carrying out their duties
in the Dorval tower. The regulations on this point are very
clear: the use of French is forbidden, even in ground to ground
communications, when controllers are dealing with instrument
landings. It's a question of safety and discipline, stated Otto
Lang, who concluded after an inquiry, that the suspensions
were justified in view of the fact that the individuals concerned
had received numerous warnings.

Mr. Lang, in a statement yesterday, indicates he may be
willing to accept a change. Studies are underway, he said, to
extend the use of French for ground-to-ground communications in cases involving instrument flights. But for the moment
the regulation must be applied says Mr. Lang, who is of the
same mind on this point as Mr. Trudeau who considers that
breaking the regulations in this area will not advance the
course of the French language. Can the Prime Minister seriously maintain that the government would have accelerated
francization in aerial communications, as it is now getting
ready to do, if at the start of the debate, the francophone pilots
and controllers had not run the risk of ignoring an unreasonable and unjust regulation? There had to be a starting point in
order to alert public opinion, enlist the Québec government,
unite francophone members in Ottawa, encourage the creation
of the 'Gens de l'Air du Québec' and trip up those who nur-
ture a nostalgia about the dominance of English. When a
francophone civil servant is forbidden the use of his language
in Québec by a federal regulation five years after the adoption
of a federal law which someone has neglected to extend to his

area his only choice is to disobey the regulation in order to denounce its absurdity. Mr. Trudeau would once have done the same.

Pilots Are Right

THE TORONTO SUN
June 22, 1976
EDITORIAL

The wildcat strikes by pilots and air controllers must be among the most unnecessary and stupid walkouts in labor history. And this time it is not the doing of some boneheaded, bloody-minded union leader flexing muscles, but the work of a bone-headed, bloody-minded federal government determined to shove French down throats.

The basic issue in this case is *not* bilingualism or Quebec nationalism, but safety. Frankly it doesn't matter a hoot what the cabinet or courts say. The cabinet and courts don't fly or land planes. Whatever is safest—we want.

If pilots say the use of French on the airwaves complicates and heightens the risk of flying—and they do—then that's good enough for us. And for most people who fly. In fact it doesn't much matter if the use of two languages really makes flying more dangerous or not. If most pilots think it does, that's it. Or should be it. Scrap French.

Otto Lang, Mr. Trudeau's tame Transport Minister in charge of wheat, has utterly discredited himself (and his integrity?) by flip-flopping. Last year he thought English was the only safe language to use in the air. But after a lecture by the Franco-phone powers of cabinet and caucus, Lang grovelled and re-versed himself and brought in the French fact. His switch was without logic or shame. It is a bad, dangerous, idiotic law.

English is the international language of the air. Transcripts of ground-air conversations are available that clearly show the dangers of mixing two languages. As pilots point out, part of the safety factor when flying is knowing where other aircraft are at all times. This is impossible if a pilot doesn't know the second language.

We even have a transcript of an Air France pilot radioing in English, then being told to switch to French, and then having difficulty understanding the Quebec accent.

Whatever the courts or Parliament may rule, the public surely is with the pilots and controllers. If they are stubborn against government, their cause is just. What more do Trudeau and Lang need as proof—a mid-air collison or crash, with a few hundred dead? If they keep it up, that's possibly what they'll get....

Professionals?

THE EDMONTON JOURNAL
June 22, 1976
EDITORIAL

Airline pilots, judging by their recent behavior in their frantic efforts against bilingualism in air services have disregarded the public's right to service, and are acting in a rather unprofessional way by attempting to blame air traffic controllers for the current airline stoppage.

The airways, say the pilots, are no longer safe because controllers are preoccupied with the bilingualism issue. The controllers have admitted no such preoccupation, at least to the extent that it would affect their job performance, but the pilots have walked out anyway.

This is not to say that pilots shouldn't concern themselves with any mistake made by controllers, especially when it leads to near misses, as charged by the Canadian Airline Pilots Association.

Nine such near misses, including two over Edmonton involving PWA aircraft, occurred in Canada in the past month, according to CALPA. According to the federal transport ministry, eight of 11 "close calls" occurring so far this year came within the past month.

It seems hard to believe—as the pilots would have us believe —that Canada's air traffic controllers would be so unprofessional as to be derelict in their duties because the French-English issue is on their minds. Without proof to the contrary,

it appears that the pilots are unnecessarily tarring all controllers with the same brush.

Not that controllers are lily white, in the work stoppage
issue. Not reporting for work in the face of an injunction—in
effect, striking when prohibited—is equally irresponsible and
undeserving of public support or sympathy in the bilingualism
controversy.

But to say they suddenly become incompetent when worrying about bilingualism would be unfair. The pilots surely
would take great objection to being accused of letting the same
issue interfere with the clear thinking that is essential to their
duties.

Canadian air travellers ought to be reassured that professionalism still reigns supreme, in the control tower and in the
cockpit. Ending the smear campaign by one group, and the
illegal strike by both groups, would do much to convince the
public that such professionalism still exists.

Unjustified Disruptions

THE OTTAWA JOURNAL
June 22, 1976
EDITORIAL

The simple fact remains. There is no justification for strikes or
walkouts by air line pilots or air traffic controllers on the issue
of air safety at present.

Despite what the public has been told by these groups—and
it hasn't been told enough by any side in this damaging dispute
—the issue of bilingual air traffic control is still essentially a
potential problem. The government hasn't gone far enough in
implementing its bilingual program to create the immediate
danger cited by the Canadian Air Line Pilots Association in its
incredibly disruptive strike.

By disobeying injunctions against strikes, many pilots and
controllers have successfully made the rule of law the issue
rather than bilingualism and air safety. By adopting tactics far
in excess of those appropriate to the problem, these people

damage their own cause. The full weight of the law must be brought to bear against those who wilfully ignore it. . . .

The fundamental challenge is to get the issue out of the political arena. It may be an impossible goal, but it must be attempted. An acceptable substitute for the John Keenan, the inquiry commissioner who resigned because of the political pressure before even looking at the safety issue, must be found. Both sides in the dispute must end their narrow political activities—and that includes strikes and walkouts.

Mr. Lang in particular must watch his words carefully in future. He has done more than anyone else to provoke pilots and controllers into rash and irresponsible actions. It doesn't matter how correct Mr. Lang may feel he is in what he says— the point is not what history decides on bilingual air traffic control but what happens in the next few months. Unless both sides in the dispute show better judgment and a lot more patience, it could be a sorry time for the air transport industry and the country that relies so greatly on it.

How to Fan a Fire

THE GLOBE AND MAIL, *Toronto*
June 26, 1976
EDITORIAL

Canadian air traffic is at a standstill as pilots, controllers and Government argue over the use of French in Quebec control towers. With rhetoric rising, the hopes of getting things moving grow dimmer.

Yesterday Prime Minister Pierre Trudeau told the Commons, "This country is in danger of very seriously being divided on this issue as it has not been for 34 years." Outside the House he spoke of sensing a "deep and underlying mistrust of the principle of bilingualism".

This kind of hyperbole will solve nothing. Worse, it will escalate an already emotional argument into a dangerously divisive national donnybrook in which opportunistic extremists of every persuasion will be the only winners. Comparing this issue with the Second World War conscription crisis could be a self-fulfilling prophecy. Crying wolf or Henny-Penny is not becoming work for a Prime Minister. . . .

There is no virtue in kidding ourselves—there are some people who have involved themselves in this confrontation because they think it is an acceptable way of demonstrating prejudices they would normally deny. The Prime Minister should not help them have their way. He should speak over them to the great majority of Canadians who are secure in their attitudes to bilingualism. Secure enough to feel that they can raise and debate such issues as safety without fear of being labeled flies in the ointment of unity.

The worst crisis in 34 years?

Not unless we work at it.

Repatriate the Control Tower

LE JOUR, *Montréal*
June 22, 1976
EDITORIAL BY YVES MICHAUD

Whatever the results of efforts by Air Canada and Canadian Pacific to force their pilots to return to work and regardless of whether or not the pilots obey the injunction of the federal court, it will have been made clear that federal bilingualism policy is a dismal failure.

The work stoppage by members of the Canadian Air Line Pilots Association (CALPA) does not merely reflect the problems of employer-employee relations, but calls into question the basic political organization of this impossible country. Mr. Trudeau's official language law, naive but well-intentioned, has added nothing to the harmonious co-existence, within the same geographical area, of the two main linguistic and cultural communities which compose present-day Canada.

The strike by anglophone pilots demonstrates this with striking force. Their spectacular refusal to heed the federal language law, their marked hostility to all forms of bilingualism is exactly the same attitude as that of the many anglophones who refuse to see Canada as a bilingual country. And, with reason.

What kind of logic is it that would have a quarter of the
population impose on three-quarters of the population the use
of a language which is useless to it. Once Québec has reached
political maturity French will become the language of common
usage and of commerce, in communication as much as in all
other areas of our national life. The airline pilots will have to
accept this, for reasons of increased security, as they do over
France's air space. It's amazing how fast one can learn when
one has to. In a sense the refusal of anglophone pilots to allow
the use of French in air communication and the stubborn
unilingualism of Air Canada and Canadian Pacific, to cite only
two of the best known examples, are much stronger arguments
for the political sovereignty for Québec than any that could be
presented in the most brilliant of speeches.

For more than one hundred years now our Control Tower
has been in Ottawa. It is about time we began to think of
bringing it home to Québec.

*No single interest group in Canada can react with greater speed
or indignation to unwelcome developments than the business
community. The Prime Minister learned this at New Year's when
he managed to throw the business world into a great flap by
stating the obvious: the system of pure capitalism is dead. It did
not matter that Mr. Trudeau had demonstrated over the past
seven years as Prime Minister that his economic actions were
consistently to the right of his rhetoric. The business community
and large segments of the press saw the new socialist dawn
arriving and they were frightened.*

Shock Waves

THE DAILY GLEANER, *Fredericton*
January 8, 1976
EDITORIAL

Prime Minister Trudeau's "interventionist state" message at the
year's end has caused shock waves across the nation, including

mutterings from his own party. The ship of state is in heavy
seas. Scylla and Charybdis lie dead ahead.

When the Prime Minister told a CTV audience that the free
market system is not working, that the "interventionist state" is
here, it was expected that opposition members would howl,
that business and labor would object. But much of the latest
criticism has come from within the Liberal Party itself—a
plaintive "say it isn't so" cry of frustration and fear.

Just what did Mr. Trudeau say in his interview to cause such
consternation?

He was quite explicit.

Speaking of his anti-inflation program, the Prime Minister
said: "It's a massive intervention into the decision-making
power of the economic groups and it's telling Canadians we
haven't been able to make it work, the free-market system."
And, he added, there is no way that the free-market system can
be made to work now or when the anti-inflation program ends.

That is explicit enough. He warned that the government has
other control measures it can impose, and will do so if necessary. But, he admonished, increased government intervention
does not contradict his liberal principles.

"There's no longer a belief in the absolute liberal state," he
said. "It's an interventionist state which intervenes to make
sure that the strong and the powerful don't abuse their
strength. Controls on large institutions—industry, unions and
government—indicate an advance in liberalism.

What the Prime Minister is proposing, it seems, is an authoritarian "state." He may believe that Canadians—harassed by a
proliferation of strikes, by inflation, by political unrest—are
ready for strong leadership. To be sure, they are not only ready
for it, they have been demanding it. But it is unlikely that they
are prepared to hand over the country to Big Brother Pierre or
any other Big Brother. . . .

Government by Conversation

THE FREE PRESS, *Winnipeg*
January 21, 1976
EDITORIAL

As the prime minister has demonstrated, government by conversation is a hazardous business which may be productive of great confusion. Mr. Trudeau's address was essentially a remedial exercise intended to clear away the misunderstandings generated by his televised musings of a month ago. A careful exposition of the December theme had, indeed, become a matter of some urgency, for the rambling and sometimes contradictory year-end remarks were open to a variety of interpretations, not all of them conducive to general confidence. There is doubtless a good case for promoting public discussion of what is to happen at the end of the control period. But if this is to be valuable, it is not only important, as Mr. Trudeau says, that we keep our feet firmly planted on today's reality, but we should also know what we are talking about, which hasn't latterly been the case.

In explanation of his earlier remarks, the prime minister relied heavily on the distinction between free enterprise, which the government supports, and the free market which, as he said in December, won't work. What would have been the point, however, of a warning against a return to the "pure, free market economy" which, at this date, is almost impossible to imagine? Of course, we have long had a mixed economy, what Mr. Trudeau now, more carefully, describes as a "modified free market system." Some may find it rather fanciful to trace this back to CPR land subventions in the Macdonald era. After all, we borrowed the system in vogue at that time from our American neighbors and the great period of rail construction in the United States has been referred to as the era of the robber barons. It may be more realistic, therefore, to consider our mixed economy as a rather more recent development. This system, Mr. Trudeau tells us, hasn't worked. Further, it won't work three years hence unless the government, while protecting the free market small business sector, modifies it in other respects. The more we change our current attitudes, the less intervention will be necessary.

Although the prime minister has thus clarified his message (which, as he explained earlier, was implicit in the government's decision to invoke controls), he hasn't altered it much. In one respect, his argument is highly defensive. The appeal—"Let's stop wasting our time looking for villains"—immediately follows a suggestion that criticism of the government (for excessive increases in the money supply, excessive spending and excessive interference in the market-place) raises a "phoney issue." Similarly in December, Mr. Trudeau spoke of the importance of government, contrasting the good things that come from it with the "baubles or multi-colored gadgets" of the private sector. It would be silly to suggest that the federal government is the only villain. But the argument that the government can do little through fiscal and monetary policy to stabilize the economy is implausible, if only for the reason that the government until recently exerted little effort in this direction. It did spend excessively. It did run huge deficits. It gave the Bank of Canada no choice but to inflate the money supply. In this sense, its villainy was at least as notable as that of the private sector which, in addition to offering us baubles, still provides us with most of the things we need.

A Difficult Time for Mr. Trudeau

LE DEVOIR, *Montréal*
January 22, 1976
EDITORIAL BY MICHEL ROY

The Canadian Chamber of Commerce has gone crazy and a kind of collective hysteria has gripped business circles. Is it possible and believable that this strange phenomenon was provoked solely by Mr. Trudeau's comments in the now-famous televised interview of December 28 and by his speech this week before Ottawa's Canadian Club? It is more likely because the centres of big business, disturbed by inflation, are made nervous by the thought of a more rigorous control and more numerous interventions in the economy by the State.

This is still only a thought since the Prime Minister, in his Ottawa speech, neglects to define political directions and limits himself for the moment to exhortations, which everyone knows will be ignored by all.

Mr. Trudeau sought to reassure public opinion Monday night. The reaction expressed on all sides, left and right, indi-

cate he has not suceeded. If he cannot soon control the situation he may find himself dealing with a leadership problem
that could provoke a political crisis. Yesterday a reporter from
the Canadian West, aware of the trends in federal politics and
familiar with business circles, confided that the latter "have
had enough of Mr. Trudeau" and are thinking of replacing
him as soon as possible. He went as far as to say that in the
eyes of these men Finance Minister Donald Macdonald would
be an acceptable replacement.

Is the Pope Catholic?

SATURDAY NIGHT
March, 1976
ROBERT FULFORD

This winter the Pope announced that he was against premarital
sex, homosexuality, and masturbation. All across Canada—and,
I imagine, all over the western world—newspaper headlines
screamed this startling information to the presumably as-
tounded masses. TV carried it as the leading item of the day,
and so did radio. But it was, surely, a classic item of non-news.
If a man biting a dog makes news, then this was a case of a
dog biting a man. What did the media people expect? That the
Pope would come out in *favour* of premarital sex, homosexuality, and masturbation?

Yet the fuss made over the Pope's declaration was no
stranger—and no dumber—than the uproar produced by Prime
Minister Trudeau's statements on the economy on December
28. The prime minister said (though not quite in these words)
that the free market economy won't work anymore and that
perhaps we are moving towards other forms of social organization. At one point he said:

"The government is important . . . there's going to be not less
authority in our lives but perhaps more."

This caused even more excitement than the Pope's statements on morality. Across Canada editorial writers thundered,

writers of letters-to-the-editor denounced the prime minister for heresy. Businessmen called the statement dangerous and Orwellian. The country shuddered in frightened anticipation. What would this madman say next?

In fact, he said nothing but the obvious. The free market economy hasn't been the working principle of our society for a good many years and anyone who doesn't know this just hasn't been looking. Since the Second World War, successive Canadian governments have taken it upon themselves to manipulate Canadian society—and they have done so with the tacit or the explicit agreement of the voters. Taxation policy has encouraged or discouraged every kind of economic activity from automobile manufacturing to home construction. Control of the money supply has exerted profound influence on everyone's life. Government control of immigration, regional development, labour laws, and education has shaped the style and structure of social life in the country. All those rich people who now feel threatened by the prime minister's apparent radicalism were in fact made rich by government policies which the prime minister is merely making slightly more explicit. All those free souls now threatened by what they fear as government "control" actually owe their present freedom to the intricate network of laws and practices developed by governments.

Prime Minister Trudeau is not, to judge by his speeches and his extemporaneous remarks over the last eight years, a strikingly articulate man. He has a good speaking style but he seldom knows precisely what he wants to say. He thinks out loud, like a professor in a late-afternoon seminar or a man talking over the day's events with his wife at dinner. He possesses, so far as his speeches indicate, nothing that could be called a social philosophy.

What was important about that TV talk was not what Trudeau said but the national reaction to it. Our society is so dedicated to not thinking about its own nature, so committed to hiding its own actions beneath layers of meaningless clichés, that even the modestly phrased and tentative comments of our prime minister terrify us. If we ever happen to get in the prime minister's office a man who can actually figure out his own beliefs and then state them, the country will go berserk.

The Trudeau government in its later years has been repeatedly accused of political opportunism, but one issue on which it clearly acted without regard for the public opinion polls was capital punishment. Despite the polls, the Prime Minister strongly defended abolition, and helped ensure the bill would pass.

Criminal Law Amendments

THE DAILY NEWS, *Truro*
March 1, 1976
EDITORIAL BY ARCHIE MCNEIL

The package of criminal law amendments is obviously intended to make it easier to "sell" to Parliament the abolition of capital punishment, to convince Canadians that there should be gun controls, and that the task of police in investigating crime be made easier by relaxation of controls on use of electronic devices. . . .

Perhaps, as the Government suggests, the death penalty is not the cure-all for murder. Then, again, is society being best served by putting a man in prison for 25 years, housing, feeding, clothing him at public expense and even, as has been suggested in the past by some government authorities, providing him with Unemployment Insurance and other benefits? . . .

Possibly we are "civilized" despite our evident enthusiastic endorsement of abortion, our shameful treatment of our native peoples and our too often indifference to our aged, our physically and mentally handicapped, and our attitude of "me-first" and the heck with you.

If we ARE truly civilized then we should abolish capital punishment.

If we do, however, let's put the shoe on the other foot. When capital punishment—with the present non-enforced exemption—was abolished in the 1960s it was for a trial period. Wouldn't it be fair if a similar time limit—assuming the amendments are passed—be placed on aboliton of the death penalty.

Parliament could amend the legislation—or the part having to do with capital punishment—to provide that after a period of five (10?) years the legislation again come before the Commons.

If the incidence of illegal life taking showed a dramatic rise, serious consideration would be given to restoring the "ultimate" penalty. If it did not rise to any appreciable extent, then maintain the "civilized" law.

The Infamous Penalty

LE JOUR, *Montréal*
June 21, 1976
EDITORIAL BY EVELYN DUMAS

Tomorrow's vote in the House of Commons on the abolition of the death penalty is of great importance not only to Canada but for everyone who seeks, often under confused circumstances and through many gray areas, to support a greater respect for life, based upon compassion and hope rather than fanatacism and violence. Capital punishment must be abolished in Canada not only out of consideration for criminals but because such a decision is a significant step towards a better world. Mr. Trudeau's speech in the Commons on this subject last Tuesday stressed this point. He emphasized that available statistics don't conclusively support the effectiveness of capital punishment as a method to dissuade criminals from committing murder.

Since there is no proof of its effectiveness, Mr. Trudeau said, the only reason for maintaining this penalty, which is nothing less than vengeance, are arguments based on emotion and visceral reaction. Mr. Trudeau, like many Canadians and Québécois would rather let the uncertainty weigh in favour of humanism and the respect for life. The fact that he has not always followed this rule in his political acts is no reason for disagreeing with him today.

Because It Doesn't Work

THE OTTAWA JOURNAL
June 21, 1976
EDITORIAL

Some members of Parliament have argued that they must vote for the retention of capital punishment tomorrow because, in effect, it will make the majority of their constituents feel better. It won't help reduce the murder rate—at least, nobody has ever been able to demonstrate that it has in the past. But it will be good therapy for those whose sense of outrage about violent crime has grown to the point where nothing less than the taking of lives will satisfy them.

If that is a harsh perspective on the capital punishment vote to be held in the House of Commons tomorrow, so be it. It is a harsh matter at issue.

Let there be no doubt, however, that the public's feelings are an important aspect of any decision taken by MPs. The majority's perception of its own safety and of the state's sincerity in trying to ensure that safety is extremely important. If enough people believed strongly enough that the state was putting a lesser value on their lives than on the lives of killers, then social order would be gravely threatened. A law to provide for the widespread use of capital punishment might then become necessary on an emergency basis. . . .

People who aren't potential murderers can imagine all they want about what prevents murder, but it's an irrelevant exercise. The important thing isn't what normal, non-homicidal persons believe but what actually happens with the abnormal and tiny minority of persons who can and do commit murder.

It would be foolish to argue that a murder is never prevented by the existence of capital punishment. There are, no doubt, persons who declined to kill someone because they decided not to risk hanging. Or at least they say that's why they declined to kill. But what about the incentive to kill that capital punishment might just as easily create for other potential murderers? Suicidal types without the ability to kill themselves who murder others in order to risk their own death;

demented glory-seekers who would revel in the publicity of
being executed by the state; persons who have killed once and
believe there is no reason not to kill again rather than risk
capture and the death sentence. . . .

Abolition

THE TORONTO SUN
June 23, 1976
EDITORIAL

At least the 133-125 vote in Parliament to abolish the death
penalty for all forms of murder, enables the federal government to cease the hypocrisy and deceit it's been practicing on
the Canadian people for the past 14 years.

By having death on the books for killers of prison guards
and police, and then violating the spirit of its own law by
commuting every death sentence since 1962, the Liberal government has set an unforgivable example of contempt for
elected authority. Better to do away with death altogether than
perpetuate a mockery.

What has consistently bothered us—and should bother all
Canadians who adhere to certain principles and ethics—is not
only the Trudeau government's eagerness to flout its own laws,
but its almost casual, elitist, dogmatic disregard for the wishes
of most Canadians.

How can a democratic government, representing the people,
pay so little heed to what the 80% plus majority think is wrong
and oppose. If five more MPs had voted for retention, the
people would have been served—and Trudeau would have
another vote next year!

We shall see what happens now. Will the mandatory 25 year
sentence for premeditated murder be a deterrent, as Trudeau,
Allmand & Co. insist? In fact the spectre of 25 years in a cell
with no hope of parole for at least 15 years is enough to drive
men to desperate measures. It also reveals a cruelty and lack of
compassion by the state that is worse than the death penalty. It

may soothe liberal consciences to keep a person alive in a cage, but it can be prolonging torture and violently inhumane.

A man facing 25 years may take all sorts of chances to escape or evade capture. What Trudeau may have done by his law is to guarantee violence, encourage contempt of government and its laws, and to demoralize police and the people.

MPs dread the thought of possibly executing an innocent person far more than they worry about a criminal victimizing an innocent citizen, raping a child, murdering or beating some unsuspecting person. Parliament's decision yesterday was a vote for vengeance not for justice, compassion or rehabilitation.

Eight years of uninterrupted power were beginning to show their effects during the calm that preceded the Québec election of November 1976. Trudeau, his policies and his government were seen to be running out steam.

The Battle to Save Canada May Be at a Turning Point

THE TORONTO STAR
July 16, 1976
JOHN SAYWELL

The summer of 1976 could emerge as a turning point in the Canadian battle against internal dissolution.

It was 11 years ago that Pierre Trudeau, Jean Marchand and Gerard Pelletier came to Ottawa to attempt to halt the growth of ultra-nationalism and separatism in Quebec.

Their policy to keep Quebec in the federation was not to yield to perpetual provincial blackmail. They did not want to let Quebec slowly become a province different from the others and slide off into some special status that bordered on a quasi-sovereignty. Instead they proposed to bring Quebec closer to the rest of Canada by enabling Quebeckers to feel for the first time in history that Ottawa was a capital and Canada a nation in which they could live freely as French-speaking Canadians.

Success depended upon establishing a highly visible French presence in Ottawa and persuading English Canada to accept French as a working language in federal and provincial institutions.

The first was readily achieved with Trudeau as Prime Minister; his Quebec colleagues in many of the key cabinet positions; and francophones running Air Canada, the Economic Council, the Canada Council, the Canadian International Development Agency, the CBC and a host of other federal agencies.

The second came more slowly and aroused more opposition —in Ottawa where the civil service was concerned about the new rules of the bilingual game and in the big wide world of English-speaking Canada where the idea of bilingualism and biculturalism was as unpopular as it was misunderstood.

But the recent pilots and air controllers crisis may have ended all this, and the waiting game may be over. In English Canada the press and the politicians have had an avalanche of mail.

Only the most blatant sophistry can disguise the fact that this widespread support for the pilots and controllers had little to do with safety and a lot to do with bilingualism. Probably not one Canadian in 20 knew or cared whether ground-to-air communication or cockpit or control-room conversation was in English, French or Swahili. Not one in 20 stopped to think that those same pilots flew into European and Asian airports where both the national language and English were used.

But whether there is a real safety factor or whether English-speaking air controllers in Montreal are so privileged that they don't have to suffer the inconvenience of working in a bilingual environment and can escape the intent of the federal Official Languages Act, which seeks to extend bilingualism, or

Quebec's Bill 22, which is determined to make French the working language, is beside the point.

The point argued and understood in Quebec is that English Canada has not really changed. Lip service to the goals of bilingualism and biculturalism has not altered the fundamental view outside Quebec that Canada is an English-speaking nation, cosmetically pluralistic as long as the cosmetics are washable.

Quebec can be tolerated as a unique cultural property and an economic necessity, and its imperatives accepted as long as they do not visibly and grossly challenge certain Canadian assumptions about the English language and majority rule.

French Canadians learned long ago that their language and culture were safe only in Quebec, and that the majority assumed and sometimes legislated that, like Indians, French Canadians lost their rights when they left the reserve.

French Canada learned, too, that the English-speaking majority could unite—regardless of party lines—on racial and linguistic questions. When it did the minority was powerless.

Whatever the merits of the individual cases, French Canadians watched the majority use its power over an almost completely agreed minority with the execution of Louis Riel, participation in the Boer War in 1899, and conscription in the two world wars.

The current crisis does not have the same dramatic proportions as the earlier ones, yet all the ingredients are there. One English-speaking group opposed the application of the law of the land, and were supported by a second predominantly English-speaking group. A government which initially refused to yield finally negotiated with what the French-Canadian press term the hijackers.

The danger is that as both the Liberals and the PQ sound increasingly alike, many Quebec voters may well decide that if they are going to vote for Levesque's nationalism they might just as well vote for his party.

That is, unless English Canadians somehow reveal dramatically that it really was only air safety they were concerned about after all.

That Trudeau's Such a Lovely Guy: So Loyal to Those Who Work for Him

MACLEAN'S
October 6, 1976
ALAN FOTHERINGHAM

The British have a lovely word called "nouse." Nouse means intelligence combined with common sense. Horse sense. It is useless having a burnished intellect that sends out its own pure beam of light if there is no sense attached to it at the lower end. The lack of nouse is the outstanding feature of the Trudeau government.

People with nouse do not grant themselves 33⅓% pay increases while attempting to exhort the grubby unwashed to a policy of restraint. People with nouse do not slip back into arrogance, with the ease of pulling on fireplace slippers, as soon as they achieve majority government once again. People with nouse do not insult the public with the cynical payoff to a prime minister's principal secretary, rewarding 43-year-old Jack Austin's 15 months of service by giving him a lifetime guaranteed income in the Senate—32 future years at $29,300 per for a total of $937,600.

The nouse-less Trudeaucrats. It is their shining characteristic, their neon-lit trademark. Run your eye down the list of Trudeau ministers and it is the consistent quality that pops up in this uniform cast of technocrats.

The image of the group of automotive technicians who run Ottawa has disguised a remarkable facet of Pierre Trudeau: he lacks the ability to be—in another British political phrase—"a good butcher." He cannot bring himself to prune and hack the congenital stumblers and fainthearted clots who clutter up his ministry.

It is generally unrecognized that Trudeau (mainly because of the artful change of life he goes through every few years: *i.e.,* the recycled swinger, the reincarnation of Laurier, the home-body and suburbanite daddy) has passed both John Diefenbaker and Lester Pearson in length of service. By the time his current term is up he will have passed Louis St. Laurent and will be well into the full gallop in pursuit of Mackenzie King (John Turner knows how to count too). This longevity through three elections (and four mental costume changes) has been established with a cast of characters that drifts on untouched by the supposedly tough hand of Himself. The intellectually rigorous product of Jesuit mental discipline finds himself unable to wield the axe even in the face of his proud boast, when he formed his first ministry, that his ministers would have to "produce or else."

We all believed it at the time. "Nothing is permanent," the new Prime Minister warned ominously in 1968 when he picked the largest cabinet in Canadian history, a collection of 29 supposedly nervous souls. Instead, we waited two years for his first cabinet "shuffle." Where was the chop, the famed Trudeau uncompromising lust for excellence? It produced not a single new face in the cabinet, with two of the ministers going back to the jobs they held under Pearson.

Ah, the Pearson years. Soft, nice guy Mike Pearson, who was too kindly and old-shoe to jettison familiar friends. Do you know that Pierre Elliott Idealist has existed for more than seven years with the core of his cabinet picked by Pearson? He has yet, despite the readjustment forced on him by John Turner's farewell, to put his own stamp on the cabinet.

After that coitus interruptus in the long-awaited 1970 shuffle, we had to wait four more years before there was a bloodletting. The ruthless one was six years in power, in 1974, before sacking *anyone*. At that, the only two of any note were the feckless Herb Gray, who has since discovered more bravery outside the cabinet than he ever did in it, and the handsome Bob Stanbury, terror of the Ottawa stenographic pool.

So what are we left with in 1975? Men who have long since proven their inability to shoulder the burdens thrown them, men who have bent and stretched the Peter Principle to unreasonable limits, men who—even taking into consideration the demands of regional, racial and religious quotas—have no business surviving in this government.

James Richardson, the poor little rich boy who will live forever in political folklore for Marci McDonald's description of him falling out of his bunk all night on one of his defense ministry ships because his naval officers "neglected" to tell him to strap himself in.

Judd Buchanan, the insensitive prize-winning insurance salesman, unleashed upon the native people of the land as Minister of Indian Affairs, regarded in the north as a beardless boy attempting to learn as quickly as possible the time-tested Liberal gifts of waffle, shuffle and mumble.

Can anyone take seriously a government that maintained for seven years dear old Mitchell Sharp, foot-in-mouth Mitchell Sharp, author of the famous reply when asked about the 1968 Russian invasion of Czechoslovakia: "Disappointing."

There are so many: Hugh Faulkner, who always appears as if he would be more comfortable in an Oscar Wilde play, Alastair Gillespie, that interchangeable TV face, the silver-haired executive from Central Casting who so pleases those interested in industry, trade and commerce. Robert Andras, the very image of a northern Ontario service club recording secretary masquerading as a manager of a very important Canadian ministry.

Even the heavies in the Trudeau cabinet have that bloodless, technocrat cast that forces one to look back with fond vigor on such as Judy LaMarsh. There is Marc Lalonde, an honest man who still can't understand what was wrong with Air Seagram, the only man in Ottawa, in the words of the Press Gallery's Marjorie Nichols, "with an IQ of 200 and the political judgment of Justin." There is Otto Lang, who can never concede he is wrong (as he was on Morgentaler) and who manages the formidable feat of appearing to be to the right even though he is surprisingly progressive.

Can anyone recall a single memorable phrase that will live beyond any of these ministers? Is "eat shit" to survive as the only quotable epitaph of this government? Those who leave, a Hellyer, a Kierans, a Turner, are allowed to sidle away. The strong resign. The weak are never sacked.

It is ironic that Pierre Elliott Trudeau, who came into politics and shook our minds as the greatest individualist within memory, ended up swallowed by the system, whittled down by the machinery, diminished, just another cog unable to move the bureaucratic wheel of party politics. In the art of jaded politics, he is a prime exhibit. He is demeaned. The system of cabinet tenure, squatters' rights, has not changed. He has changed.

CHAPTER 6

NOVEMBER 15 AND BEYOND 1976-78

IF I KEEP ON IGNORING HIM, MAYBE HE'LL GO AWAY...

AISLIN 77
MONTREAL GAZETTE

327

On the night of November 15, 1976, the people of Québec and Canada were faced with an astonishing set of election results: the Parti Québécois had captured 71 of the 110 seats in Quebec's National Assembly, and reduced the previously mighty Liberal government of Robert Bourassa to an embarrassed and leaderless 26-member opposition. In the process the PQ had captured 41 percent of the popular vote, just one percent less than that received by the federal Liberals in the election of 1974. Québec's separatist party had catapulted from splinter group to governing party in eight short years. The Canadian and international press reacted immediately.

The Victory of the "White Niggers"

LE MONDE, *Paris*
November 17, 1976
ANDRE FONTAINE

In 1960, while on an official visit to Canada, de Gaulle received no more than a lukewarm greeting in Montréal. A good portion of the population of the city at that time had more in common spiritually with the mentality of the old Vichy regime than with the Free French. But when he returned in 1967, he did so in a triumphant march that took him via the "King's Road" to the balcony of Montréal's city hall where he launched his famous "Long live free Québec!" in the midst of indescribable enthusiasm.

Many of those who were scandalized at what they considered an unacceptable intrusion into the internal affairs of a sovereign country recognize today that this deliberate gesture, that brought Franco-Canadian relations to the breaking point, has contributed considerably to the cause of Quebeckers.

Pierre Elliott Trudeau has very capably maintained the exact opposite of the Gaullist thesis, arguing that only a united Canada is capable of resisting the American elephant: "It is only at the federal level that their (Québec's) language, their culture, their institutions, their most sacred traditions, and their lifestyle can escape assaults from the outside and conflicts from within." And Mr. Trudeau certainly would never have managed to install his "Quebec mafia" in power if a good proportion of Canada's anglophones hadn't understood that the time had come to make a larger place for their fellow citizens of the French language.

But even though a good deal of his political support comes from francophones, Mr. Trudeau hasn't really succeeded in mobilizing them in his favor. This isn't simply because he is still criticized for the brutal way he reacted to the kidnapping and assassination of Labor Minister Pierre Laporte by the Québec Liberation Front in 1970. Above all, this is because for the vast majority of citizens of "la belle province," their nation is Québec and not Canada. Their National Assembly is in Québec City and not the House of Commons in Ottawa.

Only the future will tell what will become of Québec after the victory of the separatists and the "white niggers" the Quebeckers have often felt they were in the eyes of the "damn English." The PQ has put quite a bit of water in the wine of independence in the course of the last several years. Otherwise it wouldn't have been able to carry the whole thing off. And the majority of Quebeckers today still seem hostile to the idea of independence. It therefore seems unlikely that Canada will have to submit to the amputation of its Québec limb—an operation that would sooner or later lead to Canada's absorption by the United States, leaving francophones in the other provinces to quietly disappear in the English sea. At the same time, it is hard to see what miracle can breathe life into Pierre Elliott Trudeau's ambition of building in the north of America the first harmoniously bilingual nation in history.

Ottawa Is Responsible for the Future of Canada

LA PRESSE, *Montréal*
November 18, 1976
EDITORIAL BY IVAN GUAY

When the Leader of the Opposition asked Mr. Trudeau Tuesday what he will do to reassure the business community following the PQ victory in Québec the Prime Minister answered that he has no intention "of negotiating any form of separation with any province." This would seem to be a statement of principle. But the statement was not politically correct.

It's understood that Mr. Trudeau wasn't elected to dismember Canada. But having said that, what difference does it make? Politics is not a game of principles but an art that attempts to reconcile the diverse interests of a population. This is very much the case in Canada where the federal system allows the 10 provinces to each elect a political party which may differ from the party in power in Ottawa. Québec has elected the Parti Québécois. Irrespective of the reasons for which the voters elected this party we must, in order to respect the rule of democracy, accept this verdict without bitterness. The tone and style of Mr. Trudeau's statement indicated quite the contrary. It may seem excessive that a political party should aspire not only to power but to the creation of another country. It is nonetheless the right of a people to decide its own future.

In a federation like Canada the withdrawal of an important province like Québec poses serious problems which are of great concern to the federal government and the rest of the provinces. But we have not yet reached that stage. In fact the people of Québec, a huge majority of whom are federalists, have placed their confidence in Mr. Lévesque because he has promised not to provoke secession without their consent. So where is the real problem? Without being simplistic one can claim that Québec has for a number of years felt itself constrained by the federal government, which it considers too centralist. It therefore demands more power in fiscal and cultural areas. It's up to Ottawa to negotiate accommodation in these areas.

No matter what Mr. Trudeau may say Québec is not a province like the others. The French Canadians who inhabit Québec are a real nation and not simply an ethnic group. This is more than a linguistic nuance. Mr. Trudeau's rigid position does not, unfortunately, take into account this basic sociological reality. If Paris was worth a mass, as Henry IV said, Canada must surely be worth a few fiscal and cultural concessions.

Especially since they would be made to one of the country's two founding nations.

This is a time for openness of mind. It is a bad time for defenders of federalism to make intemperate statements. Statements like that of Mr. Bryce Mackasey, just elected a Liberal Member in Notre Dame de Grâce, who said Tuesday in Winnipeg that "Mr. Lévesque is a dangerous man" and that we "must not allow ourselves to be fooled by his Gallic smile." These words of an agitator, spoken in the West where there is already much intolerance for Québec, betray a stunning lack of judgment for a former federal minister. When we know that the attitude of anglophones to francophones has to a large degree contributed to the birth of the separatist movement, it becomes clear that any action or statement which might worsen the situation is clearly irresponsible.

The federalist parties will have to muffle their loudspeakers of agitation. Ottawa's policy must be flexible rather than rigid and intolerant. Federalism can only gain from this, as can Mr. Trudeau. The Prime Minister should not forget that his electoral base is still in Québec.

The Quebec Election

THE VICTORIA TIMES
November 16, 1976
EDITORIAL

If Britain won the day on the plains of Abraham so long ago it was a hollow victory which came back to haunt us on Nov. 15, 1976. More than 200 years of indifference, bigotry and an economic order that put French Canadians on the lower steps has resulted in a resounding victory for Rene Levesque's Parti Quebecois. In Canada today many people will use the victory of the separatist party to foster their own aims, Naysayers and western separatists will be vocal in coming months. Parti Quebecois policies will severely test the eroded good will of English Canadians. But Levesque's decisive victory does not signal the imminent balkanization of Canada.

As Prime Minister Trudeau stated Monday night, "They've been granted a mandate to govern, not a mandate to separate." Shrewd politician that he is, Levesque played down the separatist angle, concentrating on economics and corruption in Quebec. The final poll before the election showed that only 18 per cent of Quebecois supported separatism. That means that many voters chose the Parti Quebecois in spite of its separatist plank, not because of it. It is also clear that Levesque's victory rests on slightly more than 40 per cent of the popular vote, indicating about 60 per cent of the electorate is adamantly opposed to separatism.

It would be foolhardy, however, to interpret the results as business as usual in this country. Canada will never be the same after this historic election. Overnight the smug complacency of an insular English Canada has been swept away and replaced with an agonizing period of uncertainty. A Francophone prime minister who came to Ottawa in 1968 with the intention of unifying the country has watched his credibility erode in English Canada this past eight years. Today it is obvious he has little credibility on his home ground. The alternative to Trudeau is an untried Anglophone whose party has negligible support in Quebec.

If these be grim portents for the future of Canada, there are positive aspects to this election too. A large minority of Canadians had the guts to take a risk after years of being given a choice between separatism or various parties of entrenched vested interest. The last minute hysterical threats of the Charles Bronfmans and Liberal hacks who warned of industries leaving Quebec and economic chaos were despicable tactics reminiscent of the 1972 British Columbia election. In effect the Quebec contest was not fought on the separatist issue. It was not a constitutional fight as Robert Bourassa tried to prove. It was the culmination of a class struggle that has been going on in Quebec since the days of Maurice Duplessis. An egalitarian Quebec is more frightening to some elements in this country than the spectre of separatism.

After 109 years of avoiding their history Canadians will now be forced to confront themselves. It will be a catharsis the likes of which this country has never seen. But every country, every philosophy, is forced to test its mettle. Rene Levesque has taken a deliberate, moderate, patient route to a democratic electoral victory. In a similar vein, the prime minister has promised to co-operate with Quebec as long as it abides by the constitution. This is not a time for fear or doubt. Rene Levesque will hold his referendum on confederation. The result must be respected in accord with our democratic traditions. Meanwhile, all thoughtful Canadians must redouble their efforts to forge a new Canada. We must not quit at the eleventh hour.

No Reason for Panic

THE CAPE BRETON POST, *Sydney*
November 16, 1976
EDITORIAL

Despite opinion polls predicting it, the Parti Quebecois' stunning victory in yesterday's Quebec general election appears to have caught English Canada by surprise. But while there may be surprise, there is no reason for panic.

The nature of the P.Q. victory and the campaign that preceded it, as well as the tone of P.Q. leader Rene Levesque's comments following his victory, should be enough to ease fears expressed in some quarters about the impending destruction of Canada.

For while the voters of Quebec elected a party whose main tenet is one of separate nationhood for the province, almost everything about the way the victory was achieved makes the P.Q.'s mandate ambiguous, at least as far as the party's separatist aspirations are concerned. The voters did not so much sweep-in Mr. Levesque as throw out Mr. Bourassa. In many respects, the defeat was richly deserved.

For three general elections, the Liberal party in Quebec has gone to the voters relying on little more than the fear of separatists' hopes to propel them into power. In 1973, this strategy worked so well that Mr. Bourassa's Liberals secured 102 of the 110 seats in the National Assembly, one of the broadest mandates in Canadian political history.

But this year, Mr. Bourassa cried wolf once too often. His last-minute attempt to incite panic among the voters failed to sway the results. The voters were not impressed with the way Mr. Bourassa handled his mandate. They were sick of corruption, scandals, the Olympic fiasco, and the aloof, arrogant style of the Bourassa regime.

Mr. Levesque capitalized on this voter disenchantment by refusing to campaign on the issue of separatism. Instead, he ran a good government campaign, insisting to the end that separatism was not an issue to be decided in this election. The voters took him at his word. . . .

The gracious nature of Mr. Levesque's victory statement is further evidence of this strategy. Last night he reiterated his promise that separatism had not been decided in the election, and expressed the desire for friendly relations with all Canadians.

The fact remains, however, that whatever strategy may be employed to get there, Mr. Levesque is committed to separatism. We can assume that his government will work in that direction. In the end, this may not be a bad thing for Canada. The long festering question of Quebec's status within confederation should be settled. Quebecers must decide, once and for all, what they want to do, and just as importantly, English Canadians must decide what price they are willing to pay to keep Quebec in the fold.

If it takes a head-on confrontation with a separatist government to accomplish that, Canada may eventually be the better for it.

Critical Years Ahead for Canada

THE FREE PRESS, *London*
November 16, 1976
EDITORIAL

The gloomy interpretation of the Quebec election is that for the first time since Confederation, a separatist government is in power in Quebec.

The optimistic interpretation is that the Parti Quebecois does not have a mandate to preside over the separation of Quebec and that the popular vote is still a majority for federalism.

Somewhere in between lies the truth, which may not emerge clearly until there is a referendum to decide whether the people of the province wish to separate from Canada.

Whatever the real meaning of Monday's startling vote, it's obvious that Canada faces troubled times, certainly for the two years before the promised PQ referendum. Dangerous and difficult times lie ahead if the referendum favors separation or even if Quebec votes clearly to remain part of Canada.

The results are a dramatic demonstration of how fast an insensitive, arrogant government can fall. There is nothing comparable in Canada's political history to the Bourassa government's fall from an overwhelming majority to a struggling second party in three years. It has mainly itself to blame. Its arrogance, patronage, and corruption have been monumental.

The next two years will be critical for Canada. The PQ's election does not mean the inevitable breakup of the country. Economic issues played a key role in its victory. But it is a turning point for Quebec and the rest of Canada. The question of whether Confederation survives must now be clearly and realistically faced. Patience and understanding can still reassure Quebec that its future lies with a united Canada.

A Letter to Mr. Trudeau

THE GLOBE AND MAIL, *Toronto*
November 18, 1976
GEOFFREY STEVENS

Rt. Hon. P. E. Trudeau   Ottawa
24 Sussex Drive
Ottawa

Dear Prime Minister:

This has not been a good week for you—or for any of us who count ourselves as federalists, who regard ourselves as Canadians first and Ontarians, Albertans or Quebeckers second. None of us takes any pleasure from your predicament. Canadians elected you in 1968 because they saw you as a man who could unite the country. We will all be losers if you go down in history as the Prime Minister who presided over the disintegration of Canada.

What bothers me is the tone you have adopted since Monday night. It compares most unfavorably, I believe, with the tone assumed by René Lévesque. Of course, Mr. Lévesque can afford to be magnanimous and accommodating in victory. Even making allowances for that, however, he has struck the right chords. He says his Parti Québécois government will behave like a normal provincial government until such time (if ever) as a majority of Quebeckers choose independence. He promises the referendum on independence will be unbiased. In the meantime he will revise Bill 22 to protect minority language rights. Very calm. Very cool.

The premiers of the other nine provinces have, on the whole, responded to the election of the PQ with moderation and reasonableness. But your words, Prime Minister (and I can understand why you feel the way you do), have been tough, uncompromising, ungenerous, glacial.

Your message to Mr. Lévesque was the sort of letter a bill collector might write to a chronic deadbeat. Your salutation— "Sir:"—was more than curt; it was rude. You and René Lévesque have known each other for many years. At one time, you were close. Although you have long since gone your separate political ways, don't you think you could have unbent enough to have addressed him as "Dear René" or "Dear Mr. Lévesque"?

In the letter you said: "Your party has won in Quebec in a democratic way and it is in the spirit of democracy that I recognize its victory. There's no doubt about the legitimacy of the government that you will form. In strict terms of the constitution and in the exclusive framework of the Canadian federation, it will of course benefit from the full co-operation of the central government." Mr. Lévesque must have gotten frostbite when he opened the envelope.

Would it hurt all that much to acknowledge that Mr. Lévesque's victory was a very considerable achievement? Or to

observe that, quite apart from separatism, the election reflects
the economic and social concerns of Quebeckers; that you, as
fellow Quebecker, understand these concerns; and that you, as
Prime Minister, are equally desirous of finding remedies?

... The important thing is to proceed in a spirit of goodwill.
We must look to you to set the tone. You are, after all, the
only Prime Minister we have.

Apprehensively yours,

A Bad Start

LE DEVOIR, *Montréal*
November 18, 1976
EDITORIAL BY MICHEL ROY

On Monday night Pierre Trudeau was able to accept calmly
and with a sense of realism the blow of the Parti Québécois'
accession to power. He said only what needed to be said. On
the following day René Lévesque faithfully reassured the
Prime Minister and all those disturbed by the advent of a PQ
government in Québec: all the rules of democracy will be
scrupulously observed, said Mr. Lévesque, who in addition
committed himself to govern Québec within the context of the
federal system. Such will be the case so long as the people of
this "province" have not selected another option through a
"clear, explicit and democratic" agreement. The real debate on
the major item of the PQ's political program was not dealt with
Monday and will not be dealt with for at least two years. The
winning party's election campaign, its publicity and its commitments attest to that fact. Federalists of every color have been
warned that there will some day be a confrontation. It is only
natural that the partisans on either side will start preparing
immediately.

This has already begun in Ottawa. Parliament is gripped by
apprehension. The Conservatives are no less shaken than the
Liberals.

But Mr. Trudeau is off to a bad start. He is on the verge of
committing errors which could have serious consequences. It is
clear that the analysis of the election by the cabinet and the
East Block is incomplete and superficial. Those who are for a
strategy of confrontation have scored points. Those who seek
to defend too firmly one idea of federalism will compromise it.
Those who seek to corner the Parti Québécois and its leader
before he has even moved into his office and formed his
government risk disgusting the people of Québec and thus
isolating a province they seek to hold. . . .

A Kick in the Pants

BUENOS AIRES HERALD, *Argentina*
November 18, 1976
EDITORIAL

Rarely has an electorate given a ruling party such a mighty
kick in the pants as that delivered by the people of Quebec to
the Liberal party in Tuesday's elections. The results sent a
shock wave round the world because the triumphant Quebecois
party believes in separating French-speaking Canada from the
rest of the country. The mandate of the separatists, in terms of
votes, is overwhelming. They won 66 seats in Tuesday's elections, compared with barely ten in 1973. The ruling Liberal
party saw its power dwindle from 96 seats to only 27.

On the face of it, Tuesday's election is a rude awakening for
the many Canadians who thought that the separatist issue was
dead. It is clearly alive: but it may not be as serious as the
election results suggest. The Prime Minister, Mr. Trudeau, immediately announced that the election had not been won on
the issue of separation from English-speaking Canada. He attributed the massive vote against his own Liberal party to
"economic and administrative questions."

Mr. Trudeau was trying to put the best possible appearance
on a stunning electoral defeat which undoubtedly reflects on
his own performance as national leader. He would have been
more truthful if he had admitted that the people of Quebec
had taken advantage of the elections to register a massive

protest vote against the Liberal party, as the embodiment of what they see as a national policy of discrimination against the French-speaking people, and against the Prime Minister of Quebec, Mr. Bourassa, for failing to represent them. . . .

Mr. Levesque and the people of Quebec are now in a position to ask some questions of the national government. On the answers they receive depends the future of Quebec and of Canada. More vigorous efforts must be made to make Canada a bi-lingual country and not one in which the English speaker is naturally predominant. This does not mean that every Canadian must be forced to learn French as well as English: but it does mean that every Canadian must be educated to appreciate the fact that the country's heritage is one of two cultures and two languages—and that this is an advantage and not a disadvantage. This process of education will take time. It means recognizing minority rights. It means ending discrimination and making equality a fact of life throughout Canada. It will be a long time before prejudice is eliminated entirely and French Canadians feel themselves no differently towards the English-speaking majority than German-speaking Swiss feel about their French or Italian-speaking countrymen. But the government of Mr. Trudeau will not be so smug about discrimination against French-speaking Canada after the humiliation of Mr. Bourassa. Tuesday's elections have woken up the national government. They promise to have a healthy effect on all Canada.

Quebec to the Separatists

THE DOMINION, *Wellington, New Zealand*
November 18, 1976
EDITORIAL

The separatist movement's election victory in the big, historic French-speaking Canadian province of Quebec will bring home to all Canadians what they should have realised all along: that this province is tired of being merged into a multi-national identity that would shed its unique cultural and language background, that it is sick of being vilified by many

English-speaking Canadians as anti-monarchist or language fanatics, and that it is determined to preserve Quebec as a viable
economic unit whatever becomes of the remainder of North
America.

In voting the Parti Quebecois (the party belonging to
Quebec) to power, with its promise to hold a referendum on
separation, Quebecers would have had no feeling that they
were deserting Canada because they feel that they are Canada
—the old Lower Canada of the original constitution. And far
from staging any act of reprisal they would see it as a matter of
survival that they tackle their frightening 9.3 per cent unemployment rate, high taxes (provincial tax eight per cent in
addition to the federal levy) and North American inroads on
their culture, without the shackles of the federation. If an
east-west economy is stultifying, and a north-south one would
suit Quebec best, that will be a major consideration.

Canada and Quebec

THE WASHINGTON POST
November 18, 1976
EDITORIAL

A separate and independent Quebec is still a rather remote
prospect—although not quite so remote as it seemed before
Monday's election. Quebec's voters have now put in power an
explicitly and determinedly separatist movement, the Parti
Quebecois. Whether the PQ can translate its victory into a
genuine majority for independence, over the coming years,
remains very much an open question. But there is no question
at all that this vote is a disaster for Canadian Prime Minister
Pierre Elliott Trudeau and his Liberal Party.

The immediate effect of the Quebec provincial election will
be to force Mr. Trudeau into a deeper preoccupation than ever
with purely domestic business. Ever since he came to power
eight years ago, his first concern has had to be the unity of his
disparate country. Now it will become very nearly his only
concern. At a time when his personal standing is declining and
his long dominance of Canadian politics appears to be coming
to an end, his government is confronted with this unprece-

dented constitutional challenge. The United States and Canada have a long agenda of unspectacular but important matters to settle between them. There are negotiations on trade—the heaviest flow of trade, by far, between any two countries in the world. There is the allocation of the seabeds, the protection of water purity along the borders, and the transit of natural gas from the Arctic southward. It is necessary to expect that all of these things will now become very minor matters in Ottawa.

The language quarrel throughout Canada has now reached a point at which any concession to one tradition immediately becomes an unforgiveable insult to the other. This conflict is the kind of luxury in which a country can engage when it is rich, well-fed and safe from foreign threats. It is part of a world-wide pattern of national fragmentation along ethnic and regional lines.

But whether there are actually deep and irreconcilable differences of political rights and constitutional practice in Canada, on a scale justifying the dissolution of a major nation, has not yet been demonstrated. The question is now left to a couple of years of debate between Quebec and the rest of Canada, to be followed by a referendum in Quebec. Canada is still far from that dire decision. But it has to be said that, after a lull of several years, events are again moving in the separatists' favor.

After the initial shock of the PQ victory had subsided, the nation's press and public looked to Ottawa for a response to the crisis in Confederation. They received it November 24 as Mr. Trudeau, followed by the three opposition leaders, spoke to the country on national television.

The Right Words from Mr. Trudeau

THE MONTREAL STAR
November 25, 1976
EDITORIAL

To the extent that words can settle a country's problems, Prime Minister Trudeau's address last night made the right contribution to the national mood in the wake of the Quebec election.

He proposed an open, generous and reasonable approach to the province's new Parti Québécois government. He struck a decent balance between alarm and complacency for the rest of the country. And he administered a cool dose of reason to any remaining Canadians who might still imagine that force of arms is the way to keep the country together.

In the immediate future, as the prime minister pointed out, the job of the new Quebec government will be to tackle the province's internal problems and to carry on the existing complex and intimate relationships with Ottawa and the other provinces. The job of the federal government will be to co-operate in those continuing relationships without imagining that every future federal-provincial clash, over money, policies or jurisdiction, is the beginning of the end of the country.

At the same time, all Canadians who believe in the future of the country, must accept the fact that the actions and the attitudes needed to hold it together must be taken now—not merely at the time when the PQ decides to bring the issue to a head.

When he turned to those actions and attitudes, the prime minister displayed his customary blind spot, an exaggerated faith in the value of official bilingualism as a national adhesive.

While agreeing to renew discussion on a more flexible federalism, Mr. Trudeau pointed out that "a new sharing of power between Ottawa and the provinces . . . will never make a Francophone feel more at home in Toronto or in Vancouver than he does in Quebec."

He is quite right, it will not. But neither, let's face it, will bilingual wickets in the Vancouver post office. French-speaking Canadians living outside Quebec should be given government services in their own language because it is right. No one should expect that, however, to put an end to separatist sentiment. The sense of being at home in a country is too broad to be created by an official languages act.

Mr. Trudeau's appeal, of course, went well beyond language policy. He stressed the need for efforts to increase social justice

and reduce regional disparity, areas in which his own government's efforts have been marked more by good intentions than
good results. But his overall message was one of balance and
sanity, and it deserves a positive response from the country.

That is more than can be said for the efforts which followed
from the leaders of the three opposition parties. The contrast
was inevitable. Mr. Trudeau spoke as the prime minister of the
country. The others spoke as opposition politicians and their
contributions were bound to sound partisan, self-serving and
carping. Joe Clark's efforts to edge into René Lévesque's lime-
light are a continuing source of embarrassment.

Why the three opposition leaders jumped at the chance of
air time is hard to imagine. Whatever their rage at the prime
minister's free public exposure they simply had nothing useful
to offer last night. The best that can be said for Mr. Clark, Mr.
Broadbent and Mr. Fortin is that they missed a splendid opportunity to shut up.

The Prime Minister's Remarks

THE VICTORIA TIMES
November 25, 1976
EDITORIAL

If a person from another planet watched Canada's four political leaders explain the need for national unity Wednesday
night Prime Minister Pierre Trudeau would tower above his
antagonists from a detached viewpoint. The word "antagonists" is used here because opposition leaders paid little more
than lip service to national unity in their self serving attacks on
a man who is deeply committed to saving this nation from its
own greedy excesses. Yes, Trudeau and his floundering administration have serious faults, faults that could result in their
defeat at the next election. But in Canada today we are not
talking about internecine political shadings, we are not comparing images. The survival of our nation state, our Canada, is
at stake.

Given this most urgent premise, it is shocking to hear Con-

servative Leader Joe Clark say the answer to confederation is a
healthy economy and increased job opportunities. He almost
winked adding that he and Rene Levesque could work together "as two men who have no old scores to settle." Canadians want "to restore a sense of competent management to our
national economy." The country faces the gravest crisis in its
national history and this neophyte whistles about a realignment
in the boardroom.

New Democratic Party Leader Ed Broadbent wasn't much
better. Sounding flat and trite, he admitted it was foolish to
place all the blame for our current contretemps on the Trudeau government, and then proceeded to personally castigate
the prime minister. As for Social Credit leader Andre Fortin,
the less said the better. Yet all three of these men, who quite
properly demanded their share of national television time at
this sombre moment, used it for partisan political purposes. To
employ this issue as a soap box for individual political ambi-
tions diminishes their stature as Canadians and demeans our
political process. All three should hang their heads in shame
today.

And then we come to the prime minister. He was eloquent,
emotional and oddly moralistic. If only he could bring the
same high mindedness to dealing with an auditor general's
report as he does to our survival. In an oblique warning to
Anglophone provinces who hope Rene Levesque's victory will
result in a more decentralized federation (that is more money
for the provinces) Trudeau said it is an illusion to think separatists will abandon their goals for new powers. How true. Why
is it that Canadians both individually and collectively will pros-
titute even their country for a short term buck?

But it was when he spoke of Canada that the mind of Pierre
Elliott Trudeau flashed like the northern lights. "I'm speaking
to you about a deeper brotherhood than blood, a fraternity of
hope and charity in the biblical sense. Our two historically
intertwined cultures have become the source of our individual-
ity and the very cornerstone of our identity as a people." It is
not often a politician gets the last word in this space but the
prime minister deserved it November 24. "Our forefathers
willed this country into being and we must continue to will it
every day."

Mr. Trudeau Speaks

THE CALGARY HERALD
November 26, 1976
EDITORIAL

The prime minister's address to the nation Wednesday didn't do much to advance discussion of the problems facing Canada in the wake of the Quebec election.

Perhaps his request for national network television time raised unreasonable expectations about what he would have to say. The fact remains that what he did say was not especially novel.

He urged calm in a nation that is already calm, if not apathetic. He said that he would not use force to keep Canada together. Has anyone suggested that he do so? For that matter, has he enough force at his disposal?

The prime minister's call for love and understanding, and for a recognition that the "brutal question" of the country's survival must be faced, are not to be scorned. However, moral exhortations tend to be judged as much by their source as their content. As the leader of a government that is widely perceived as cynical and inept, Mr. Trudeau is not well-placed to mobilize Canadians' finer feelings.

The prime minister's understanding of Quebec might be an asset in the difficult times ahead, if only it were matched by a similar understanding of the West.

He is concerned that Quebecers don't feel fully at home in Canada. He doesn't seem to understand that many Westerners feel the same way, perhaps less intensely.

Quebec separatism is not by any means the only strain on Confederation, though it is currently the most severe and obvious one. It is time to wonder whether Mr. Trudeau and his strongly centralist idea of federalism are the solution or part of the problem.

This point was well made by Opposition Leader Joe Clark in a short address immediately following the prime minister's. It was one of Mr. Clark's better efforts since he became Conservative leader, and helped diminish the suspicion that he is a light-weight with no real ideas about Canada's future.

Considering the problems ahead, and the performance of the Trudeau government, evidence that there is an acceptable alternative is welcome.

Mr. Trudeau's Sortie

LE DEVOIR, *Montréal*
November 26, 1976
EDITORIAL BY CLAUDE RYAN

Listening Wednesday night as Mr. Trudeau presented on television his reaction to the election of a PQ government in Québec, one could not help but feel a certain uneasiness stemming not from his comments but rather from the medium through which he chose to communicate what he had to say. Mr. Trudeau had in effect reserved for himself the period of prime time on all major radio and television networks.

After having heard him put forth the bare details of what his government intends to do, one wondered honestly if this was really worth the extraordinary arrangements that surrounded the Prime Minister's statement. Given the little he had to say, Mr. Trudeau could have easily contented himself with using the Parliamentary press gallery or any other forum that would have been willingly offered to him by many people across the country.

Poor Judgment and Wise Fools to Blame for Trudeau's Collapse

THE OTTAWA CITIZEN
January 22, 1977
DOUGLAS FULLERTON

... No one has come to high political office in Canada more gifted than Pierre Elliott Trudeau—a first-class intelligence, great fluency in both our main languages, a degree of personal appeal and histrionic skills that carried his party to power in three federal elections.

Perhaps it is because we expected so much from him—as we do from our most talented people—that the dimensions of his failure as a prime minister seem all the greater.

But he *has* failed, and failed most in the area in which he had the highest hopes—bringing English and French in Canada closer together.

Failed because of his total rejection of the emotional needs of his fellow Quebecers for a larger say in their own affairs; failed because his own impeccable Cartesian logic led him to conclude long ago that French-Canadian nationalism was a kind of sickness that had to be stamped out—or cured by its conversion into a larger Canadian nationalism, somehow more legitimate.

Failed because his answer to Quebec's felt needs was an organized effort to make Quebecers feel more at home in public service and in the rest of Canada. Launched with the best intentions in the world, his bilingualism policy, as a result of political and bureaucratic mismanagement, alienated English-speaking Canadians in government and across the country —and all for objectives which have never had much popular appeal in Quebec.

Failed because his hard line on constitutional issues has immeasurably strengthened the will of the separatists, polarizing opinion and forcing Premier Rene Levesque and his supporters into ever more uncompromising positions—as rigid as those of Mr. Trudeau himself. . . .

How could any prime minister have made so many mistakes? For one thing, bad judgment in choosing the people around him, his praetorian guard, most of them like himself, academic and legal in background, bright—yes, very bright indeed—but knowing little of the real world, a collection of wise fools.

Some of them like Mr. Trudeau, born with a silver spoon in their mouths—unsoiled by contact with ordinary people, but assuaging their sense of guilt about their wealthy origins by the massive spending, and wasting, of public money.

Prime Minister Trudeau, the man to keep Quebec in Confederation? One separatist put it to me—"Just give us two more years of Trudeau in power, and independence is assured." And I have yet to meet a Quebecer, of any political stripe, who does not believe that Trudeau's hard and inflexible line, his repeated assertions that "separatism is dead," his inability to understand the needs of his own people, have contributed materially to the rise in separatist strength in the province.

If the recent Gallup poll means anything, the people of Canada realize this too. Will our prime minister accept their verdict? Or must we wait for internal stresses and strains in the Liberal party, or an election, to bring his removal about?

In April 1977 the Prime Minister journeyed to Winnipeg to set out his vision of a unified Canada and the West's place in it. Then several days later he helped engineer the most surprising political defection of the decade.

Talking to the West

THE STAR-PHOENIX, *Saskatoon*
April 20, 1977
EDITORIAL

Western Canadian attitudes toward Quebec and Confederation are, to rework a saying, either part of the problem or part of the solution.

A growing body of westerners, some of them even respectable, believe their attitudes to be part of the solution. That is, they have grievances and they feel alienated for what they feel are good reasons. Some of these reasons are related to the concentration of bureaucratic and economic power in one province.

Whether they exaggerate this or not, perceptions rank high in politics. Their sense of alienation, therefore, becomes an important part of the solution of Canada's constitutional problem because the redress of grievance will rally people to the country, not only in the west, but in Quebec as well.

On the other hand, many Canadians, equally respectable and not all resident in central Canada, believe such attitudes to be part of the problem. They do not deny a basis for grievance, but they do believe the whole to be greater than the sum of its parts. Canadian unity is a far better prize than the satisfaction of regional complaints; moreover, they might say, those complaints would not loom so large if the people making them were more outward looking.

Into this latter category, Prime Minister Trudeau naturally falls, and his remarks in Winnipeg Monday night were directed to the proposition there is something more important at stake today than the complaints of westerners and, more to the point, the feelings of westerners toward French-speaking Quebecers.

And by comparing the grievances of western Canadians to those of Quebecers, he astutely struck an empathetic chord.

No doubt the great tragedy of Canada is the failure of many English-speaking Canadians to accept the reality of the French fact, and to be more accommodating to official bilingualism.

The success of Mr. Trudeau's Winnipeg address will largely be measured by the impact of his plea for understanding on behalf of those five million Quebecers who speak only French and do so as their legitimate right.

It was not so much a historical or constitutional legitimacy, he argued, but a political one.

He did not say so, but he implied thereby that if there were five million people speaking Ukrainian as their first language, Ukrainian would too be made official.

If reason can prevail, there should be little problem with western Canadians accepting the legitimacy of French-Canadian grievance. Moreover, there should be little problem identifying with it.

But, here we come back to what may be behind the grievances of both regions, and behind the grievances of the Atlantic provinces and British Columbia as well, the belief that this country is too centralized.

If Quebec and western Canada move closer together as the prime minister has urged, will not the area where capital and power are concentrated be more threatened?

A common grievance is, perhaps, the greatest unifying influence this country could enjoy. But such a common grievance could not be pressed for long without something having to give.

Useless Raiding

LE DEVOIR, *Montréal*
April 21, 1977
JEAN-CLAUDE LECLERC

After their fall last year to the bottom of the Gallup Poll the federal Liberals have, with the unexpected election of a separatist party in Québec, regained the hope of beating the Conservatives and staying in power. But to ensure against a resurgence of popular disapproval and so as not to take any chances they and their emissaries are attempting to dismantle the Official Opposition.

Yesterday, Jack Horner crossed the Rubicon. Maybe tomorrow Claude Wagner will return to the Bench. All, of course, in the name of national unity which is, it seems, more important than the political vitality of the country or its democratic equilibrium.

These raiding tactics would not have succeeded and would not have been attempted so intensely by ministers if the Conservatives and most of all their leader Joe Clark had been able to create within their party the cohesion that was granted them from the outside by the polls predicting their future victory. The Liberals who are now rejoicing are not in any better position. It's not with the Member from Crowfoot that they will regenerate their party and re-establish the authority of the government. This game of Parliamentary musical chairs is a spicy episode for a House which rarely sins through an excess of enthusiasm. It will however do nothing to raise the confidence of the electorate in partisan traditions and in the leadership of the federal government.

All of this is astonishing coming from a capital which seeks to rekindle the trust of Québec and the West in Canadian institutions. Is it perhaps that Canada is as badly served by the ruling party in Ottawa as Québec was up to last November 15? Mr. Trudeau would be correct to see in the results of the last Québec election a call to social progress and change.

Pierre Trudeau, judging from the welcome he accorded his new representative from the West, doesn't seem to realize that a significant improvement is not possible without a sweeping change at the top.

Margaret Trudeau had kept pretty much in the background during her first years as Canada's first lady. But increasingly, particularly after the 1974 election, her discontent with the role of prime minister's wife became apparent as her public behavior became more and more erratic. When the break came it held little surprise.

A Matter for Compassion

THE GAZETTE, *Montréal*
May 31, 1977
EDITORIAL

The Trudeau family deserves a period of quiet sympathy from all Canadians. Marital breakup in itself is no longer a cause for either political scandal or setback, simply for personal sorrow on the part of the people directly involved.

The prime minister now has three sons to raise by himself. This is a problem he will have to deal with as he wrestles with issues such as the economy, national unity and development of the Canadian north.

Beleaguered as he is, he has shown admirable restraint in not discussing his private life in public. This alone should strike a responsive chord with the Canadian public.

It should also bring sympathy from those Canadians who find themselves in the same situation. According to the latest reports from Statistics Canada, one out every 10 Canadian families is headed by a single parent: that figure is growing at a rate which will result in one family in five—or twice today's level—having only one parent by the end of the next decade.

The effects of a marriage breakup cannot, unfortunately be limited strictly to the man and woman concerned. In the present situation when a prominent couple is involved along with their children, some degree of public interest is inevitable. It is to be hoped this interest will combine restraint and compassion.

A Chance to Keep Quiet

LE DEVOIR, *Montréal*
June 4, 1977
MICHEL ROY

It has been impossible not to note the discretion, the respect and even the modesty which the francophone press in Québec, written, spoken and televised, has shown towards the personal affairs of Mr. Trudeau. Certainly, public information and official statements have been published; this is normal. But on the whole, French-language newspapers have studiously avoided a casual display of the various events which preceded and which followed the separation. It is not usually the French-language correspondents who, during his press conferences, belabor the issue with the Prime Minister. And he, with a dignity that does him honor, has replied in an appropriate manner to the sometimes embarrassing questions addressed to him.

Certain of our colleagues in Toronto or Winnipeg all too easily criticized the journalists of Québec for having demonstrated what they thought was an excessive caution towards Mr. Lévesque when he was involved in a car accident last February. Granted that Mr. Trudeau's separation and Mr. Lévesque's accident are not comparable. But in each case, to varying degrees, there arises the issue of privacy. Other colleagues conclude this discretion is probably due to a kind of solidarity among French-speaking Canadians or a secret Québec deal that transcends political beliefs. Yet when Otto Lang had problems in the Commons as a result of a domestic affair involving the hiring and transporting of an English nanny in a military aircraft, the Québec press refrained from exploiting this minor, personal incident.

The knowing and subtle analyses of the life and behavior of Mrs. Trudeau which we have read in the English-language press in the last few weeks are often unfair towards this young woman and tend, especially since their separation, to depict Mr. Trudeau as the heroic husband, brutally abandoned by an ungrateful wife. Such judgments are caricatures and it is good that Mr. Trudeau himself, during his press conference, thought it time to remind us that Margaret is a "good person" unjustly manipulated by the gossips who exploit such situations.

If it was a question of examining in all its dimensions the real problems of a politician's wife the analysis would have to be pushed much further. It is precisely because we are dealing with a public figure, the leader of the government, and with a woman who became famous despite herself that it is best to avoid setting oneself up as a judge or psychoanalyst.

Mrs. Trudeau might also contribute to this discretion by refraining from reciting to any reporter who comes along details from her married life which, reproduced boldly in the columns of the popular magazines, can only feed the rumor mill. In short she must, as her husband has learned to do over the years, take the occasions that are offered to her to remain silent.

This silence will become contagious to the point where even the press will not succumb to the temptation to repeat all the inanities it hears.

On Losing My Taste for the Lady

BILD AM SONNTAG, *Hamburg*
June 12, 1977
HANS HABE

"Current Culture" is the heading of this page and therefore justifies the question of what the estranged wife of the Canadian Prime Minister Pierre Elliott Trudeau has to do with culture.

More than one is inclined to believe—as can be proved.

When the fifty-year old statesman married the twenty-year old flowergirl, the "Anti-Parliamentarian-Opposition-Culture-Revolution" was in full swing. It could be that the aging politician did not marry the pretty flowerchild because he wanted the young person, but rather because he wanted to win the young people. Seen in a cultural-historical perspective, this was a marriage as political-opportunistic as any arranged marriage between the children of princes in the 18th century. It was bound to fail.

After the wedding, the demonstration-girl went on demonstrating, and since Margaret could not now wave black or red banners, withal she wore holes in her pantyhose during state-receptions. She followed the Rolling Stones, well known for their drug affairs. She told a curious world that she possessed "strong sexual energies," that she could not live "in a golden cage."

I don't find fault with the substance of this, however I do not like the sequence. Even a flowergirl cannot believe that the Prime Minister's residence in Ottawa is a disco. Someone who fights for her "private life," as the international left-wing press chirps admiringly, does not marry a prime minister. Margaret Trudeau is just a little careerist who wants both luxury and excitement.

The hippie-girl is interesting for other reasons, too. "She is not seeking sex, but only herself," Hamburg's red "Stern" wrote. How touching!

Today immaturity has become an ongoing excuse for the do-nothings, and good-for-nothings in the streets and the fashionable salons. Working women, and wives of workingmen have no time "to seek themselves." We all have problems. But the man or woman who has not discovered his "identity" at thirty, is simply using the search for his or her own personality as a pretence to fill the emptiness inside.

I find this obsession with the question "Who am I?" especially repulsive in one who already has brought three children into this world. I am not saying that a mother of three children has no right to her own personal difficulties and there may be good reasons to leave husband and children. But if that is done, lackadaisically, in order to "find oneself," the flight becomes cowardly desertion.

It is hard to find one good hair in the beautiful head of Margaret Trudeau. The flowerchild who deemed "unbearable" the "lusty old men"—meaning visiting statesmen—and who allegedly fled the "wolves of the press," today does not hawk home-made jewelry on streetcorners, but skips from one party to another with her friend, the princess Jasmin Ali Khan, tries to dethrone Bianca Jagger as jet-set Queen, collects alimony, and sells back to "the wolves of the press" her amateur photographs which no one would think of buying if it weren't for her self-provoked notoriety. Now psychologists probe the "riddle of Margaret Trudeau" and talk about "endogenous depressions," but nobody gives one hoot for the "endogenous depressions" of women who have not hooked the Canadian Prime Minister.

Apart from Quebec-Ottawa relations, the leading political issue of 1977 was the RCMP. News of the federal police force's illegal activities over the preceding four years came into the open: break-ins at PQ headquarters in 1973, illegal wiretapping, mail openings, and prying into confidential personal records. An atmosphere of Nixonian paranoia began to descend on the nation's capital as press and public wondered aloud at the extent of the Trudeau government's involvement.

In Parliament, the Prime Minister denied any such participation in the RCMP's illegal activities while defending the Force's basic integrity. As independent provincial inquiries into the RCMP got under way, notably the Keable Commission in Québec, the Prime Minister announced the appointment of the McDonald Royal Commission on July 6 to investigate the entire affair.

RCMP-Liberal Tangle

THE PROVINCE, *Vancouver*
July 7, 1977
EDITORIAL

At last the Trudeau government has done what should have been done months ago—appointed a royal commission to look into the "extent and prevalence" of illegal activities by the RCMP.

Solicitor-General Francis Fox announced the inquiry in the Commons Wednesday, saying that RCMP Commissioner Maurice Nadon, who had earlier opposed the appointment, now agrees that some of the allegations "might have some basis in fact."

Allegations of RCMP's involvement in unauthorized break-ins have formed the basis for hard questioning recently by the opposition parties. Throughout that period the government has maintained it did not know of the raids and that an inquiry was not needed.

Now inquiries into RCMP activities are underway in Alberta, New Brunswick, Quebec and Ontario. Both Quebec and Ontario are inquiring into unauthorized break-ins. Information from one of them probably formed the basis for the list of the so-called "unofficial opposition."

Belatedly, the federal government is following the provinces' lead.

Mr. Fox said it appeared that some members of the RCMP in protecting national security could well have had been involved in actions which were neither authorized nor provided for by law.

He went on to say the rule of law and the requirements of national security were difficult to reconcile in a democratic society. Maybe, but the law provides the police with considerable power if they care to use it wisely. It seems that, in Montreal at least, no attempt was made to use the law at all.

As we have said . . . a royal commission into the RCMP's activities is needed to protect the reputation of our national police force. But the inquiry should go beyond the break-ins and make searching investigations into the tangled relationship between the RCMP and the Liberal government. In particular it should examine the degree to which the government knew of the break-ins. Mr. Fox should expand the terms of reference of the commission at once.

Probe RCMP and Politicians Too

THE TORONTO STAR
July 7, 1977
EDITORIAL

The royal commission inquiry into illegal investigative practices by members of the Royal Canadian Mounted Police, announced last night by Solicitor-General Francis Fox, is the best way to preserve the force's reputation.

The public needs to be assured that members of the force have not been acting as if they are above the law and that there are clearly understood rules of procedure that members of the force must follow in conducting any investigation.

But the inquiry should not stop at RCMP headquarters. The force, after all, is under political control through the Solicitor-General's office.

The public should know whether that political control has been properly exercised and, more important, whether there have been political pressures by the cabinet on the RCMP to conduct certain types of investigations.

The Mounties should not be allowed to become the scapegoats if fault rests higher up the ladder.

Fox contends the inquiry's terms of reference permit the investigation to go right to the top. But the opposition does not feel assured on this point and it would be worthwhile for Fox to revise the terms of reference so that the point is clear.

Calls for an inquiry arose out of an illegal break-in, in 1972, by members of the RCMP, along with Quebec and Montreal police officers, into the offices of a politically oriented news agency in Montreal. Police officers were charged but they were acquitted by a Montreal judge.

This was followed by charges that the RCMP was somehow involved in the theft of documents from a Toronto-based social activist group known as Praxis.

Both these cases are now under investigation—the Montreal one by the Quebec government and the Toronto one by the Ontario government.

But there was a need for a broader inquiry which Fox, until yesterday, had refused to order. Now he says new information suggests illegal activities by some members of the force may have been more widespread than he thought, hence the turnaround.

The inquiry has two responsibilities: To uncover the facts on past behavior, all the way up to the political masters of the RCMP; and to advise the government on what procedures the RCMP should follow in future.

In a free society, police forces are in a delicate position, for they have to provide protection against groups and individuals who may want to destroy that freedom by terrorist activities or political subversion.

But the health of a free society depends on police and government following the rules. If the rules are not adequate to the task, then the political process can change them.

The inquiry announced by Fox provides a chance to clear the name of the RCMP and to come up with strict rules, arrived at in public discussion, for the future undercover behavior of the RCMP.

Intolerable Abuses

LE DEVOIR, *Montréal*
October 29, 1977
EDITORIAL BY CLAUDE RYAN

The Solicitor General of Canada, Francis Fox, referring yesterday in the Commons to the latest of the illegal acts of the Royal Canadian Mounted Police of which the government has become aware, tried to indicate two extenuating circumstances which should, according to him, urge the Canadian public to judge these incidents less harshly. We can agree with Mr. Fox that in committing illegal acts of a purely political nature agents of the RCMP were pursuing noble aims. Before subscribing however to the verdict of acquittal which is almost suggested by the Solicitor General's words, we cannot help being astonished by the incredible ease with which some were able to mock the law and the rights of citizens within an organization whose name until now has always been synonymous with professional competence and respect for the law.

Cabinet Accountability

THE OTTAWA CITIZEN
November 1, 1977
EDITORIAL

Both Prime Minister Trudeau and Solicitor-General Francis Fox have been glib and facile in their explanations of illegal conduct by the RCMP Security Service. Theirs is the predictable reaction of government leaders who have abrogated their responsibilities.

The official government line, as enunciated by Trudeau and Fox, is that violation of the law in the name of the law is inexcusable, so maybe the law should to be changed to legalize what has heretofore been illegal.

That is Nixonian logic by any measure.

The facts of RCMP break-ins, buggings and theft have been slow in coming, for obvious reasons. But what is emerging as more and more details do come out is a consistent pattern of failure of government officials to get to the bottom of what was happening. . . .

The information available now indicates that high-ranking officers within the RCMP ordered their subordinates to bend, stretch or break the law in the zealous pursuit of their objectives.

Maybe, as the prime minister has said, critics of the RCMP and the government must remember the mood of the times in which RCMP illegal acts are alleged to have occurred. Of course, it is hard to forget the over-reaction of the federal, Quebec and Montreal governments to the FLQ crisis of 1970. The imposition of the War Measures Act was a dramatic weapon to use in a case where police were unable to solve two kidnappings and a subsequent murder.

Perhaps what the prime minister wants people to believe is that the RCMP believed that the government's actions in 1970 were tantamount to a *carte blanche* for subsequent investigations. Maybe the War Measures precedent led the RCMP to believe that the end justified the means.

That isn't so in a democracy. But what is more frightening is to hear the prime minister and solicitor-general saying that now the police may need more power.

And Nothing Else

THE DAILY GLEANER, *Fredericton*
November 9, 1977
EDITORIAL

No doubt some Canadian journalists would like to see a scandal in this country as sensational and far-reaching as the one which toppled Richard Nixon. However, the cries of "Watergate" in relation to illegal RCMP activities are dangerously misleading.

A list of Parti Quebecois members was obtained illegally. But there is no evidence this information was used to disrupt the activities of the PQ. This is a far cry from the dirty tricks of Nixon's men who manipulated the race for the Democratic leadership to make sure the weakest candidate won.

The RCMP broke into the office of a left-wing news agency in Montreal. This is a far cry from some of the Nixon tactics, such as stirring public opinion against the "new left" by hiring phony demonstrators to make a spectacle of themselves at a Billy Graham evangelical rally.

Watergate comprised a vast web of intrigue in which millions of dollars and some of the most brilliant minds in the country were turned to one objective—keeping the Nixon administration in power. There is no evidence that the RCMP was being used in a similar fashion to prop up the Trudeau administration.

The tactics of Watergate were far more devious, vicious and successful. Reputations were destroyed, and victims were left "to turn slowly in the wind." We have yet to learn of serious harm that has occurred to any individual or group as a result of the RCMP activities in question.

The current situation would suggest that, with enemies like the RCMP Security Service to impede its rise to power, the PQ didn't need any friends.

If the Mounties had stolen the files of a political leader's psychiatrist, to give a far-fetched example, then the parallel with Watergate might be justified.

If they had sent out hate literature under the letterhead of Ed Broadbent, as Nixon's men did under the letterhead of Edmund Muskie—the parallel would be justified.

But as it is, the universal outrage which the RCMP revelations have provoked is hard to understand. Certainly there are serious issues at stake and the facts should be brought to light and debated but Canadians should also keep their perspective on the situation.

The thing to do now is to divorce the RCMP from subversive tactics and allow them to do the job they were created to do—maintain law and order. That and nothing else.

Integrity Threatened

THE CALGARY HERALD
October 18, 1978
EDITORIAL

The federal government has again chosen to duck questions concerning its dispute with the McDonald commission into RCMP wrongdoing.

In passing off inquiries concerning whether the government would go to court to prevent cabinet ministers testifying before the commission in public, Ottawa has chosen to delay the issue and label it hypothetical, when in fact such questions are anything but hypothetical. They strike at the very heart of the Canadian inquiry system.

The government is merely delaying the inevitable, for high-ranking RCMP officers and senior cabinet ministers begin appearing before the commission October 24. The commissioners, and through them, the public, have a right to know whether or not the guidelines set down by the government for the inquiry will be honored, or set aside. And they have a right to know exactly what the government will do before that Tuesday rolls around.

At issue is whether evidence of cabinet ministers and cabinet documents will be produced in public, or in closed session. And also at issue is the commission's mandate to make that decision.

In spite of government obfuscation, the fact remains that it has changed position since setting up the commission, and has taken to itself the final say in protecting cabinet secrets and national security.

Without a drastic change in government position, Alberta Judge David McDonald may be put in the position of having to resign to protect his reputation and that of the other commissioners and even the entire process of inquiry.

The fact that the commission is essential is undeniable.

The fact that its integrity has come close to being compromised is also undeniable.

The Liberal government has chosen to apply one law for cabinet ministers and top-ranking officers, another for lower ranks in the RCMP. There was little fuss from Ottawa when lower-ranking RCMP officers testified, revealing the Mounties had been involved in such questionable acts as barn burning, breaking and entering, and theft. Now, with the prospect of cabinet ministers and cabinet material coming under scrutiny, the government is doing some fancy talking, covering up their change in position with rhetoric....

A year ago, the government appeared to have faith in the integrity of royal commissioners. And when that integrity is stripped from men appointed to the sensitive and difficult task of looking behind the closed doors of a police force and probing into the backroom workings of a government, they have been stripped of the very reason for that appointment.

Canadian royal commissions have carried clout because the people believed in their independence and integrity in investigating the matter at hand, without coercion or collusion.

In its threatened move to muzzle democracy, as Opposition Leader Joe Clark so aptly stated, the government casts doubt on findings of any commission—if it gets away with it.

On April 6, 1978, Pierre Elliott Trudeau observed his tenth anniversary as leader of the federal Liberal Party, and on April 20 his tenth year as Prime Minister of Canada. Numerous press assessments of the man and his performance in office began to appear in Canada and abroad.

The Canadian press has changed its view of Mr. Trudeau quite radically and with some regularity over these years. From the Trudeaumania of 1968 to the virtual Trudeauphobia of 1978, with stops at several points between, the press has now come full circle.

The Agonising Dilemma of Two Just Men

THE OBSERVER, *London*
February 19, 1978
CONOR CRUISE O'BRIEN

Quebec today appears to be in some danger of breaking up Canada without really intending to. . . .

In the long uncertainties of the pre-referendum period, pressures and resentments seem likely to intensify. The wording of the referendum will be designed by the Government of Quebec. Its exact form is not yet known, but it will probably not include the word 'independence' and certainly not the word 'separation.' It is likely to be based on the Levesque formula of 'sovereignty and association.' This sounds attractive (in Quebec).

In the January 1978 survey already cited, one question gave three options: independence, sovereignty/association, and remaining part of Canada. Faced with those choices, only 6 per cent chose independence, 36 per cent chose sovereignty/association, and 55 per cent were for remaining in Canada. It may be, as the Parti Québécois appears to assume, that the support for sovereignty/association will increase as the content is more fully explained and that at the coming referendum—or, failing that, some later referendum—there will be a clear majority in favour of this formula.

Even so, the troubles of Canada and of Quebec would not end there. Quebec may vote for 'sovereignty/association,' but the rest of Canada seems to think that this formula wraps together two conflicting concepts between which Canada has to choose. The rejection by the rest of Canada of the formula approved by Quebec would represent a singularly unhappy deadlock, propitious to revolutionary violence—especially if these uncertainties are attended by further decline in the Quebec economy.

But the prospect, if 'sovereignty/association' is defeated in

Quebec, is hardly much more attractive. The defeat would be likely to be blamed on the Anglophones resident in Quebec—already sometimes identified as not being real Quebecois. These feelings, reflected in the course of further referenda, could involve intimidation of Anglophones, an accelerated exodus, and a drift towards the independence of an isolated and impoverished Quebec.

The world is greatly indebted to Canada for the patient, skilful and unassuming work of her statesmen in many international contexts, including the United Nations. Few countries can have attracted more genuine admiration, respect and liking, for their contribution to international affairs.

It is to be hoped that the remarkable qualities which Canadians have shown in helping the rest of the world will enable M. Trudeau and M. Levesque—two men of goodwill and notable intellectual gifts—to surmount the dark problems now facing the great country which contains these two men and should, in some manner, be enabled to continue to contain them.

The Loneliness of the Long-Distance Premier

THE OBSERVER, *London*
March 30, 1978
EDITORIAL

When Pierre Trudeau came to power, just 10 years ago, Lyndon Johnson was President of the United States, Harold Wilson was Prime Minister of Britain, Charles de Gaulle was President of France. The first and last are dead, and Wilson, only four years older (62 against 58), is very much the elder statesman. Trudeau is preparing for his fourth federal election, and is the favourite to win.

The outlook, however, both politically and personally, is very different from the heady scene of a decade ago.

The country has fallen on hard times: its economy is in a

mess, with unemployment at a record million, inflation high and the dollar sagging badly against America's. Scandal has dimmed the legendary image of the Royal Canadian Mounted Police, which, it appears, has been guilty of illegal break-ins, wire-taps and harassment.

In Quebec, the secessionist Parti Québécois, led by Trudeau's fellow French Canadian, René Levesque, threatens the break-up of the Federation. And, while no one in the colourless Conservative Opposition seems anywhere near him in political standing, a rival star has just appeared within his own party: Claude Ryan, the new provincial Liberal leader in Quebec, another French Canadian.

Under Trudeau, said one Ottawa commentator, Canada has had 'some of the best government Canadians have ever known —and some of the worst.' Certainly there has been progress. Capital punishment has been abolished. Divorce and homosexuality laws have been reformed. (A group calling itself Pilgrims of Michael the Archangel described Trudeau as 'the Beast of Sodom,' and cast reflections on his heterosexuality.)

Before he took office, the Federal Civil Service was a very English affair. Now the number of French speakers reflects, reasonably accurately, their proportion (27 per cent) of the national population. Federal civil servants have to be proficient in French. Products must be labelled in both languages—when a politician from Western Canada complained about having to look at the French on his packet of breakfast cereal, Trudeau told him brusquely: 'Turn the damn box round.' . . .

Critics say Trudeau is out of touch with his own people, the Quebeckers, and fails to realise that, while most of them do not want to secede, they are dissatisfied with both the *status quo* and his ideas on constitutional reform. What they want is structural and political change.

Trudeau's most vulnerable point, however, is the economy. 'Pierre seems to have no ability to grasp this subject,' a leading economist has commented. 'He persists in believing that unemployment is not the result of Government policy but something workers inflict upon themselves through laziness or self-destructiveness. His assumption that one million people can occupy the 80,000 jobs available suggests his maths need brushing up as well.'

Trudeau's defence is to blame world trends—and the rise to prominence of Levesque and his Parti Québécois. His own ethnic background is aptly reflected in his name: Pierre Elliott Trudeau. His father was a Montreal millionaire (thanks to a string of petrol stations), the descendant of a carpenter who emigrated from France 10 generations ago in 1659. His mother's family was of Scots descent.

He married in 1971. His bride, Margaret Sinclair, daughter of a British Columbia politician, was 30 years younger than himself. The wedding was in March and on Christmas Day that year they had their first child, a boy. Two years later, again on Christmas Day, another son was born. A third followed. It all seemed rather idyllic, almost too good to be true. It was.

Spiritually, Margaret Trudeau was one of the flower children of the sixties. In 1974 she went into hospital for treatment of what she told reporters was 'severe emotional stress.' Later, on television, she said she wished her husband would get out of politics. That November, apparently misunderstanding an Opposition question in the House of Commons as referring to the possibility of a divorce in his family, Trudeau called the questioner a son of a bitch and stalked out of the chamber.

Newspapers began to carry stories about Mrs. Trudeau's goings-on in New York; in particular, her enthusiasm for Rolling Stones concerts and her friendship for Mick Jagger and Keith Richard. She is now a New York photographer. Trudeau lives with his three young sons in the Prime Minister's official residence in Sussex Drive, Ottawa (almost certainly the world's only single-parent ruler). . . .

He clearly enjoys the exercise of power and—thanks largely to the mediocrity of his Conservative opponents—looks set fair to keeping it. The unhappy marriage has won him sympathy. Levesque's victory in Quebec has increased support for Trudeau as the foremost defender of the 110-year-old Federation. All this suggests victory in the next election, though with a reduced majority.

The one achievement no one can deny him is in foreign affairs. Despite Canada's residual inferiority complex about its big neighbour, relations with the US are more relaxed; Trudeau gets on particularly well with President Carter. In the

Third World, through his early recognition of China, his ties with Cuba (both of which he visited as a young man), and his discouragement of new investment in South Africa, he has strengthened Canada's 'Scandinavian' reputation. His dream of utilising his country's unique bi-cultural quality has been enhanced by the presence of Canadians in every United Nations peace-keeping force since the organisation was founded.

Above all, there is his own personality. People have never forgotten his determination, even ruthlessness, in dealing with the outbreak of terrorism in Montreal in 1970, when the British Trade Commissioner was kidnapped and a Quebec Minister murdered. After proclaiming a state of emergency and sending in the Army, Trudeau was asked how far he was prepared to go. With a look that could have sliced steel, he replied. 'Just watch me.'

After a decade, Canadians no longer need an invitation to watch Pierre Trudeau. He remains a very watchable man.

Pierre Elliott Trudeau's Spring; 10 Years Later

SOUTHAM NEWS SERVICES
April 5, 1978
CHRISTOPHER YOUNG

> *"Bliss was it in that dawn to be alive.*
> *But to be young was very heaven!"*

Ottawa—Canadians tend to be shy about expressing themselves in romantic language. Otherwise, Wordsworth's lines on the French Revolution might have been written about the first week of April, 1968.

Here in Ottawa, there had been a lot of snow that spring. The contenders for the Liberal party leadership had been campaigning via executive jets through the February blizzards and the winds of March.

With the first days of April, the winter broke. When the Liberal delegates began to assemble at the Ottawa Civic

Centre, a brilliant sun was making the snowpiles run in rivers across the asphalt parking areas. With that marvellous exhilaration that every Canadian experiences once a year, people went out for the first time in 1968 without the woolly burden of an overcoat.

Pierre Trudeau, whose leather coat had become a trademark and symbol that winter, quoted a saying of Napoleon's mother to the effect that it was great as long as it lasted.

It has lasted now for 10 years—not the dizzy euphoria of Trudeau's triumph, not the adulation of those April days, not the pathways strewn with flowers and kisses, but the power—which was what it was all about.

Among the Liberals who opposed Trudeau (1,149 to 1,203 on the last ballot), it was common to say then that he was a flash in the pan, a dilettante who had never stayed long at anything and who would quickly tire of political power.

It seems a ludicrous judgment now, with Trudeau Canada's fourth longest-serving prime minister and, if he wins the next election, closing in on Laurier's 15 years. (Coincidentally, that's about as long as it lasted for Napoleon as well.)

In retrospect, it might have been better for Canada, for the Liberal party and for Prime Minister Trudeau if the Conservatives had won the election of 1972, as they so nearly did. A term or two for Robert Stanfield would have provided a healthy change and plenty of time, if the voters had so decided, for Pierre Trudeau to return to office in the later '70s.

If we give the Liberals another majority, we are stuck with them well into the 1980s. Not only would we be giving Trudeau a potential 15 unbroken years, as Laurier had through four elections at the turn of the century, but we would be giving the Liberal party a potential 20 years from the last turnover in 1963.

The record 22 years of Liberal power under King and St. Laurent from 1935 to '57 would then begin to seem like a normal pattern, with a five-year Tory break once a generation when things got really awful.

That is less a criticism of the Liberals than it is of the Conservative party, whose utter failure to sustain a reputation for competence and cohesion has forced the Canadian voter to turn again and again to the same political party, regardless of his discontent with specific policies, individual leaders or local candidates.

Clearly it is not a healthy pattern for a democracy, and the electorate is going to have to look more seriously at Joe Clark and his Tories in the next two or three months than we have done to date. . . .

From the "Just Society" to Pierre Trudeau

LE DROIT, *Ottawa*
April 8, 1978
EDITORIAL BY PIERRE TREMBLAY

An ideal took power 10 years ago. The entire country except for several skeptics who were quickly left behind by events responded to the call for action to create a "just society." A leader had won because people thought he belonged to that new breed of politicians who would lead their countries down the road to the post-industrial era.

From the start two themes were taken as the definition of the "just society." Give to the two societies (French and English) the elementary justice of recognizing the equality of their means of expression—their languages—at the levels of government and administration, and give the regions the possibility of participating, with the help of Ottawa if necessary, in the economic progress of the country. This was translated into action in 1969 by the adoption of the Official Languages Act and by the creation of the Department of Regional Exonomic Expansion. In addition, universal social programs would reduce individual inequalities which would also be dealt with by a system of guaranteed annual income. And the relations between individual and state? They would be based upon a participatory society, which would be open to and altered by radical means if necessary—as was the case with the support given The Company of Young Canadians and other social animation services. Ten years later, what has become of this great social project and all it entailed?

The official languages have been recognized by all the political parties but the law hasn't been accepted by a vast segment of the population which, some say, has not properly understood it. Federal institutions were to become "functionally" bilingual.... However in the last several years the realization of this aim has become increasingly difficult. The Royal Commission on Bilingualism and Biculturalism proposed more than this kind of bilingualism. It wanted to see an adjustment of the country's political structures to fit the reality of "two solitudes" mutually connected but often living according to different values. Trudeau didn't believe that. He felt that protection of the French language was enough.... As for culture, it was left to the domain of personal excellence. However one question this does not solve is that of the French minorities outside Québec. This fact alone is proof positive of the weakness of Trudeau's theories.

Have regional disparities diminished? The ministry created to deal with them has turned into a grant-giving machine. The social programs from unemployment insurance to social security have produced equal disillusionment. Recent independent studies have shown their weakness if not their complete failure. The latest study of the Canadian Council on Welfare of taxation and the distribution of income demonstrates clearly that the gap between rich and poor has been widening at the same time as government social programs are costing the taxpayer more and more. This is obvious proof of badly structured social programs.

As for the relations between the individual and the state, have they become more civilized in the face of mounting bureaucratic control? Government information remains subject to arbitrary secrecy. The police have been endowed with ever-increasing powers of investigation, with the October Crisis serving as a demonstration of their "necessity." ... We were promised a participatory society ten years ago. What has become of it?

We have seen 10 years of power based upon the weakness of the opposition and clever election publicity—a power in which the occupants of the Langevin Block (the Prime Minister's Office), the real seat of government, hold sway over the politicians in the House of Commons; a quasi-presidential power that is obliged to negotiate only by the stubbornness of the provinces, and still a power based upon the ideal of the just and participatory society.

No—this is a personal power, held together by a powerful palace guard. Ten years ago an ideal took power. Today it is Pierre Trudeau who holds it.

Getting to Know the Unknown Canadian

THE SUN, *Vancouver*
April 12, 1978
BRUCE HUTCHISON

No leader in Canada's history, it is safe to say, has been so thoroughly examined by his compatriots as Pierre Trudeau and none less understood. At the end of his 10 years in office and the start of his fourth election all Canadians fancy themselves as trained psychoanalysts well qualified to diagnose the patient on the couch.

Mr. Trudeau has become a kind of native phenomenon like the weather, a parlor guessing game, a creature sui generis, a mutation in our breed, a myth, an obsession with his worshippers and haters alike.

In the first serious attempt to plumb this mystery George Radwanski has written an excellent biography of the prime minister and tried hard to escape the hypnotic fascination of his subject. His book, *Trudeau* (Macmillan of Canada) will not be reviewed here but everyone interested in national affairs should read it while remembering John W. Dafoe's acid comment, in the case of a book on Laurier, that if men fail to be heroes to their valets they are more successful with their biographers....

Mr. Trudeau knows more than any of his predecessors about the theory of government, the endless conflict of ideas, the philosophies and religions of ancient and modern times. He knows far less than Mackenzie King, St. Laurent, Laurier or Macdonald, for instance, about the nature of ordinary people, the decisive factor in politics throughout the ages. They are a riddle to him as he is to them.

Intellectually, he has studied and mastered the strange chronicle of our species and realizes its fragile grip on a tiny planet but all his economic training has never taught him how to save a dollar of public money, to meet a payroll, or balance a budget. He imagined, planned and expected more wealth than the Canadian economy could provide, more justice than society was prepared to accept, more reason than the real world allowed, but he did not foresee the cost of his miscalculation.

He has a mind of peculiar brilliance—reckless, daring in action—all the necessary talents except the common touch and except the most important thing of all, that visceral intuition, that mere hunch which must finally govern nations and persons. For brilliance and learning are no substitute for wisdom and horse sense in the great turning points of life, public or private.

With his abundant mental equipment, his innocent faith in flow charts and blueprints, his astounding memory, his excessive working hours, and his boyish charm when he cares to use it, why has his government made so many mistakes? Why has everything turned out so differently from his plans and expectations as if the central computer of Ottawa had slipped a gear to derange the whole governing apparatus?

On the other hand, why is it that the nation has failed, in the last decade to produce his equal and why, after his indefensible economic record, does the public, as reflected by the opinion polls, still prefer him to any alternative?

The first questions are easily answered. Mr. Trudeau made the mistake of depending on the infallible Cartesian logic studied in his youth at many universities. As a lawyer he counted on the old legal doctrine of the "reasonable man" only to find that voters are not necessarily, or even usually reasonable.

When he attempted, in the disastrous election of 1972, "to speak the language of reason," as he recalls, "I don't think I got through to the people...Next time I may be more impassioned and a little less rational."

So he was in the election of 1974 and won it. No doubt he

will follow the same method in 1978. He must go through the motions, the kissing routine and the fixed smile of the quadrennial sun dance but it is alien to his nature because he is shy; he cringes from direct human encounters; he does not like to hurt anyone or accept favors; he grossly mismanages such personal clashes as the resignation of John Turner and he cannot bear to expose his real self.

Or so Mr. Radwanski assures us and argues that the public image of the unfeeling man is quite wrong. In truth, Mr. Trudeau is so sensitive that he must erect a high dam of pretended indifference lest his emotions overflow, as they always overflow, in tears, at the funeral of any friend. His struggle is not with his public enemies but with his own several personalities, always at war.

The second question—why he remains the giant of our politics despite his misjudgments—is not so easily answered but at least half of his electoral strength is sheer luck. If the opposition had discovered, and the nation perceived, a better alternative the Trudeau government would be doomed by now.

Whether it is doomed anyhow we shall find out. In the meantime nothing could be more improbable, with less relevance to our immediate practical business, than an election fought primarily on a curious love-hate complex between the man and the nation, not on the hard issues of the day, not on Cartesian logic, but on the talents, the flaws and the churning psyche of a leader whom the people admire or abhor and will never understand.

Trudeau in Power

THE CANADIAN FORUM
July, 1978
DENIS SMITH

For ten years Canada has been led by a strong and combative prime minister with an increasingly weak cabinet. George Radwanski, in his useful new book *Trudeau*, concludes that "he has governed intelligently in a difficult time, and his record thus far makes him not a failed prime minister but an unfulfilled one." Radwanski's depiction of the prime minister's character—proud, shy, strong-willed, competitive, erratic—is the best that has yet been written; but his analysis of the Trudeau government is less satisfactory. It is difficult to understand what being "unfulfilled" can mean for a prime minister who has governed through three parliaments over ten years, most of that time with an obedient majority and a compliant public, whose party program has sagged into quietism, who has failed to cope with economic decline and constitutional malaise—except that he has failed. It would be asking too much of the Canadian public, in the face of that record, to suggest (as George Radwanski implies) that Mr. Trudeau should now be given the chance to fulfill himself in office. What has he been waiting for?

The prime minister has done what he could do in his way, and there is no reason to believe that he can bring any fresh vision to the country in 1978. His reforming interest never extended much beyond bilingualism, administrative rationalization and subsidization of poor regional economies in Quebec and the Atlantic provinces. Too much was expected of, or claimed for, those programs, and their inadequacies were doggedly ignored for too long. On the two subjects of central importance to the country, the economy and the constitution, the prime minister has been disastrously wrong, out of a combination of ignorance and dogmatism. His unexplained liberal faith has led him to ignore the problems of a foreign-dominated economy, and in desperation to preach the very addiction to foreign investment which is at the root of our economic decline. And in a decade that called for unusual feats of constitutional imagination, the country has been governed by a constitutional conservative bound by his sterile definitions and engaged in a game of manipulation aimed at the maintenance of the *status quo*. Meanwhile the edifice has been crumbling around him.

The decay of talent from the federal cabinet since 1968 offers a key to understanding the prime minister's inability to face and adapt to the realities of the country's condition. One by one the men of character have gone, and Trudeau has done nothing to keep them. Radwanski puts this down to the prime minister's pride and insecurity: "Trudeau has a fundamental belief that it would be a misuse of power for him to use the moral authority of his office to pressure any individual because, as he puts it, 'the individual destiny is more important than the institution.' Unwilling to have anyone impose fetters on his own freedom of choice, he cannot bring himself to do it to others. But his sense of freedom also plays a role in another way: to express a vital need for any individual is to become beholden to him if he agrees to stay on, and that debt of gratitude would strike Trudeau as a limitation on his own independence."

A prime minister who refuses, out of misplaced personal pride, to engage in politics in his daily relations with colleagues is also a prime minister who cannot alter his deepest convictions about the country he governs, even when those convictions are based upon fantasy. The country in his mind is not *our* country—it is rather a country of illusion—but the prime minister has apparently never recognized the disjunction.

The tight self-control, the imposition of rational order at the expense of connection with the real world of politics which usually governs his acts, is not something that the prime minister can always sustain. When passion breaks through the barriers of his will it too comes in excess, and we are then ruled by a careless demagogue or a buffoon. This happens in frequent flashes in the House of Commons; it happened in the October Crisis; it happens in Mr. Trudeau's systematic depiction of the Parti Québécois as subversive and of the federal opposition parties as conspirators in that subversion. Impulsiveness and dogmatic reason are the two poles of his political character; and we are all the victims of his failure to balance reason and passion in serenity. "Quarry the granite rock with razors," wrote John Henry Newman, "or moor the vessel with a thread of silk; then may you hope with such keen and delicate instruments as human knowledge and human reason to contend against those giants, the passion and the pride of man." Pierre Elliott Trudeau's combat should henceforth be a private one that does not buffet half a continent.

For the Record—Economic Ineptitude

THE OTTAWA CITIZEN
August 25, 1978
DON MCGILLIVARY

... If we are on the brink of an election campaign in which the government will try to bedazzle the voters with public relations tricks, the voters will need to keep its record firmly in mind:

1. This is the government that increased its annual spending by $18 billion a year or 62 per cent since the last election. It is the government that has increased its spending by $37 billion a year or 370 per cent since the present prime minister took office 10 years ago. Its boasted cuts are minor compared to its increases.

2. This is the government that allowed the money supply to grow by 13 per cent in 1971, 14 per cent in 1972 and 14.5 per cent in 1975. If a ballooning money supply has anything to do with inflation, as monetarist economists claim, then the Trudeau government cannot blame inflation on factors beyond its control.

3. This is the government that brought most of the major items in Canada's food production under marketing board control designed to push prices up. It cannot claim a total lack of connection between that policy and the fact, as the prime minister put it, that "many Canadians, the old especially, cannot cope with world price increases in food."

4. Having followed policies that promoted inflation, and having seen the inflation rate jump into the double-digit range

in the spring of 1974, the government ran an election campaign that year designed to reassure Canadians that all was well and none of its policies needed to be changed except in the direction of increased government spending.

5. After the election, with a majority mandate, the government allowed things to drift for more than a year in which inflation reached a peak of more than 12.5 per cent and the output of the Canadian economy dropped, instead of rising, for 12 months.

6. Finally taking alarm at the inflation rate in the fall of 1975, the government put into effect a series of policies which reduced output and employment rather than inflation. The result was that the recovery from recession was aborted in Canada. After one quarter of good growth—the first three months of 1976—the government's squeeze on the incomes and investments of Canadians took effect and the recovery died.

7. Policies that choked the life out of Canada's recovery were kept in effect in the budgets brought down by Donald Macdonald in May, 1976, and March, 1977.

8. In Jean Chrétien's mini-budget of October 20, 1977 and his first full budget of April 10, 1978, he set a pattern of little shots of stimulus for the economy which were too small and short-term to get it moving but which frittered away his ability to give it any major, general stimulus.

9. When the present prime minister took office the cost of living was rising at 4.1 per cent a year. Despite his many claims to have "beaten" inflation or "wrestled it to the ground" the latest 12-month inflation rate is 9.8 per cent. Unemployment—4.5 per cent of the labor force when he took over—is 8.4 per cent.

These are only a few salient points in the government's economic record. It deserves to be remembered.

The policies advocated in the past—and present—by the Opposition parties deserve to be examined as critically, of course. Would what they proposed have worked any better than what the government did? In many cases they would not. But that is no excuse for a record of government economic mismanagement and ineptitude.

Confidence at Stake

THE OTTAWA JOURNAL
September 13, 1978
W. A. WILSON

It is a commonplace that a large part of this country's problems involve the question of confidence. It is not merely a matter of confidence at home, among the people of the country, the workers, the businessmen, the investors. It is equally a matter of how we are seen by others outside the country.

At the present time, the signal coming from the world's financial markets is that this country is not viewed with confidence. That is the basic reason why the Canadian dollar is falling to levels that are causing true concern here and why it has failed to respond to the periodic bursts of relative strength in the American dollar.

There are several reasons for this. One is that the uncertainty over Quebec is part of the general Canadian background. . . .

The two big deficits—one that of the federal government at home, the other part of the nation as a whole in its external accounts—are probably a larger factor than the Quebec situation.

These have become perennial and it must be said that at the political, if not the official, level the government was extremely slow in coming to grips with them.

It is only a couple of years since a very senior member of the government asked this correspondent one day what was wrong with running a large payments deficit and covering it with exceptionally heavy borrowing abroad.

Presumably, looking at the state of the dollar since shortly after that, he has observed the answer in practice.

It was at about that same time that I asked one of the strong men who had left the Trudeau ministry his view of that situation.

He replied that it was extremely dangerous, that the first crack would be a sharp decline in the dollar and that it would probably not stop sliding above 85 cents.

Now it is in doubt whether it will stop at that level, the psychological barrier which no longer seems substantial.

For Proof That Power Tends to Corrupt Look No Further Than Pierre Trudeau

MACLEAN'S
September 18, 1978
ALLAN FOTHERINGHAM

What is so astonishing, in this sour fall of 1978, is the shift in mood and perception. The mood belongs to Pierre Trudeau and his face toward the public: it is cynicism. Relationships between the unwashed and those on high always are bound to alter, but the most remarkable thing about Pierre Trudeau's link with his subjects in this autumn of our discontent is that it is so diametrically opposed to the original understanding. The public can perhaps comprehend and absorb the fact that the leader chosen is not really as bright as first perceived—as in Jimmy Carter. Or that, for all his fire and idealism, he essentially doesn't know how to run anything—as in John Diefenbaker.

It is somewhat harder for a public to swallow the fact that its chosen hero has had a complete mental (more correctly, perhaps, ethical) reversal of field. That is the current view of the electorate toward the chameleon Trudeau, the man who captured the imagination of the country one decade ago because of his frankness, his appealing innocence in decrying personal ambition, his apparent honesty in allowing that he really didn't seek the job and regarded the whole exercise, in his own words, as a bit of "a joke" on the public and press. Now, 10 years later, we have the most jaded, insulting appeal for public support since the days of "Boss" Tweed. Some of the recent Liberal tactics appear almost a caricature of ward-heeler methodology. Look at the editorial columns across the land and you consistently come across one word: cynical.

What is so remarkable about the whole degrading process of the last few months is that the prime minister, encased in that intellectual cocoon that shields him from real life, appears astonishingly immune to the rising contempt of the electorate. He is vaccinated against reality.

There's a reason for this insularity. The Liberal party seeps through the underbelly of this country like a nuclear submarine in the deep. In 1955, when the Liberals modestly acceded to the 20th anniversary of uninterrupted rule in Ottawa, the shrewd political scientist Paul Fox noted that: "The Liberal government aims at operating noiselessly, like a respectable mammoth business operation which fears nothing more than making people aware that it is there. The shadows flit silently along the wall, as in Plato's cave, and the citizen is never sufficiently disturbed to turn his head."

In truth, a business operation. As a sample, in the 1935 election just five firms contributed 26 per cent of the campaign funds for the key Toronto Finance Committee: Labatt's, Imperial Oil, Laura Secord Candy Shops, Canadian General Electric, National Breweries. Forty per cent of the money came from just 12 sources. (Liquor and gold mine interests were the prime donors.) By the 1940 election, just seven donors provided 40 per cent of the slush fund.

By 1953, 50 per cent of the Liberal party financing came from commerce and industry, 40 per cent from businessmen linked to firms and only 10 per cent from private individuals. K. Z. Paltiel, research director of Ottawa's 1964 Barbeau Committee on election expenses found that only some 350 donors piled up the $7.5-million war chest used by the Liberals in the 1957 campaign.

In this atmosphere of the Natural Governing Party, born to rule and steered by business, there has been the shrewd Liberal tactic—the recruiting of symbolic public relations figures from outside the grimy party system. Mackenzie King came from his duties as an employee of the Rockefeller family. Uncle Louis St. Laurent came from corporate law, Lester Pearson from the bureaucracy and Trudeau from the intellectual fringe. In the case of the latter three, a reasonable case can now be made that they were chips floating on the Liberal tide, the party machinery keeping them aloft. What is now becoming apparent about Trudeau, the innocent chosen over the pros, is that after a decade he has become a passenger on the vehicle. The party lumbers on and he flounders for a direction.

For a man of such inflexible personal standards, he is astonishingly pliable when the backroom operatives convince him that another tack is necessary to ensure the rule of the Natural Governing Party. Jack Horner was purchased in return for a cabinet seat. Key Tory Gordon Fairweather was lured onto neutral ground and away from the Opposition shadow cabinet with the Human Rights Commission appointment. Tory MP Bob McCleave was given a judgeship. Claude Wagner was purchased with the sweet of a Senate seat.

The spring buying of Opposition trouble spots over with, increasingly desperate plunges were needed to shore up the fall excuses for a vote. The prime minister, a philosopher seemingly taking a constant cram course in economics, decided that Helmut Schmidt, rather than Jean Chrétien, is his real finance minister. With the only strong personalities in a grey cabinet long fled—Turner, MacDonald, Mackasey, Kierans—the ebullient Chrétien was reduced to being a target for open derision from the press gallery when Trudeau's surprise "budget from Bonn" left the finance minister fumbling and naked. There is a whiff of the Keystone Kops to Parliament Hill, a smell of the last floundering Diefenbaker disaster days.

CONCLUSION

Canada's economic growth through the fifties and sixties was accompanied by progress in the creation of social programs. A basic level of services was made available to everyone through hospital and medical insurance programs. Children's allowances and the Canada Pension Plan were introduced as essential social measures.

The first Trudeau government entered the scene at a time when the basic directions of national policy needed refining. Mr. Trudeau's past record and his campaign utterances led to the natural expectation that he would, as a priority for his "just society," deal with four main issues: 1) the question of Québec; 2) reinforcement of individual rights; 3) the redistribution of personal income to bring about a more equitable sharing of wealth; 4) the curbing or reversal of the trend toward foreign control of the Canadian economy.

Mr. Trudeau's solution to the Québec problem was official bilingualism. He would create a bilingual civil service and thereby ensure that Quebeckers and other francophones could communicate with the federal government in their own language. The main flaw in this concept was that Quebeckers still perceived the government in Québec City as the main guarantor of their rights and future. Trudeau did little to change that. In fact, bilingualism came to be seen in Québec as a threat, since it asked the province to curb its drive toward protection of the French language in return for the creation of a disgruntled, officially bilingual civil service in Ottawa. The increased recruitment of young Quebeckers by Ottawa was also seen as a theft of talent from the province. The fact is that Quebeckers had always seen Ottawa as a colonial capital. The bilingualization of the capital did little to alter this perception.

Mr. Trudeau, for his part, has refused to consider alternative approaches to the French-English issue, such as redirecting money from ineffective civil service bilingualism programs to an emphasis on teaching second languages in the primary schools. He also adopted a confrontationist approach in his dealings with Québec, refusing to enter into negotiations for a redistribution of federal-provincial powers. Mr. Trudeau's rigidity and refusal to reconsider the failed panacea of official bilingualism has contributed greatly to the increased reliance of Quebeckers on the strength of their provincial government. Robert Bourassa, for example, was turned out by Québec voters at least in part for his demonstrated weakness before the will of Ottawa. On November 15, 1976, one of the reasons Québec voted in the PQ was because it knew Lévesque would stand up to Ottawa. Mr. Trudeau's years in office had reinforced the feeling that only a strong government in Québec City can safeguard the interests of Quebeckers.

What progress has resulted from 10 years of Trudeau government as far as individual rights are concerned? The fervor for individual rights began to develop in Canada in the 1960s, largely through the influence of a similar movement in the United States. Mr. Trudeau's writings and his work as justice minister led many to believe he shared their concerns. In every test since, however, he has demonstrated that given a choice between individual liberties and what he perceives as the need to safeguard "national security" he will opt for the latter. This was so with the invocation of the War Measures Act, with recent legislation allowing the RCMP to open private mail, and with the refusal of the department of justice in 1979 to consider compensation for Peter Treu, the man it had unsuccessfully hounded in a secret trial.

In economic matters it is possible to make a statistical assessment of the Trudeau decade. The redistributive economic measures implemented by the Pearson government in the mid-sixties were beginning to show results by the time Mr. Trudeau came to power. The gap between the poorest and the richest fifths of society was narrowing. Statistics show that redistribution of personal income has practically ceased since 1969. Mr. Trudeau's changing economic and social policies have worked to the benefit of the middle class in Canada while allowing the gap between rich and poor to widen.

The government's social conscience has wavered with the state of the economy and its electoral prospects. Improvements in social programs have been jettisoned in "austerity" measures. Wage and price controls, first rejected and derided, some months later became official government policy. Short-term planning of this sort shows a basic inability to deal effectively with economic problems. Rather than establish effective budgetary control and reform the tax system to produce needed revenues, the government has opted for easy but socially damaging solutions such as cutbacks in unemployment benefits and dropping the indexation of pensions.

Foreign control of the Canadian economy has been an issue in the Canadian press and with voters since the early sixties. Foreign ownership, particularly in the manufacturing sector, had come about during the rapid economic expansion of the fifties and early sixties. By 1968 nearly 75 percent of the Canadian manufacturing sector was in foreign hands, and control of other vital sectors was equally endangered. The response of the Trudeau government was to create an ineffective bureaucracy, The Foreign Investment Review Board, which would have little substantial effect on new takeovers and absolutely no effect on the foreign control that had developed before FIRA was created. Foreign control existing to that point was simply accepted by the government. Mr. Trudeau seems never to have taken very seriously the desire, especially in English Canada and particularly in Ontario, to repatriate the economy before repatriating the constitution. This is one of the main reasons for the decline of the Liberal party under Mr. Trudeau in Ontario.

Surprisingly little progress is evident, then, in the four main policy areas Mr. Trudeau was expected to deal with. Yet he deserves recognition for several lesser initiatives. Parliament, with its revised committee structure and rules of procedure is today a more efficient institution than Mr. Trudeau found it in 1968. Televised debates have brought Parliament back to its rightful position of public prominence, and the PM's regular press conferences provide better access for journalists. Despite the enormous cost and waste associated with civil service bilingualism, federal services in both languages are now more readily available than ever before. On the question of the new oil wealth, Mr. Trudeau has tried consistently to ensure that at least some of this windfall is shared among the non-producing provinces. Capital punishment has been abolished and reforms in the laws governing homosexuality and marijuana have been slowly made.

In foreign policy, the Trudeau decade has seen the establishment of diplomatic relations with China and an attempt to lessen Canada's traditional international role as an echo of the United States, by developing new diplomatic and economic ties with the Common Market and several Pacific Rim countries. Unfortunately, this flurry of mid-seventies diplomatic activity has produced few tangible results, and the absence of an effective policy on foreign ownership has left America's dominance in Canadian life largely untouched.

It should be said that the press, by default, has played a part in this long process of political disappointment. The media, particularly in English Canada, have consistently presented the Prime Minister and his government in a highly personalized way. Rather than outlining and discussing the issues facing Canada, the press has often been content to peddle empty journalistic stereotypes: Trudeau the swinger of 1968, the philosopher-king of 1972, the embattled campaigner of 1974, and the unpopular vacillating leader of 1978. The same cartoon-like treatment was given to bumbling Bob Stanfield and his football fumble and to his successor Joe Who. The Prime Minister's marriage has received more press coverage than individual rights, poverty, or foreign ownership. Shallow press coverage of this sort makes it more difficult for the public the media serves to evaluate governments, their policies, and leaders. Overall this problem is less noticeable in Québec where it is easier to find thoughtful, issue-oriented, and well researched feature articles and editorials. The combination of personality-oriented journalism in English Canada and unimpressive Conservative

Party leadership has worked to the enormous long-term advantage of Mr. Trudeau.

The astounding question that arises from an examination of Prime Minister Trudeau's more than 10 years in power is how a man so uniquely endowed with gifts of intelligence and communication could have so thoroughly misunderstood the currents active within his own country while seeming to possess a singular grasp of world movements. This misunderstanding was mutual from the start. In retrospect it seems the leadership candidate of April 1968 and the election campaigner of the following June never had a true sense of the expectations his presence and personality created in this country. Canada in 1968 was psychologically and politically ready for the type of innovative leader Pierre Elliott Trudeau seemed to be. At the moment when a majority of the voting population felt the country had matured sufficiently to break from the mould of its past, it elected a leader whose instincts were for caution, discipline, and bureaucratization. Future historians may view Mr. Trudeau's restraining influence as beneficial, but for most of those who helped elect him in 1968 and kept him in power, the Trudeau decade has proven a time of unexpected disappointment.

THE PRIME MINISTER'S FOREIGN TRAVELS

1969

January 3-17	London—Commonwealth Conference Rome—visit to Vatican
March 24-5	Washington
June 27	Massena, New York—Tenth Anniversary of St. Lawrence Seaway

1970

May 10-24	Hawaii, New Zealand, Australia, Malaysia, Singapore, Hong Kong, Japan

1971

January 5-29	Pakistan, India, Indonesia
May 17-28	USSR (Moscow, Kiev, Tashkent, Norilsk, Murmansk, Leningrad)
December 6-7	Washington—meeting with President Nixon

1972

December 2-4	London—meeting with Prime Minister Heath

1973

October 8-19	Peking

1974

Jan. 27-Feb. 11	Switzerland and Austria—Prime Minister's

	holidays and Club of Rome meeting
April 8	Paris—President Pompidou's funeral
May 12	Duke University, North Carolina
October 19-25	Paris and Brussels
December 4-5	Washington

1975

Feb. 26-Mar. 15	Netherlands, Germany, Italy, England, Ireland
April 24-May 7	Trinidad, Tobago, Barbados, Guyana, Jamaica
May 27-June 1	Denmark, Belgium, Luxembourg
July 28-Aug. 5	Finland and Poland
October 23	Washington

1976

Jan. 23-Feb. 2	Cuba, Mexico, Venezuela
June 16	Washington
June 26-8	Puerto Rico—Summit Conference
October 19-26	Tokyo

1977

February 21-3	Washington
April 7-8	Berkeley, California, and Disneyland
May 5-14	England, France, Iceland
June 6-16	London—Commonwealth Conference
September 7-8	Washington

1978

May 26-30	New York and Washington
July 16-26	Germany and Denmark
September 1-4	Rome
December 6-11	London and Paris
December 28-9	Jamaica

FEDERAL ELECTION RESULTS 1968, 1972, 1974

Party	1968		1972		1974	
	no. of seats	popular vote	no. of seats	popular vote	no. of seats	popular vote
Liberal	155	45.2%	109	38.5%	141	43.2%
Progressive Conservative	72	31.3%	107	35.0%	95	35.4%
New Democratic Party	22	17.4%	31	17.7%	16	15.4%
Social Credit (Créditiste)	14	5.2%	15	7.6%	11	5.0%
Other	1	0.9%	2	1.2%	1	1.0%

BIBLIOGRAPHY

BOM, PHILIP C. *Trudeau's Canada: Truth and Consequences.* Guardian Publishing: St. Catharines, Ontario, 1977.

COWLEY, MICHAEL. *The Naked Prime Minister.* Winnipeg: Greywood Publishing, 1969.

HARLSON, JOHN DAVIDSON. *This Is Trudeau.* Toronto: Longmans, 1968.

LAXER, *The Liberal Idea of Canada: Pierre Trudeau and the Question of Canada's Survival.* Toronto: Lorimer, 1977.

PELLERIN, JEAN. *Le Phénomène Trudeau.* Paris: Seghers, 1972.

RADWANSKI, GEORGE. *Trudeau.* Toronto: Macmillan of Canada, 1978.

STEWART, WALTER. *Shrug: Trudeau in Power.* Toronto: New Press, 1971.

STUEBING, DOUGLAS. *Trudeau: A Man for Tomorrow.* Toronto: Clarke, Irwin, 1968.

THORDARSON, BRUCE. *Trudeau and Foreign Policy: A Study in Decision-Making.* Toronto: Oxford University Press, 1972.

TRUDEAU, PIERRE ELLIOTT. *Pierre Elliott Trudeau: Portrait in Time.* Montreal: Stanké, 1977.

WESTELL, GEORGE ANTHONY. *Paradox: Trudeau as Prime Minister.* Toronto: Prentice-Hall, 1972.

WILSON, WILLIAM A. *The Trudeau Question: Election 1972.* Toronto: Paperjacks, 1972.

ZOLF, LARRY. *Dance of the Dialectic.* Toronto: James, Lewis and Samuel, 1973.

INDEX OF SUBJECTS

The following is not an exhaustive index. It is designed to enable the interested reader to find the major sections of the book dealing with the important issues and events covered in the text.